DATE DUE

Realms of Meaning

CURRICULUM AND METHODS IN EDUCATION
Arno A. Bellack, *Consulting Editor*

By the same author:

Education and the Common Good
Religious Concerns in Contemporary Education
Philosophy of Education

Realms of Meaning

A PHILOSOPHY OF THE CURRICULUM
FOR GENERAL EDUCATION

Philip H. Phenix

Professor of Philosophy and Education
Teachers College, Columbia University

McGraw-Hill Book Company
NEW YORK   SAN FRANCISCO   TORONTO   LONDON

6789-MP-9

REALMS OF MEANING

TO MY STUDENTS IN THE WAYS OF KNOWING

Preface

In the past decade educators and concerned citizens have shown renewed appreciation for the place of the organized disciplines of knowledge in education. To some extent the impetus for this interest has come from the technical and ideological challenges of the cold war. Americans have become aware of the need for the most effective possible educational system if they are to meet the demands of life in a highly precarious and rapidly changing world, and they see how important knowledge is for meeting these demands.

However, there is a far more fundamental justification for basing the curriculum upon the best available results of critical scholarship than the present crisis. This justification is found in the nature of man and of the educative process itself. There are now heartening signs that scholars and educators are drawing together in cooperative effort and in recognition of a common opportunity to make the best that is known as widely and economically available as possible.

Accordingly, the focus in modern education at all educational levels and for students of all abilities is increasingly upon excellence and adequacy of knowledge. It is recognized that knowledge does not belong to specialists alone, but that, through the agency of general education, understanding of a high order can and should be attained by everyone.

The new directions appear in many developments. Most impressive are the large-scale revisions taking place in the various school subjects, beginning with mathematics and the natural sciences, and extending to the languages, history and the social studies, and English. At the collegiate level many experiments in general education are under way which place a greater emphasis on the life of the mind than was found among earlier generations of collegians. Academic scholars and professional educationists have come to better mutual understandings through conferences on Teacher Education and Professional Standards. The 1961 Report of the Educational Policies Commission on *The Central Purpose of American Education* reflects the general concern of educational leaders for the nurture of intelligence. There are also growing signs of *rapprochement* between schools of education and the faculties of arts and sciences in colleges and universities.

Of particular importance is the work of investigators of human learning as related to the structure of knowledge and the processes of disciplined inquiry. The most widely read and influential work in this field is Jerome S. Bruner's *The Process of Education,* [1] a book that grew out of a conference of scientists who had been actively engaged in revising the mathematics and science curricula for the schools, together with a number of psychologists, professional educators, and scholars in history and classics.

In a somewhat similar vein, the present volume is an attempt to elaborate a philosophical theory of the curriculum for general education based on the idea of logical patterns in disciplined understanding. The central thesis is that knowledge in the disciplines has patterns or structures and that an understanding of these typical forms is essential for the guidance of teaching and learning. This thesis grows out of a concept of human nature as rooted in meaning and of human life as directed toward the fulfillment of meaning. The various patterns of knowledge are varieties of meaning, and the learning of these patterns is the clue to the effective realization of essential humanness through the curriculum of general education.

In the current revival of interest in knowledge there are two temptations which it is hoped this philosophy of the curriculum will help to counteract. One is the temptation to return to a traditional subject-matter curriculum related neither to the needs or abilities of the individual learner nor to the social and psychological factors affecting education. Concern for the structure of knowledge is presented here not for the sake of reestablishing "hard" traditional studies as the best basis for training mind and character, but as a means of making the most economical use of each person's capacity for learning.

[1] Harvard University Press, Cambridge, Mass., 1960.

The second temptation is to construe knowledge too narrowly in purely intellectualistic terms. The present analysis shows that meanings are of many kinds and that the full development of human beings requires education in a variety of realms of meaning rather than in a single type of rationality.

The current vogue of the "pursuit of excellence," the growing prestige of intellectual achievement, and the mounting pressures on young people to succeed academically may eventually result in a great outcry against educational formalism, like the one that seventy-five years ago ushered in the Progressive movement—the rise and decline of which is the theme of Lawrence A. Cremin's definitive history of Progressivism in American education from 1876 to 1957. [2] The educational proposals in the present book are intended to show how knowledge may be used in the curriculum in such a way as to make it unnecessary to repeat the reaction and reform cycles of the past.

This book grew out of my course at Teachers College, Columbia University, on the Ways of Knowing, in which the basic methods and representative ideas of selected disciplines of knowledge were examined to illuminate their purpose and treatment in the program of general education. I hope that the book will prove of interest to students of education, to teachers and other professional workers in education, and to the general reader who is concerned about the problems of education. The study may also have something to offer to any person, in formal education or outside of it, who seeks perspective on knowledge in the modern world and who is in search of order and meaning in his own life.

I wish to express special thanks to my colleagues Arno A. Bellack and Lawrence A. Cremin for reading the manuscript and for their valuable suggestions. I also want to acknowledge my appreciation to Ruth Greenberg for her assistance in preparing the manuscript.

Philip H. Phenix

---

[2] *The Transformation of the School,* Alfred A. Knopf, Inc., New York, 1961.

Contents

Realms of Meaning

Introduction

1

THE ARGUMENT

It is not easy to sustain a sense of the whole. Many a person pursues his own limited calling with scarcely a thought for his place in the total drama of civilized endeavor. While he may have a vague notion of the larger context in which his contribution is made, he may never engage in any sustained study and reflection about his relation to the entire pattern of civilization.

This limitation of outlook is evident even in education. All too commonly the teacher teaches a particular subject or unit within a subject without any reference to its relationships to other components of the curriculum. Similarly, the student may study one subject after another with no idea of what his growing fund of knowledge and skill might contribute to an integrated way of life. Students and teachers alike are prone to take the curriculum as they find it, as a traditional sequence of separate elements, without ever inquiring into the comprehensive pattern within which the constituent parts are located.

Since education is the means of perpetuating culture from generation to generation, it is natural that the partiality of outlook endemic in the culture generally would be found also in education. Yet, this consequence need not follow. Indeed, the special office of education is to widen one's view of life, to deepen insight into relationships, and to counteract the provincialism of customary existence—in short, to engender an integrated outlook.

If this integral perspective is to be attained, a philosophy of the curriculum is necessary. By such a philosophy is meant a critically examined, coherent system of ideas by which all the constituent parts of the course of instruction are identified and ordered.

A unitary philosophy of the curriculum is important for many reasons, among which the following four may be cited: First, comprehensive outlook is necessary for all intelligent decisions about what shall be included and excluded from the course of study. If one subject is to be chosen instead of another, it is important to know how the one differs from the other and why the one is to be preferred to the other as a constituent in the complete pattern of the learner's experience and character.

Second, because a person is essentially an organized totality and not just a collection of separate parts, the curriculum ought to have a corresponding organic quality. Since it is one and the same person who undergoes each of the successive experiences in his course of study, the plan of study can best contribute to the person's growth if it is governed by the goal of wholeness for the human being.

Third, society, as well as individual persons, depends upon principles of community; corporate life, like the life of each individual, requires some overall plan. A curriculum planned as a comprehensive design for learning contributes a basis for the growth of community, while an atomized program of studies engenders disintegration in the life of society.

Fourth, a comprehensive concept of the structure of learning gives added significance to each of the component segments of the curriculum. The value of any subject is enhanced by an understanding of its relationships with other subjects, and its distinctive features are best comprehended in the light of its similarities and contrasts with other subjects.

The purpose of the present work is to sketch a view of the curriculum for general education by showing how the desirable scope, content, and arrangement of studies may be derived from certain fundamental considerations about human nature and knowledge. It will be shown that the controlling idea of general education, imparting unity to the pattern of studies, emerges from a philosophy of man and his ways of knowing.

The main line of argument may be summarized as follows:

Human beings are essentially creatures who have the power to experience *meanings*. Distinctively human existence consists in a pattern of meanings. Furthermore, *general education is the process of engendering essential meanings*.

Unfortunately, the pathway to the fulfillment of meaning is never smooth. The human situation is such that mankind is always threatened by forces that destroy meaning. Values, purposes, and understandings are fragile achievements and give way all too readily to attitudes of futility, frustration, and doubt. Meaning is thus lost in an abyss of meaninglessness.

The perennial threat to meaning is intensified under the conditions of modern industrial civilization. Four contributing factors deserve special emphasis. The first is the spirit of criticism and skepticism. This spirit is part of the scientific heritage, but it has also tended to bring the validity of all meanings into question. The second factor is the pervasive depersonalization and fragmentation of life caused by the extreme specialization of a complex, interdependent society. The third factor is the sheer mass of cultural products, especially knowledge, which modern man is required to assimilate. The fourth factor is the rapid rate of change in the conditions of life, resulting in a pervasive feeling of impermanence and insecurity.

Since the object of general education is to lead to the fulfillment of human life through the enlargement and deepening of meaning, the modern curriculum should be designed with particular attention to these sources of meaninglessness in contemporary life. That is to say, the curriculum should be planned so as to counteract destructive skepticism, depersonalization and fragmentation, overabundance, and transience.

If education is to be regarded as grounded in the search for meaning, the primary goal of a philosophy of the curriculum is to analyze the nature of meaning. Meaningful experience is of many kinds; there is no single quality that may be designated as the one essence of meaning. Accordingly, we should speak not of meaning as such, but of meanings, or of the *realms of meaning*. Hence, a philosophy of the curriculum requires a mapping of the realms of meaning, one in which the various possibilities of significant experience are charted and the various domains of meaning are distinguished and correlated.

Six fundamental patterns of meaning emerge from the analysis of the possible distinctive modes of human understanding. These six patterns may be designated respectively as *symbolics, empirics, esthetics, synnoetics, ethics,* and *synoptics.*

Each realm of meaning and each of its constituent subrealms may be described by reference to its typical methods, leading ideas, and characteristic structures. These features may be exhibited both in their uniqueness for each realm or subrealm and in their relationships and continuities with the other types of meaning. Leaving the details to be elaborated in subsequent chapters, the six realms can be broadly characterized as follows:

The first realm, *symbolics,* comprises ordinary language, mathematics, and various types of nondiscursive symbolic forms, such as gestures, rituals, rhythmic patterns, and the like. These meanings are contained in arbitrary symbolic structures, with socially accepted rules of formation and transformation, created as instruments for the expression and communication of any meaning whatsoever. These symbolic systems in one respect constitute the most fundamental of all the realms of meaning in that they must be employed to express the meanings in each of the other realms.

The second realm, *empirics,* includes the sciences of the physical world, of living things, and of man. These sciences provide factual descriptions, generalizations, and theoretical formulations and explanations which are based upon observation and experimentation in the world of matter, life, mind, and society. They express meanings as probable empirical truths framed in accordance with certain rules of evidence and verification and making use of specified systems of analytic abstraction.

The third realm, *esthetics,* contains the various arts, such as music, the visual arts, the arts of movement, and literature. Meanings in this realm are concerned with the contemplative perception of particular significant things as unique objectifications of ideated subjectivities.

The fourth realm, *synnoetics,* embraces what Michael Polanyi calls "personal knowledge" and Martin Buber the "I-Thou" relation. The novel term "synnoetics," which was devised because no existing concept appeared adequate to the type of understanding intended, derives from the Greek *synnoesis,* meaning "meditative thought," and this in turn is compounded of *syn,* meaning "with" or "together," and *noesis,* meaning "cognition." Thus synnoetics signifies "relational insight" or "direct awareness." It is analogous in the sphere of knowing to sympathy in the sphere of feeling. This personal or relational knowledge is concrete, direct, and existential. It may apply to other persons, to oneself, or even to things.

The fifth realm, *ethics,* includes moral meanings that express obligation rather than fact, perceptual form, or awareness of relation. In contrast to the sciences, which are concerned with abstract cognitive understanding, to the arts, which express idealized esthetic perceptions, and to personal knowledge, which reflects intersubjective understanding, morality has to do with personal conduct that is based on free, responsible, deliberate decision.

The sixth realm, *synoptics,* refers to meanings that are comprehensively integrative. It includes history, religion, and philosophy. These disciplines combine empirical, esthetic, and synnoetic meanings into coherent wholes. Historical interpretation comprises an artful re-creation of the past, in obedience to factual evidence, for the purpose of revealing what man by his deliberate choices has made of himself within the context of his given circumstances. Religion is concerned with ultimate meanings, that is, with meanings from any realm whatsoever, considered from the standpoint of such boundary concepts as the Whole, the Comprehensive, and the Transcendent. Philosophy provides analytic clarification, evaluation, and synthetic coordination of all the other realms through a reflective conceptual interpretation of all possible kinds of meaning in their distinctiveness and in their interrelationships.

The symbolics, which have been placed at one end of the spectrum of meanings, encompass the entire range of meanings because they are the necessary means of expressing all meanings whatever. Similarly, the synoptics, which have been placed at the other end of the spectrum, also gather up the entire range of meanings by virtue of their integrative character. Between these two realms of symbolics and synoptics lie the realms of empirics, esthetics, synnoetics, and ethics as four essentially distinct (though interdependent) dimensions of meaning or modes of significant human relatedness to the world and to existence.

The six realms thus charted provide the foundations for all the meanings that enter into human experience. They are the foundations in the sense that they are the pure and archetypal kinds of meaning that determine the quality of every humanly significant experience. From this viewpoint, any particular meaning can be analyzed as an expression of one of the fundamental meanings or as a combination of two or more of them. In practice, meanings seldom appear in pure and simple form; they are almost always compounded of several of the elemental types.

Despite this complexity in practice, it is useful for purposes of curriculum analysis and construction to distinguish the basic ingredients in all meaning and to order the learning process for general education in the light of these elements.

If the six realms cover the range of possible meanings, they may be regarded as comprising the basic competences that general education should develop in every person. A complete person should be skilled in the use of speech, symbol, and gesture, factually well informed, capable of creating and appreciating objects of esthetic significance, endowed with a rich and disciplined life in relation to self and others, able to make wise decisions and to judge between right and wrong, and possessed of an integral outlook. These are the aims of general education for the development of whole persons.

A curriculum developing the above basic competences is designed to satisfy the essential human need for meaning. Instruction in language, mathematics, science, art, personal relations, morals, history, religion, and philosophy constitutes the educational answer to the destructively critical spirit and to the pervasive modern sense of meaninglessness. Moreover, all of these elements are necessary ingredients in the formation of a mature person.

Because the realms of meaning form an articulated whole, a curriculum based upon them counteracts the fragmentation of experience that is one of the sources of meaninglessness. The various meanings do not merely occupy separate and isolated domains; they are interrelated and complementary, forming parts of a single hierarchical system of meaning. The symbolic and the synoptic fields, especially, serve as binding elements running through the various realms and welding them into a single meaningful pattern.

In addition to decisions about the scope of studies, the planning of the curriculum requires decisions about the ordering of content. With respect to the sequence of studies three factors are of major importance. The first is the previously discussed factor of integrity, which suggests that every student at every stage of his learning career should receive some instruction in all six of the realms of meaning. In this way continuous progress toward wholeness of meaning may best be assured.

The second factor in sequence is the intrinsic logical order of the various kinds of meaning. Clearly the languages, being essential to expression in all the other fields, need special initial emphasis. On the other hand, the synoptic fields, depending upon a substantial fund of other meanings to be integrated, can most profitably be pursued at a later stage in the learner's career. The descriptive sciences may be entered upon with less prior preparation than can the moral disciplines, which gain significance only with the assumption of real responsibility. The esthetic and synnoetic disciplines are intermediate in the degree of experience required for most effective learning. Thus, the logical interrelations of the realms of meaning have some bearing on the optimum sequence of studies.

The third factor in ordering studies is that of human development and maturation. Empirical studies show that the growing person becomes ready for different types of learning at different stages of growth. These levels of preparedness should be taken into account in planning the sequence of instruction.

Beyond the scope and sequence of studies, curriculum making requires principles for the selection and organization of content.

Given the enormous volume of knowledge available to be learned, the educator is faced with the task of choosing a minute fraction of this total cultural stock for inclusion in the course of study. It was pointed out above that surfeit of knowledge is one of the causes of frustration and the sense of meaninglessness in the present-day world. If some defensible criteria can be found for reducing the mass of material to assimilable proportions, a major contribution can be made to the quest for meaning.

It will be recalled that another source of meaninglessness is the rapidity of change in modern life, which soon renders much that is learned obsolete. Again, a signal contribution can be made to fulfillment of meaning if curricular content can be selected so as to have a measure of permanence amid pervasive changefulness.

Four principles for the selection and organization of content are suggested as means of ensuring optimum growth in meaning. The first principle is that the content of instruction should be drawn entirely from the fields of *disciplined inquiry*. The richness of culture and the level of understanding achieved in advanced civilization are due almost entirely to the labors of individual men of genius and of organized communities of specialists. A high level of civilization is the consequence of the dedicated service of persons with special gifts for the benefit of all. Every person is indebted for what he has and is to a great network of skilled inventors, experimenters, artists, seers, scholars, prophets, and saints, who have devoted their special talents to the well-being of all. Nobody, no matter how capable, can make any perceptible progress on his own without dependence on the experts in the various departments of life.

It follows that the teacher should draw upon the specialized disciplines as the most dependable and rewarding resource for instructional materials. While he should seek to make the disciplined materials his own, he should not presume to originate the knowledge to be taught, nor should he expect the fruits of learning to come forth as if by miracle from the shared experience of the students or as the products of common sense.

This term "discipline" is not meant to refer to an unchanging set of established fields of knowledge. New disciplines are regularly coming into being, such as cybernetics, parapsychology, theory of games, astronautics, and the like. New combinations, such as biochemistry and history of science, are forming. Also, many established disciplines are undergoing radical internal transformations: modern physics, music, history, and theology, to mention only a few. In fact, there is scarcely a field of study that is not today different in important respects from what it was only a few decades ago. Hence the present proposal to use materials from the disciplines does not constitute an argument for education to return to a traditional subject-matter curriculum. It simply argues for the exclusive use of materials that have been produced in disciplined communities of inquiry by men of knowledge who possess authority in their fields. Given the developments in disciplined inquiry, the proposal to use knowledge from the disciplines favors a modern rather than a traditional type of curriculum.

The second principle for the selection of content is that from the large resources of material in any given discipline, those items should be chosen that are particularly *representative* of the field as a whole. The only effective solution to the surfeit of knowledge is a drastic process of simplification. This aim can be achieved by discovering for each discipline those seminal or key ideas that provide clues to the entire discipline. If the content of instruction is carefully chosen and organized so as to emphasize these characteristic features of the disciplines, a relatively small volume of knowledge may suffice to yield effective understanding of a far larger body of material. The use of teaching materials based on representative ideas thus makes possible a radical simplification of the learner's task.

A third and related principle is that content should be chosen so as to exemplify the *methods of inquiry* and the modes of understanding in the disciplines studied. It is more important for the student to become skillful in the ways of knowing than to learn about any particular product of investigation. Knowledge of methods makes it possible for a person to continue learning and to undertake inquiries on his own. Furthermore, the modes of thought are far less transient than are the products of inquiry. Concentration on methods also helps to overcome the other two forms of meaninglessness earlier considered, namely, fragmentation and surfeit of materials. Every discipline is unified by its methods, which are the common source of all the conclusions reached in that field of study. As this common thread, the characteristic modes of thought are included in the category of representative ideas, which, as indicated above, allow for the simplification of learning.

A fourth principle of selection is that the materials chosen should be such as to arouse *imagination*. Growth in meaning occurs only when the mind of the learner actively assimilates and re-creates the materials of instruction. Ordinary, prosaic, and customary considerations do not excite a vital personal engagement with ideas. One of the qualities of good teaching is the ability to impart a sense of the extraordinary and surprising so that learning becomes a continuous adventure. According to this principle, ordinary life-situations and the solving of everyday problems should not be the basis for curriculum content. The life of meaning is far better served by using materials that tap the deeper levels of experience. Such materials reveal new perspectives on old problems by throwing familiar experiences into fresh combinations and showing old beliefs in novel contexts. Such imaginative use of materials generates habits of thought that enable the student to respond to rapid changes in knowledge and belief with zest instead of dismay and to experience joy in understanding rather than the dead weight of ideas to be absorbed and stored.

Such, in barest outline, is the argument to be elaborated and illustrated in the following pages. This philosophy of the curriculum for general education centers on the idea of *meaning* as the key to distinctively human experience. Hence the processes of teaching and learning are to be guided by reference to the major varieties of meaning. Six fundamental patterns of meaning are found to cover the spectrum of significant human experience, and each of these can be analyzed into constituent disciplines. These domains of understanding comprise sources from which curricular materials are to be drawn. The sequence of studies and the selection of materials is to be based on the logic of the realms of meaning, the psychology of human development, and certain content criteria that minimize the following principal enemies of meaning:

destructive skepticism, fragmentation, overabundance, and transience.

In the foregoing summary nothing has been said explicitly about the social factors in the formation of the curriculum. Surely the conditions and needs of society do and ought to play an important part in educational decision making. Why, then, is no specific reference made to these factors in the present analysis? There are three principal reasons.

First, the basic concept of meaning, around which this study is focused, is itself inherently social. Meanings are relational. They are shared. No one can have a significant life in isolation. The community of meaning applies to all the realms without exception. Every pattern of meaning is a shared way of understanding. Hence, a curriculum of general education constructed on the basis of the fundamental patterns of meaning necessarily incorporates the realities and ideals of life in relation to others.

Second, particular social factors are more relevant to the curriculum of specialized education than of general education. The nature of a society is reflected in the character and distribution of its specialized occupations. These functions vary from society to society more than do the qualities of meaning that a person needs in any society to fulfill his being as a person. It follows that particular social needs have less relevance to the curriculum of general education than to the curriculum of specialized education, which is not covered in the present work.

Third, no claim is made that the principles herein recommended provide a complete basis for the construction of the curriculum even of general education. The considerations presented are intended to give only a broad framework within which specific curriculum decisions can be made by taking account of many other factors relating to particular personal and cultural situations. The special needs and resources of the society in which and for which education takes place are among the additional factors pertinent to what is taught in the institutions of learning.

This philosophy of the curriculum for general education is thus intended as a comprehensive but not exhaustive guide to the fulfillment of human existence through education. It may perhaps be regarded as a contribution to what James Harvey Robinson called "the humanizing of knowledge." [1] The fruits of inquiry by professional scholars are largely beyond the comprehension of the layman, even though he may be intelligent and formally well educated. Also this knowledge may appear to have little pertinence to the vital concerns of any except those who are professionally committed to it. There is a great need for the best insights of civilization to be made available to people generally and for its humane significance to be made clear. "Popular culture" need not be mediocre and trivial. Meaning is lost both when knowledge is abstruse and inaccessible and when it is commonplace and superficial. The present philosophy of the curriculum is dedicated to the proposition that the finest treasures of civilization can be so mediated as to become a common inheritance of persons who are seeking to realize their essential humanness.

[1] See his book by this title, 2d rev. ed., George H. Doran Company, New York, 1926.

Part One

Meaning

and Human Nature

2

HUMAN NATURE

Since education is a means of helping human beings to become what they can and should become, the educator needs to understand human nature. He needs to understand people in their actualities, in their possibilities, and in their idealities. He must also know how to foster desirable changes in them.

For the required understanding one naturally turns to the scientists and scholars who have made the study of human beings their concern. It is evident at once that there are many different classes of investigators interested in the exploration of human nature and that no one type of expert has a monopoly on knowledge about man. Each kind of investigator sees man from a particular perspective. Each is well equipped to elucidate certain aspects or dimensions of what human beings are.

Physicists and chemists usually do not study man as such. They usually assume that he is part of the general matter-energy system of nature and that a person as a material structure conforms to the same physicochemical laws as rocks, plants, animals, and all other existing things. However, some physical scientists hold that the phenomena of mind, which are not found in developed form except in man, need to be considered even within natural science in order to explain the observed nonrandom organization of energy in the natural world.

Biologists consider man as one species of animal, the most highly developed of all forms of living things within the evolutionary sequence. They draw attention especially to the extraordinary adaptive powers of Homo sapiens that result from the extensive elaboration of his nervous system.

Psychologists divide into two principal groups in their view of human nature. One group, oriented toward the biologists, concentrates on the physiological, chemical, and neurological structures and functions required to explain human behavior. The other group approaches the study of man from the standpoint of his inwardly perceived mental states, using such concepts as consciousness, intention, purpose, value, choice, and the like. Both kinds of psychologists see man as an organism with mind. They differ in the ways in which they interpret the meaning of mind and the data they use to explicate it.

Sociologists and social psychologists see man as a social animal, and they describe and try to explain the many patterns of social organization and transformation that human beings exhibit.

Economists describe man as a producer and consumer of material goods and services, with wants that always outrun resources, and hence, with the need to invent social mechanisms for the allocation of the limited resources.

Political scientists see man as a seeker after power or influence, and they describe the many ways, such as force, reason, propaganda, threats and promises, and economic and social pressures, in which people influence and are influenced by one another.

Anthropologists describe the many types of human beings, with regard to both physical characteristics and cultural patterns. They study the varieties of languages, customs, beliefs, rituals, laws, and forms of social organizations that man has developed. They see human beings as having certain basic biological and social needs which are satisfied in a great many different ways, according to the circumstances of environment and historical development.

Linguists view man in his distinctive capacity for speech. They describe the many different ways human beings have invented to communicate with one another, and they analyze the formal patterns that characterize the languages of mankind.

Geographers study man in relation to his earth habitat. They show how human behavior is conditioned by such factors as climate, food supply, ease of transportation, distribution of natural resources, and population.

For the most part, the natural and social scientists are concerned with describing the distinctive behavior of classes or kinds of human beings, rather than of individual persons. They are also not generally concerned with the inner or subjective life of man except as a means of explaining observed behavior. Other groups of experts on human nature are interested in understanding man more directly from the inside, as it were.

Artists see man as a being with a rich and variegated life of feeling, and they attempt to objectify the most significant kinds of human feelings through various types of works of art, including musical compositions, paintings, sculptures, buildings, dances, poems, plays, and novels. Artists also regard man as a creative agent, and they exemplify the range and power of human creativity through their own works.

Biographers set forth the unique individuality of the person, showing how, through the interplay of many factors, a singular life develops toward its particular consummation.

Moralists portray man as a moral agent, with a consciousness of right and wrong. They see him as free and responsible, fashioning his own destiny through a continuing series of moral decisions. They describe the great moral visions of mankind, by the light of which the way of each person is illuminated and judged.

Historians see man as a being living in time, with memory of the past, anticipation of the future, and the freedom of a creative present in which both past and future meet. They try to understand the real meaning of past events by imaginatively reconstructing the conscious life of the persons who brought these events to pass.

Theologians regard man as dependent for his being upon God and as having a spiritual nature rendering him capable of

entering into relationship with the divine. They believe that
human beings possess the power of infinite self-transcendence,
living in nature but also able by virtue of imagination to look
upon natural existence from a transcendent standpoint.

Thus, men of knowledge investigate human nature using a
variety of methods and from a great many different perspectives.
The natural scientists, by and large, are interested in types of
observable human behavior, and they refer to the inner life of man
chiefly to render the outer phenomena intelligible. The humanistic scholars, on the other hand, are more immediately concerned
with the inner life, and they consider the outer conditions of
existence mainly as the background and context for understanding
the particular forms of subjectivity. Yet all the different groups of
investigators are concerned with the same human reality. What,
then, is man?

It is the special task of the philosophers to attempt a comprehensive interpretation of human nature, incorporating and coordinating the work of inquirers from other scholarly specialties
with the results of their own reflection. A comprehensive view,
first of all, must allow for the many-sidedness of man. Man is
everything the various special inquiries show him to be: He is a
complex energy-system; an intelligent adaptive organism with
highly developed neurophysiological mechanisms and the power
to perceive, think, and purpose; an organized social animal with
demands for goods and power that need intelligent allocation; a
maker of culture and a user of language; a being who lives in a
natural and social environment with which he must cope; a
creature of feeling and a creator of interesting forms to objectify
them; a unique self; a doer and judge of good and evil; a dweller
in time, who remembers, anticipates, and celebrates deeds done;
a creature of God partaking of the divine nature through the
power of boundless self-transcendence.

Is this all the philosopher can say of man, that he is the sum
of all the things that specialists say of him? Is there any unifying
idea of human nature of which the experts' testimonies are partial
aspects? A classic philosophical answer is that man is a rational
animal, that his unique property is the ability to reason, that his
distinctive quality is in the life of mind. According to this view,

each of the aspects of man described by the various specialists is a manifestation of the life of mind. Even as a matter and energy system, man is of a peculiar sort, determined by the power of thought. His organic adaptations are based on thought. His social and cultural forms are expressions of reason. His arts, his individuality, his morality, his history, his worship—all are embodiments of reason. This power of thought distinguishes man from everything else in the creation. In human nature reason is of the essence.

This philosophical answer suffers from the limitation that such ideas as rationality, reason, and mind tend to be too narrowly construed as referring to the processes of logical thinking. The life of feeling, conscience, imagination, and other processes that are not rational in the strict sense are excluded by such a construction, and the idea of man as a rational animal in the traditional sense is accordingly rejected for being too one-sided.

This difficulty can be avoided by using a unifying concept that expresses the broader connotations of the idea of reason. The concept proposed is *meaning*. This term is intended to express the full range of connotations of reason or mind. Thus, there are different meanings contained in activities of organic adjustment, in perception, in logical thinking, in social organization, in speech, in artistic creation, in self-awareness, in purposive decision, in moral judgment, in the consciousness of time, and in the activity of worship. All these distinctive human functions are varieties of meaning, and all of them together—along with others that might be described—comprise the life of meaning, which is the essence of the life of man.

The proposed philosophic answer to the question about the nature of man, then, is that humans are beings that discover, create, and express meanings. Moreover, human meanings extend across a broad spectrum, encompassing all the unique qualities of mind described by the scientists and scholars who study human nature.

The import of this fundamental concept may be made clearer by explaining four dimensions of meaning.

The first dimension is that of *experience*. A meaning is an experience, in the sense that it pertains to human consciousness.

It refers to the inner life, or the life of mind. This inner life has the peculiar quality of *reflectiveness,* or self-awareness. Automatic reaction to environmental stimuli is not the characteristic human mode of response. The unique human response is one in which the person is aware of his responding. He acts consciously rather than mechanically. As the psychologists say, thought is a "mediating process" intervening between stimulus and response. Reflective mediation is the basis of meaning.

As a reflective experience, meaning presupposes a basic principle of duality, or of self-transcendence. In self-consciousness a person both is himself and yet, so to speak, stands outside himself. He is at one and the same time both subject and object, knower and known, agent and patient, observer and observed. This duality is what enables a person to *know* anything at all. One knows something if he is at one and the same time distinct from and identified with what he knows. All perception of relationships is based on this duality. A relationship is identity-in-difference: two things are united in the one act of consciousness in order that their nonidentity may also be recognized.

All the varieties of human meaning exemplify this self-transcendence. It is the secret of man's unique adaptability. Because of it he can make judgments of truth and falsity, of beauty and ugliness, of right and wrong, of holiness and profanity; he can predict and control events, use tools, create interesting objects, make laws, organize socially, know the past, and project purposes. In short, this inherently dual quality of experience is the source of all that is characteristically human.

Since meanings are experiences in the inner life, the humanistic scholars give a more intuitively acceptable picture of essential human nature than do the scientific interpreters, for whom the inner life is inference rather than testimony and direct objectification. However, both are valuable and mutually corrective sources of knowledge about man. Direct readings of the inner life need to be checked against inferences from observable behavior, and the outward manifestations need to be humanized and individualized by recognition of the inner sources from which they spring. No matter which method of study is adopted, the objective is the same, namely, to understand the inner life that is the center and substance of human existence and from which all distinctively human actions spring.

The second dimension of meaning is *rule, logic,* or *principle.* The many types of meaning are distinguished from one another by some difference in characteristic form. Each type of meaning has its own rule that makes it one kind of meaning and not another. Each is defined by a particular logic or structural principle. Meaning is not an undifferentiated experience of awareness. Consciousness is differentiated into a variegated array of logical types.

Intention meanings follow a different rule from memory meanings. Social meanings have a different logic from artistic meanings. Moral meanings are based on a different formation principle from language meanings. Similarly, each item in the long, or perhaps even interminable, list of evidences of human mentality has its particular defining characteristics.

The third dimension of meaning is *selective elaboration.* Theoretically there is no limit to the varieties of meaning. Different principles of meaning formation can be devised ad infinitum. New combinations and nuances of rule can be imagined without limit. Not all of these possible kinds are humanly important. From the endless variety selection occurs. The types that are significant in actual human life are the ones that have an inherent power of growth and lead to the elaboration of the enduring traditions of civilization. These are the kinds of meaning that have proven fruitful in the development of the cultural heritage.

One could, of course, attempt an a priori analysis of possible classes of meaning and attempt to forecast which would prove most fertile. It seems far better, however, to benefit from the long experience of mankind and to regard as most significant the forms of meaning that have actually demonstrated their fecundity.

These selected types of meaning that have been elaborated into the traditions of civilization can be identified by means of the classes of specialists who serve as the guardians, refiners, and critics of the cultural heritage. These specialists consist of the scientists, scholars, savants, or "wise men" who are recognized as the authoritative interpreters of the human inheritance. Each of these men of knowledge belongs to a community that is for the most part invisible, comprised of persons bound together by common responsibility for a particular kind of meaning. Each such community has its characteristic discipline or rule by which the common responsibility is discharged. This discipline expresses the particular logic of the meaning in question.

Thus, the kinds of meaning that have been selected for their proven capacity for elaboration are to be found by reference to the world of disciplined scholarship. Each type of meaning that has demonstrated generative power is the special province of a company of experts who make the preservation and advancement of that sort of meaning their professional business.

And so for the elucidation of meaning we return to the same source to which we turned for knowledge of human nature. Earlier we asked what these men of knowledge knew about man. Now we ask more broadly what the men of knowledge know. What the wise ones know are meanings, and the varieties of productive meanings correspond to the varieties of scholarly disciplines. The operative kinds of meanings are revealed in the work of linguists, mathematicians, scientists of various types, artist-critics, moralists, historians, theologians, and philosophers, who together inhabit the world of scholarship.

It should not be assumed, of course, that the universe of meanings is exhausted by the particular collection of meanings that have been elaborated in any given civilization at any given stage in its history and that are represented by a corresponding collection of scholarly disciplines. Meanings wax and wane, as do the disciplines responsible for them. On this account, any conclusions drawn about man and his meanings on the basis of actual cultural elaborations must be regarded at tentative and incomplete.

The fourth dimension of meaning is *expression*. Meanings that have civilizing power are communicable. They are not private property. The communication of meanings takes place through symbols. Symbols are objects that stand for meanings. The possibility of symbolization is dependent on the unique human power of self-transcendence, for the dual quality of reflective awareness is required to understand a symbol. The essence of a symbol is that it is both identified with its referent and distinguished from it. For example, the word symbol "tree" is not a tree, and yet by the power of thought the symbol stands for a tree. Symbolization also presupposes self-transcendence in the awareness of a common world, for the symbols are taken as having the same or similar connotation to oneself as to others into whose being one imaginatively projects oneself.

The symbolic expressions of meaning are of particular concern to the communities of scholars representing the various types of meaning. Each kind of meaning has its distinctive expressions, the symbolic forms of each corresponding to the peculiar rule or logic of the type. The symbols of the disciplines are essential to scholars for analyzing, criticizing, and elaborating their domains of meaning.

Summarizing, these are the four dimensions of meaning: the experience of reflective self-consciousness, the logical principles by which this experience is patterned, the selective elaboration of these patterns into productive traditions represented by scholarly disciplines, and the expression of these patterns by means of appropriate symbolic forms. These dimensions all pertain to the idea of meaning and help to explicate it.

If the essence of human nature is in the life of meaning, then the proper aim of education is to promote the growth of meaning. To fulfill this aim, the educator needs to understand the kinds of meaning that have proven effective in the development of civilization and to construct the curriculum of studies on the basis of these meanings.

In order to simplify this task of curriculum planning it is necessary to divide the many scholarly disciplines into broad categories so that a balanced allocation of studies may be made. There is no single basis of categorization that any body of material forces on the investigator. Classifications are to some extent arbitrary, depending on the uses for which they are intended. Since the purpose of classifying meanings in education is to facilitate learning, it is desirable to organize the disciplines along lines of general similarity of logical structure. In this manner certain basic ways of knowing can be described, and these may be used to allocate studies for general education, that is, for the education of persons in their essential humanness.

A study of the logical patterns of the disciplines shows that they may be divided into nine generic classes on the basis of logical structure. This can be demonstrated as follows: Every cognitive meaning has two logical aspects, namely, *quantity* and *quality*. That is to say, knowledge consists in a relation of the knower to some range of things known, and each such relation is of some kind. Now there are three degrees of quantity: *singular, general,* and *comprehensive.* That is, knowledge is either of one thing, of a selected plurality, or of a totality. Furthermore, there are three distinct qualities of meaning, which can be designated as *fact, form,* and *norm.* In other words, the meanings may refer to what actually exists, to imagined possibilities, or to what ought to be.

The nine generic classes of meaning are obtained by pairing the three quantity aspects with the three quality aspects in all possible combinations. Each of the nine classes may now be briefly characterized and associated with the discipline or disciplines to which it applies.

1. *General form.* This class includes the disciplines that are concerned with the elaboration of formal patterns for general application in the expression of meanings. They comprise the various symbol systems of ordinary language, of mathematics and logic, and of gesture, ritual, and other nondiscursive symbolic conventions. Together they constitute the realm designated "symbolics."

2. *General fact.* When general forms are related to actuality, they express the kind of knowledge that is the special province of the sciences. These disciplines, designated by the term "empirics," are concerned with material truth expressed in the general laws and theories of the actual world as studied in the natural and social sciences.

3. *Singular form.* This class includes meanings perceived in imagination, without any necessary reference to actual fact, and as embodied in unique particular objects. This class of meanings is basic to the various arts and is designated by the term "esthetics."

4. *Singular fact.* These meanings arise out of concrete existence in direct personal encounter. They are reflectively elaborated and expressed in existential philosophy, religion, and psychology,

and in those parts of the literary enterprise designed to portray the uniquely personal dimensions of existence. Individual psychology and the various types of individual psychotherapy, counseling, and guidance also aim at an understanding of singular fact. All these disciplines, or parts of disciplines, may be designated by the term "synnoetics."

5. *Singular norm.* This class comprises particular moral obligations within a given situation where one seeks for knowledge of what he really ought to do. The discipline of morals is concerned with the methods of making and justifying such decisions.

6. *General norm.* Generalizations concerning moral conduct and the development of moral principles are usually assigned to the discipline of ethics. Knowledge of singular norms and knowledge of general norms are commonly associated closely since the latter is appealed to in justification of the former, and the former is considered as the necessary source for the latter. Both singular and general norms are distinguished by the quality of obligation, setting them apart from both facts and formal conventions or constructs. While the ethical realm is not commonly divided into constituent disciplines, such a division is possible for theoretical analysis. For example, the methods and categories of social ethics differ from those of personal ethics, and each of these domains may be divided into ethical disciplines dealing with decisions in various aspects of life, such as family, business, intellectual pursuits, technology, and political affairs.

7. *Comprehensive fact.* The study of actuality from a comprehensive standpoint, including both the singularity of the unique event and the relationships of that event with other events, is the province of the discipline of history. The historian integrates symbolic, empirical, esthetic, and ethical meanings into a synoptic perspective on what happened in the past.

8. *Comprehensive norm.* When all kinds of knowledge are comprehended within a synoptic perspective controlled by the normative quality, the resulting discipline is religion. Religious knowledge is regarded as an apprehension of the Ultimate Good —a Harmony of the Whole, a Complete Truth—that is not contained in any of the more limited ways of knowing. Religious knowledge is usually thought to require an act of faith by which

a total commitment is made to whatever is regarded as ultimately worthy of devotion. In this essentially normative act all the various classes of knowledge are synthesized.

9. *Comprehensive form.* A formal consideration of knowledge in all its kinds belongs to the discipline of philosophy. The philosopher's task is to interpret meanings in any realm or discipline by the use of concepts of wide generality, thus affording a synoptic view of all the ways of knowing.

In the present analysis the two normative classes will be treated together under the category designated "ethics" and the three comprehensive classes will be treated together under the category designated "synoptics," thus yielding six realms of meaning. The resulting logical classification of meanings is summarized as follows:

Logical Classification of Meanings

Generic classes		Realms of meaning	Disciplines
Quantity	*Quality*		
General	Form	Symbolics	Ordinary language, mathematics, nondiscursive symbolic forms
General	Fact	Empirics	Physical sciences, life sciences, psychology, social sciences
Singular	Form	Esthetics	Music, visual arts, arts of movement, literature
Singular	Fact	Synnoetics	Philosophy, psychology, literature, religion, in their existential aspects
Singular	Norm	Ethics	The varied special areas of moral and ethical concern
General	Norm		
Comprehensive	Fact	Synoptics	History
Comprehensive	Norm		Religion
Comprehensive	Form		Philosophy

It is evident that disciplines are not always clearly assignable to a single realm of meaning. Some disciplines have inner tensions that incline some scholars working in them toward one logic of meaning and other scholars toward another. Part of the confusion in the social sciences is due to the fact that some social scientists are committed to a rigorously empirical program, while others believe they should also be concerned with ethical meanings. Some psychologists incline toward the synnoetic realm in their concern for individuals in their subjective life, while others hold to a strong empirical line. Historians likewise differ as to whether their discipline belongs in the empirical social sciences or in the synoptic class with philosophy.

In this chapter we have attempted to show the intimate connection between education, the nature of man, and the scholarly disciplines. Education can only be conducted effectively on the basis of knowledge about human nature in its actuality and possibilities. A survey of the relevant fields of scholarship shows that there are many different critical perspectives on man. A working philosophical synthesis of these different perspectives may be achieved by modifying the classic formula that man is a rational animal to read that man is an animal that can have meanings. The variegated content of meaning is contained in the various distinctive aspects of human nature exhibited by the many specialized studies of man.

Analysis shows that the meanings by which human nature is defined are conscious experiences with structural principles, some of which prove capable of elaboration as cultural traditions with corresponding symbolic expressions. These traditions of significant meaning may be found in the most refined and articulate form in the various scholarly disciplines. For purposes of education these disciplines may be assigned to six basic logical classes, or realms of meaning, indicating the general kinds of understanding a person must have if he is to function well within the civilized community. The purpose of the present study is to explicate these ways of knowing and to show how they may be used in the curriculum of general education.

3

MEANINGLESSNESS
AND MODERN MAN

The meanings that constitute the proper content of human experience do not appear automatically by a process of natural growth and development. The singular quality of human life is a product of deliberate nurture. It is not a gift of nature; it is a creation of culture. This is another way of saying that meaningful human life is necessarily social. It is only through the educative power of human community that genuine persons are brought into being.

Regrettably, however, society and culture are by no means perfect. Nor are human beings necessarily responsive to whatever beneficent influences are brought to bear on them. People both resist and deny meanings and seek and affirm them, and cultures both destroy meanings and create them. Moreover, quite apart from individual or social threats to meaning, the perfection of human life is limited by the finitude of human existence. Because men are fallible, weak, and mortal, no person can experience in his lifetime more than an infinitesimal fraction of possible meanings.

The educator, therefore, needs to understand human life as a complex of meanings and to know what the various realms of

30

meaning are. He also needs to be aware of the enemies of meaning that arise within the human situation and to organize instruction in such a way as to overcome or minimize the threatened meaninglessness.

The present chapter describes some of the evidences of the modern sense of meaninglessness in various phases of cultural life. The picture presented here is deliberately one-sided. In the next chapter some evidences of a contrary tendency—toward the creation, affirmation, and preservation of meaning—will be presented. The largely negative paragraphs below should be read with this intended contrast in view, as a background and foil for the description of positive factors to be presented subsequently.

A great deal of attention is devoted by contemporary writers to the loss of meaning. The Viennese psychotherapist Viktor Frankl holds that the secret of all worthwhile human existence is found in meaning and that the basic cause of human deterioration is loss of meaning. He has devised a system of treatment called "logotherapy," the aim of which is to restore meaning to those who have lost hope and faith in the value of life. In this way he seeks to renew the courage to struggle for right and to endure whatever suffering is entailed by the accidents of fortune and the malice and ignorance of men.

Paul Tillich also sees meaninglessness as an important fact of modern life. In *The Courage to Be* [1] he describes the human condition as one of inescapable anxiety. He finds three principal sources of anxiety. The first, ontological anxiety, arises from the fact of human finitude. Man is anxious because he knows he must die, and all the particular fears besetting him participate in the final horror of annihilation that they symbolize and foreshadow. The second is the anxiety resulting from guilt. Man is anxious because he knows himself to be a transgressor. Consciously or unconsciously, he is aware of having violated the moral law. Do what he will, says Tillich, one can never wholly eradicate the uneasy conscience. The third anxiety is that in which man sees himself threatened by meaninglessness. He is beset with doubts no arguments can dispel, and he asks questions to which

[1] Yale University Press, New Haven, Conn., 1952.

he can find no answers and which only lead to deeper perplexities and paradoxes.

Tillich believes that while anxieties are inherent in human existence, they are intensified in periods of transformation when one era of human history is giving place to another. Moreover, the dominant character of the anxiety differs from era to era. Thus, Tillich finds that the end of the classical period in Western civilization was dominated by ontological anxiety—the fear of death—as evidenced, for example, in the Mystery religions and in Christianity by the preoccupation with immortality and resurrection. The end of the medieval period was characterized by moral anxiety, as evidenced by the concern for forgiveness and atonement in the penitential system of the Church and in the spiritual agonies of the great Reformers. The modern period, which now appears to be ending and giving way to a new "post-modern" epoch, is a time dominated by the anxiety of meaninglessness, revealed in a pervasive skepticism, relativism, aimlessness, and feeling of futility.

All three kinds of anxiety are, however, interfused in every age, including the present. Death is feared because it nullifies the meaning of life and ultimately renders every hope illusory and all striving useless. Guilt also robs existence of meaning because under its burden one cannot accept himself, and the springs of action are poisoned by a bad conscience.

This theme of meaninglessness in contemporary life has been consistently sounded in recent decades by the Existentialists. They believe that the old certainties and securities are gone, and they bid mankind give up the vain hope of progress fostered by the technical successes of science. They point to the ever-mounting social, political, and economic crises as eloquent witness to the impotence of reason in matters of genuine human significance. They see no complete cure for anxiety, no prospect for finally ending human suffering, no reasonable hope for universal safety and peace. Man's life is absurd, they say, since his natural longings and expectations are forever doomed to remain unsatisfied. According to many Existentialists, there is no answer to this human predicament. Through the power of courage, one can only go on affirming one's own being in spite of dread and nausea, creating one's own values out of nothing, and proceeding step by step through the enveloping darkness by acts of defiant and desperate decision.

For the most part the Existentialists' posture is one of general disillusionment, and the meaninglessness of which they speak so eloquently is largely undefined and undifferentiated. To make the description of modern man's situation more specific, it may be helpful to analyze the phenomenon of general meaninglessness along the lines laid down in the preceding chapter. It can be shown that each of the kinds of meaning earlier discussed is threatened by a corresponding kind of meaninglessness. In every realm of meaning there is also a realm of meaninglessness. If any progress in restoring meaning is to be made, it is necessary to distinguish these different domains. Contrary to the Existentialists, it will be our theme that durable meanings can be found and that the obstacles to meaning can be overcome when the realms of possible meaning and the conditions for their realization are well enough understood. But now let us consider briefly some of the threats to fulfillment in each of the realms of meaning in turn.

Meaning is threatened in the domain of language by the fact of ambiguity. Rarely does language convey to the hearer the meanings the speaker intends. Sincere, serious, and well-informed people are all too often unable to reach common understanding. Even professionals skilled in discourse and devoted to the Socratic ideal seem to make little progress toward secure wisdom by their discussions. In this age of propaganda it has become apparent how easily language can be used as an instrument of power rather than as a channel for truth. Battered by a barrage of words creating incompatible responses, modern man has become cynical about language itself. Flooded by a ceaseless outpouring of symbols through the mass media of communication, language has tended to become a debased currency with little relation to real values and ineffective in the creation of genuine community.

In mathematics and science, strongholds of rational demonstration and experimental proof, modern developments have also brought once secure meanings into question. The axioms of mathematics are no longer regarded as self-evident truths but as arbitrary bases for defining postulate systems, an endless variety of which can be invented. The clockwork simplicity and order of the Newtonian world have been replaced by a universe without absolute space and time, but only relations between space-time events. Statistical probabilities have replaced certainties, and even the principle of causal determination has been radically questioned. Critical scrutiny of scientific knowledge has made untenable the view that science discloses the world as it actually is and has substituted for this naïve realism a variety of operational, instrumental, and constructionist views that recognize the place of arbitrary human activity and purposes in the making of science. Science is thus no longer considered the source of complete and demonstrable truth, but as a system of convenient hypotheses, valid only within specified limits and continually subject to reconstruction in the light of new experience.

In the realm of esthetics the crisis in meaning is evident on every hand. Traditional standards have been widely discredited and many artists have declared their independence of all the conventions of the past. The result, as Richard Weaver and others have argued, is a disintegration of art caused by the destruction of a settled and accepted world for the artist to portray. To most people not belonging to the novelty-hungry and iconoclastic avant-garde, much modern art discloses only the morbidity, confusion, inanity, or plain incompetence of the artist, whether in drama, literature, music, painting, architecture, or dance. Art has become increasingly alienated from the common life, and many artists have reacted against popular hostility and misunderstanding, withdrawing into tight, self-justifying cliques. Inherent in all this confusion and separation is the widespread suspicion that art may not express anything but the private feelings of the artist and that works of art have no universal, permanent, or objective meaning.

In wide areas of modern life the meaning of personal relatedness has disappeared from view. People feel isolated and estranged from nature, from themselves, from one another, and from the ultimate sources of their being. The depersonalization and collectivization of life is far advanced. The plundering of natural resources, the destruction of living things, and the manipulation of human beings are widely practiced. Love has been displaced by lust, loyalty by expedient self-interest, devotion by avarice, responsibility by the unbridled pursuit of power, and reverence by self-sufficient autonomy. Mutual respect and trust have given way to warfare between nations and classes, personal animosity, and suspicion and cynicism regarding the possibilities of building stable and harmonious personal relationships.

Moral meanings also fare badly in the modern world. Pragmatists convincingly wage war on moral absolutes. Positivists deny any cognitive significance to moral assertions, regarding them as expressions of feeling and as disguised commands or means of persuasion. Anthropologists demonstrate the variety of moral codes in the cultures of mankind and usually disapprove of making value judgments about different ways of life. No one appears able to demonstrate the validity of any particular moral injunction so as to convince anyone not already committed to it. Allegedly universal principles seem to reveal more exceptions than rules, and moral obligations are seen as only particular personal expedients within unique specific situations. In short, contemporary life is pervaded by doubts about the basis for moral commitment, and by skepticism as to the possibility of reliable meaning in the ethical realm.

Finally, synoptic meanings are nowadays under sustained attack. Historians, acknowledging the inevitable bias of their interpretations and the limited evidence at their disposal, no longer claim to know what really happened in the past. Despite the revival of grand speculations about the total plan of history by Arnold Toynbee and other neo-Augustinian philosophers of history, the dominant mood is that of Crane Brinton, who heralds the age of "multanimity" and the demise of unanimity, and that of Herbert Muller, for whom the lesson of history is that in the final analysis there is no final analysis. Despite a recent resurgence in popular appeal, religion no longer inspires the serene faith of earlier times. Friedrich Nietzsche proclaimed that God is dead, and millions the world over believe he spoke truly. Doubt is potent even (or perhaps especially) among theologians, for whom belief wins out in the end only by a desperate "leap of faith" into an apparent abyss of meaninglessness. Philosophers, too, generally eschew large speculations about the meaning of life and the nature of reality. Metaphysics is largely out of favor, having been displaced by the more modest and manageable concerns of logic and theory of knowledge, because to many it no longer seems profitable to attempt a comprehensive synoptic interpretation of human experience.

Thus, in all the major domains of meaning modern man is threatened with meaninglessness. If educators are to counter this threat successfully, they need some understanding of the factors in culture and society that are sources of the difficulty.

One of the prime enemies of meaning, the critical spirit, paradoxically also affords a major opportunity for growth in meaning. Doubt and criticism call old meanings into question. They destroy traditional assumptions and reveal the insufficiency of simple answers to profound problems. Such destruction of the old can open the way for new and deeper meanings. On the other hand, criticism may become an end in itself without any positive effort at reconstruction. In that event the critical spirit simply negates meaning. This nihilistic attitude is, in fact, a perversion and corruption of the experimental outlook, which has been one of the mainsprings of modern scientific progress.

Another cause of meaninglessness in the contemporary world is the growing mechanization and depersonalization of life. Man has become assimilated to the machine, and in the process has lost his identity as a person. He has merged with the mass in the anonymity of impersonal organization. He is valued not for himself, but only for his contribution to the efficiency of the social mechanism. Hannah Arendt, in *The Human Condition*,[2] has brilliantly analyzed this depersonalization as an inversion of the classical human ideal, according to which the contemplative, deliberative, and constructive powers were regarded as superior to the biological functions. Modern man, by contrast, has largely lost interest in contemplation, and enlists his political and creative activities in the service of material necessities. As a consequence, the person has been degraded into an *animal laborans*, chained to an endless cycle of production and consumption, lacking any of the authentic human meanings that belong to the thinker, the artist, and the free and responsible citizen of a genuine community.

An aspect of this depersonalization is the widespread frag-

---

[2] The University of Chicago Press, Chicago, 1958.

mentation of modern life. Advanced civilization depends upon a high degree of specialization. When productive efficiency is the chief goal of society, the valuable principle of specialization degenerates into mere division of labor with each worker performing relatively simple operations without reference to the meaning of the whole. Individuals thus become personally isolated, even though they are ostensibly connected with the organizational structure.

Just as the critical spirit is both an opportunity and a threat to meaning, so also may the wealth of possibilities of meaning in a complex culture become a cause of meaninglessness. Modern man is presented with an enormous number and range of possible experiences. Our civilization is exceedingly complex, and makes demands that no one can expect to satisfy fully. The limited skills required in earlier societies no longer suffice for life in a complicated industrial civilization. Knowledge proliferates at such a rate that even specialists cannot keep abreast of everything being learned in their own fields. Moreover, they can acquire no more than the most partial acquaintance with what takes place in other fields of inquiry.

In the face of this hyperabundance of culture and the profusion of related problems, modern man feels frustrated and impotent. He is presented with more stimuli than he can possibly cope with and more experiential material than he is able effectively to organize and assimilate. Becoming bewildered and distracted, he tries to escape from the unmanageable multiplicity by taking refuge in more highly specialized activities, and he abandons hope of finding any coherence among the fragments of experience which he undergoes. In this way the consequence of cultural affluence is to reinforce the trend toward meaninglessness inherent in the depersonalization and fragmentation of life previously described.

One further significant factor in adding to the meaninglessness confronting modern man is the rapid changes taking place in every sphere of life. Transformations in the content and conditions of experience make life unsettled and precarious. Nowadays the world in which the average person dies is vastly different from the world in which he was born. Few traditions remain as unchallenged points of reference. Rarely are there settled orders around which a person can organize his hopes and expectations. Change is the only certainty, and transience pervades everything. These upheavals are a constant source of anxiety and insecurity. They diminish the value ascribed to anything that now exists, in view of the probability that it will soon be superseded. The meanings that enrich human life are found in abiding patterns persisting through time and change. It is the constant and the permanent that help to overcome the anxiety of meaninglessness. It is for this reason that the transience of modern life presents such a threat to meaning.

In this chapter we have pointed to the enemies of meaning in each of the domains of distinctively human understanding—in language, in science, in the arts, in personal relations, in morals, and in history, religion, and philosophy. We have also considered some of the factors contributing to modern man's loss of meaning in all these fields: the critical spirit, depersonalization and frag-mentation, cultural hyperabundance and congestion, and the drastic changefulness of the contemporary world.

The fact of meaninglessness presents a challenge to education to contribute to the restoration of meaning. This challenge can be met. The way lies in recognizing the centrality of meaning in human life and in creating a curriculum deliberately designed to overcome the prevalent forces of meaninglessness. This design calls for the use of instructional materials drawn from the organized disciplines of learning in which dedicated experts make progress toward significant understanding, tested by shared professional criteria of validity and excellence. As a humanizer of this knowl-edge, the educator is called upon to gain and communicate effec-tive understanding of the characteristic ideas and modes of think-ing in the various disciplines and to invent imaginative ways of mediating these fundamental patterns of meaning to his students.

4

THE SEARCH
FOR MEANING

The attacks on meaning described in the last chapter have not been without countervailing influences. Recent decades have also witnessed a sustained and many-sided search for meaning, the results of which are providing the basis for a renewal of modern man and for an educational program in which human possibilities can be amply fulfilled. Thinkers with widely different interests and orientations are converging in a remarkable way on the problem of meaning and are opening up new channels of understanding having profound influence both on professional practices and on currents of popular thought.

In 1923 C. K. Ogden and I. A. Richards published *The Meaning of Meaning,* [1] a work that has since become a classic in the field of the interpretation of language. These scholars demonstrated the widespread confusion regarding the meaning of "meaning," and they sought by systematic analysis to discard meaningless conceptions and to make proper distinctions among valid modes of interpretation. They discussed and evaluated sixteen major definitions of meaning, and formulated a new theory of signs in which the functions of language were reduced to two,

[1] Harcourt, Brace & World, Inc., New York, 1923.

namely, the referential and the emotive. By such a distinction the authors hoped to strike a decisive blow at superstition, obscurantism, and "word magic," and to provide a comprehensive, contextual, and functional basis for the whole range of language meanings. While it is doubtful whether this division of language functions into the two types—of referential and emotive meanings —does justice to the full range of meanings, there is no doubt about Ogden and Richards' contribution to a revival of concern for meaning and the stimulus they provided in this and later works to the serious study of the varieties of symbolic forms.

The most widely publicized recent movement in the field of language meaning is semantics. Alfred Korzybski's *Science and Sanity* [2] became the bible of the General Semanticists, who promised solutions to the most vexing problems of mankind through a scientific reconstruction of linguistic meanings. Charles Morris in his *Foundations of the Theory of Signs* [3] developed "semiotics," which was subdivided into the fields of "semantics," "pragmatics," and "syntactics." Popularizers of semantics, including Stuart Chase and S. I. Hayakawa, brought to the attention of the general public some knowledge of the pitfalls of language and of the methods available for the improvement of verbal communication.

Another group of investigators for whom the problems of meaning are fundamental are the analytic philosophers. These philosophers owe their inspiration to such thinkers as G. E. Moore, Bertrand Russell, and Ludwig Wittgenstein, and their movement currently dominates professional philosophy in England and America. Unlike Existentialists, who are concerned with the "meaning of life" and the problems of selfhood and decision, analytic philosophers undertake the detailed critical scrutiny of various modes of human discourse. In their earlier years the analysts were most interested in the pure constructive languages of logic, mathematics, and natural science. More recently, they have become preoccupied with the problems of ordinary language and have tried to show how most of the traditional philosophical

[2] 3d ed., International Non-Aristotelian Library Publishing Co., Lakeville, Conn., 1948.

[3] The University of Chicago Press, Chicago, 1938.

puzzles have been created by philosophers themselves in using concepts without reference to their generally accepted meanings-in-use.

Perhaps the greatest contribution of the analytic philosophers is their personal witness to the importance of meaning and their faith in the possibility of making meanings clear. Furthermore, they have shown that meanings are of different logical orders, which cannot all be subsumed under one type. By this demonstration they have countered the positivistic position limiting all meanings to those of logic, mathematics, and science, and have reaffirmed the possibility of many distinct modes of thought, each valid in its own sphere and justified by its specific human uses.

This recent philosophic emphasis on distinct logical orders of meaning and on the clarification of human understanding by the analysis of the actual uses of symbols is basic to the philosophy of curriculum set forth in these pages. While the method of treatment used herein is not predominantly that of the language analysts, the present work presupposes a similar commitment to the exposition of meanings-in-use and parallel conclusions as to the multiple patterns of human signification.

Ernst Cassirer, using methods quite different from those of the language analysts, has also established the principle of distinct logical orders of meaning. In his great *Philosophy of Symbolic Forms* [4] and his briefer *Essay on Man* [5] Cassirer shows that the characteristic mark of human activity is the creation and transformation of symbols. The whole world of human meanings, he says, is expressed in the several kinds of symbolic forms contained in such diverse fields as myth, ritual, language, art, history, mathematics, and science. Each of the types of symbolic forms has its unique and legitimate human functions. For example, ritual communicates orders of experience not expressed in speech, and the arts present meanings different in kind from those of the sciences and inexpressible in the categories of empirical description. Each symbolic form has its appropriate field of application,

[4] Yale University Press, New Haven, Conn., vol. 1, (1953); vol. 2, (1955); vol. 3, (1957).

[5] Yale University Press, New Haven, Conn., 1944.

and, though it has relationships with other systems, is not wholly reducible to any other form.

The search for symbolic meaning inherent in semantics and linguistic analysis and comprehensively outlined by Cassirer is paralleled by the inquiries into meaning in each of the other realms of human understanding. Thanks to the labors of philosophers, historians of science, and scientists reflecting on their own enterprise, both the nature of science and its limitations are becoming increasingly clear. Investigators as diverse as James Byrant Conant, Alfred North Whitehead, Bertrand Russell, Percy Bridgman, Rudolph Carnap, Stephen Toulmin, and Ernest Nagel, to name but a few, have critically examined the methods and assumptions of science, showing with precision what scientific knowledge is and what it is not. They have demonstrated the validity and the scope of scientific methods and have defined the terms in which empirical descriptions and theoretical explanations are to be interpreted.

In esthetics, too, new exponents of meaning have appeared. Against the criticisms of modern art by those who hold that the classical motifs are the only meaningful ones, and more particularly, that visual art should be representational and music should be limited to the traditional melodies and harmonies, critics like Clive Bell, Roger Fry, Igor Stravinsky, and Roger Sessions have made a strong case for a more generous conception of artistic import. Under the banner of "significant form," those who defend modern art against the charge of meaninglessness have pointed to the wider possibilities of esthetic expression provided by the new artistic forms.

Susanne Langer, taking her lead from Ernst Cassirer, whose general theme she popularized in her book, *Philosophy in a New Key,* [6] makes a particularly cogent case for the distinctively esthetic mode of understanding. She denies that a work of art is only an expression of the artist's personal feelings and argues that artistic import has its characteristic logical forms. She insists that significance is not limited to the literal meanings of factual statements, but extends also to the art symbols objectifying the patterns of feeling found in man's inner life.

[6] Penguin Books, Baltimore, 1948.

In the literary arts the renewed concern for meaning is manifest in the New Criticism in the work of men such as Edmund Wilson, William Empson, W. K. Wimsatt, Jr., John Crowe Ransom, and Ronald S. Crane. In this movement the earlier dependence of literary interpretation on psychology, philology, history, and sociology has been overcome and a fresh recognition of the uniquely literary modes of understanding has been achieved.

Turning next to the synnoetic realm, substantial progress is being made in the articulation and interpretation of personal meanings. Psychoanalysis, though grounded in the identification of unconscious and irrational factors, is primarily aimed at bringing these subterranean forces under the scrutiny and control of reason. What appear as meaningless dreams and fantasies and as inexplicable actions are shown by analysis to be symbols of unconscious meanings. These hidden meanings often reflect disturbances in relationships with other persons and in evaluations of the self. Improvement of relations with others and self may then follow the recognition of unacceptable emotional patterns and understanding of their causes.

Many different systems are employed for the revelation and clarification of these personal meanings. Sigmund Freud and his followers emphasize infant sexuality and the Oedipus complex. C. G. Jung and his school analyze the interplay of inferiority and superiority feelings. Therapists in the line of Alfred Adler find important clues to behavior in the problems of infantile dependence and the struggle for power. The approach used by Harry Stack Sullivan and his colleagues is to analyze patterns of interpersonal relations, particularly with the "significant persons" in association with whom early self-appraisals are formed. In contrast to the early analysts who regarded the period of infancy as all-important in the development of emotional life, many present-day therapists place as much or more emphasis upon experiences beyond infancy. They concern themselves directly with present behavior patterns instead of tracing everything back to the first few months or years of life.

Others, besides psychotherapists, have joined in the search for meaning in selfhood and in human relationships. The concept of personal meaning is especially important to the Existentialists.

As Paul Tillich points out, preoccupation with meaninglessness is itself evidence of a passionate concern for meaning. Rejecting the idea of the subconscious from depth psychology, Jean Paul Sartre proposes a scheme of "existential psychoanalysis," which consists of a thoroughgoing introspective analysis of the content of consciousness aimed at eliminating the self-deceptions by which one tries to avoid responsibility for his own authentic existence. Karl Jaspers, more concerned than Sartre with relationships beyond the self, finds the "way to wisdom" in the will to unlimited communication, and protests against the depersonalized mass culture that has lost faith in "Transcendence," the source of all true selfhood. Martin Buber discovers the source of truly human meaning in the "I-Thou" relation, which he contrasts with the impersonal, manipulative, objectifying "I-It" type of relation. In the act of turning from the personal emptiness of the I-It to the loving, community-creating affirmation of I-Thou, Buber believes the secret of a meaningful life may be found.

Contemporary literature provides further vivid evidence of modern man's search for synnoetic meaning. While typologically poetry, the novel, and drama are art forms communicating esthetic meanings, they can also be powerful expressions of concern for selfhood and for community among persons. In various ways such diverse writers as W. H. Auden, T. S. Eliot, William Faulkner, James Joyce, Franz Kafka, André Malraux, Thomas Mann, Eugene O'Neill, J. D. Salinger, and Tennessee Williams portray some of the deepest concerns of human beings—a concern that in its very seriousness reveals a profound faith in the potential meaningfulness of personal existence, even under conditions that seem to deny all meaning and value to life.

In the realm of ethics, subjectivism and skepticism regarding meaning are encountering strong opposition. Anthropologists are more disposed than they once were to recognize the universality of some moral principles, despite the relativity of laws and customs in the cultures of mankind. Social scientists are taking the normative aspects of human behavior more seriously than before and some are even beginning to assert that it is the proper business of the scientist not only to describe what *is* but also to investigate what *ought* to be. Leading jurists like Justice Brandeis have led jurisprudence away from literalistic interpretations of the legal tradition toward a view of law as an expression of standards for the good life in a dynamic society. Such thinkers are making increasingly clear the dependence of a meaningful social order upon moral principles rather than mere custom and tradition, and they emphasize the need for continual reexamination of laws in the light of these principles.

These developments are complemented by certain trends in ethical theory. Philosophers are largely agreed, as David Hume long ago decisively argued, that an "ought" can never be derived from an "is," i.e., that values are of a different logical order from facts. While this insight exposes the futility of trying to establish morality as an empirical science, and thus contradicts certain of the assumptions implicit in the efforts to develop a scientific ethic, it does support the autonomy of morals and prepares the way for the discovery of distinctively moral meanings. G. E. Moore, in his classic *Principia Ethica,*[7] presents a realistic theory of morals, refuting the "naturalistic fallacy" inherent in every attempt (as in egoism, hedonism, utilitarianism, voluntarism, and supernaturalism) to define "good" by reference to any matters of fact (such as interest, pleasure, utility, or the will of man or God). Later philosophic analysts, including R. M. Hare, Stephen Toulmin, and P. H. Nowell-Smith, though generally rejecting Moore's intuitionism, take seriously the principle of the autonomy of the moral realm and continue to make valuable contributions to the clarification and illumination of moral meanings.

The search for meaning in the synoptic disciplines is also yielding encouraging results. In the discipline of history, nineteenth-century scientific historians had been confident that the historian could strictly present the facts about what really happened in the past. In reaction against this reduction of history to empirical science, the subsequent Historicist movement emphasized the personal, irrational, and contingent factors in historical judgments, thus bringing into question the possibility of any reliable historical knowledge. More recently, the possibility of genuine historical understanding has once again been affirmed,

[7] Cambridge University Press, New York, 1959.

on a broader basis than that of the scientific historians. For example, R. G. Collingwood sees history as a reconstruction of past events—what must have happened—on the basis of an imaginative identification with the thought of the persons who decided the events. Herbert Butterfield, too, holds that in a larger sense than the scientific historians thought, the historian can discover what actually happened by an act of sympathetic understanding in which the historian divests himself of his preconceptions and enters into the life of the past on its own terms.

In religion theologians continue the pursuit of ultimate meanings with great vigor. Having successfully weathered the crises of faith caused by the higher criticism of the Bible, the theory of evolution, and the comparative study of religions, religious thinkers are endeavoring to assess the claims of faith in the light of new developments in knowledge and the social order. Protestant thinkers such as Karl Barth, H. Richard Niebuhr, Paul Tillich, and Rudolph Bultmann are reformulating the doctrine of revelation so as to establish an autonomous logic of religious understanding. Roman Catholic thinkers (e.g., Jacques Maritain and Etienne Gilson) offer contemporary versions of Thomistic theology, reaffirming the common sense meanings of Classical Realism within a dual framework of Natural and Revealed Theology. Interpreters of Jewish thought in all three of the leading traditions—Orthodox, Conservative, and Reform—are working out ways of making Judaism a relevant and meaningful way of life and thought in the modern world. One of the most impressive signs of the contemporary search for meaning is this development of religious thought which is taking place, despite all the forces of secularization, not only in the various branches of Christianity and Judaism, but also in Islam, Buddhism, Hinduism, and many smaller syncretistic and theosophical sects.

In philosophy, mention has already been made of the signal contribution to the recovery and expansion of meaning made in quite different directions by the logical analysts and the Existentialists. Metaphysics is recovering from the crushing blows administered by logical empiricism and pragmatism. Even some analytic philosophers are now saying that metaphysical statements may be something more than nonsense. A few adventurous spirits, most notably Alfred North Whitehead, have dared to attempt new cosmological schemes after the manner of the great system-builders of the past. In these efforts the possibility of attaining a synthesis of meanings through a comprehensive interpretation of experience is once again affirmed.

The aim of the foregoing summary sketch of some twentieth-century movements reflecting modern man's search for meaning has been twofold: first, to show that the forces of skepticism, frustration, and confusion in present-day life have by no means won the day, and second, to suggest some of the kinds of resources available for the construction of a meaningful philosophy of general education.

It is further important to relate that in the development of curricula for the schools, much work has been done since World War II on instructional materials in a number of the academic disciplines. These efforts were stimulated initially by the pressures for more efficient education to meet the urgent demands for trained manpower in an ever more tightly organized technical society geared to the needs of national defense. Mathematics was the first discipline in which radical renovations of teaching materials took place. Sweeping changes soon followed in physics, chemistry, and biology, and these were joined by economics, English, and foreign languages. Geographers, historians, anthropologists, and other specialists also have undertaken studies and discussions concerned with revisions in their teaching materials. Although the reconstructions in all these fields have been aimed chiefly at the secondary school, they have not been without effect on the curriculum at the elementary and college levels, since they represent fresh perspectives on the subjects of study themselves, regardless of the level.

These current curriculum revisions are actually more than responses to pressures for educated manpower. They belong to the general movement toward deeper and more secure meanings, aspects of which have been indicated in earlier paragraphs. Evidence for this statement lies in the fact that the new programs of instruction are not simply rearrangements of old materials, nor mere substitutions of up-to-date for out-of-date information. They are based on a complete reconsideration of the distinctive characteristics of the several disciplines in regard to content, methods, and basic concepts, and on a study of the methods for effective teaching and learning of these fundamental meanings. It is noteworthy, too, that the new teaching materials are not being produced either by the professionals in education alone or only by scholars in the academic disciplines. In a manner worthy of a serious effort to reach basic understandings, they are an outcome of the cooperative work of scholars, teachers, and curriculum specialists.

The objective of the present study is to provide a comprehensive orientation to the search for meaning in the curriculum, uniting in one coherent account the various strands both from the general thought movements of our time and from the studies going forward in the various disciplines. From the analysis of human nature and meaning outlined in this and the two preceding chapters, the major features of a philosophy of the curriculum for general education emerge.

A human being is in essence a creature who creates, discovers, enjoys, perceives, and acts on meanings. These meanings are of six general kinds: symbolic, empirical, esthetic, synnoetic, ethical, and synoptic, corresponding respectively to the distinctive human functions of expressing and communicating, describing, making and perceiving significant objects, entering into relations, deciding between right and wrong, and comprehending integrally. Each of these realms is defined by a certain general logic of meaning. Within each realm there are special fields of study, each defined by its own subject matter, typical concepts, and methods of inquiry. Yet all these exhibit the general logic of the realm to which they belong.

These special fields are designated as the various disciplines in which the authoritative systematic study of meanings by communities of experts is carried on. Disciplines are assigned to the various realms on the basis of the general logical type of meaning they exhibit. Thus, analysis of how linguists and mathematicians know shows that they share the general logical features of the realm of symbolics. Similarly, the work of physicists, biologists, psychologists, sociologists, economists, and other scientists shows certain common features permitting all to be grouped within the empirical realm, despite their many differences in detailed methods and concepts. The various different artistic enterprises may be grouped together within the esthetic category of meaning, and history, religion, and philosophy, for all their contrasts, still share a common synoptic role. The case of synnoetics and ethics is less clear because the disciplined pursuit of meanings in these realms is not organized as definitely along distinct professional lines, but is carried on by special groups of experts from other disciplines, such as psychology, literature, and religion. However, these expert contributions, though differing in detail, have the same basic logic within each realm, of relational intuition or normative judgment, as the case may be.

A philosophy of the curriculum based on meaning is thus constructed by ascertaining the essential distinct logical types of human meaning, as exhibited by the successful fields of disciplined inquiry. The next task is to analyze each of the disciplines so as to exhibit its particular structure, organizing concepts, and methods.

In this manner the entire range of basic meanings may be charted, and the structures and interrelationships of the various realms and disciplines within each realm may be comprehensively viewed. Such an understanding of the fundamental patterns of meaning enables the educator to make a successful attack on the various sources of frustration in learning, such as fragmentation, surfeit, and transience of knowledge, by showing what kinds of knowledge are required for full understanding and how the essential elements may be distinguished from the unessential ones in the selection of instructional materials. In this fashion the curriculum may become a means for the realization of the distinctively human potentialities.

Part Two

Fundamental

Patterns of Meaning

Introduction to Part Two

Chapters 5 through 20 are devoted to an exposition of the fundamental patterns of disciplined understanding. Before entering upon these chapters it is important that the reader be entirely clear about their intended purpose, so that he may understand what they are and are not designed to convey.

The chapters in Part Two are intended to show that the various fields of knowledge exhibit distinctive structures or patterns of meaning and to indicate the nature of these characteristic designs in the basic disciplines of general education. The main questions to be answered in each case are: What does it mean to know in this discipline? How is knowledge gained in this subject, and how is it validated? How does knowledge in this discipline differ from and agree with knowledge in other disciplines?

The aim of these expositions is to describe the characteristic *logic* of each discipline. Each has a particular outlook, style of thinking, and organization of ideas. These logical patterns have been developed by experts in the course of inquiries in the areas of their specialized competence. The purpose of the interpretations below is to outline these logical patterns in the main disciplines of knowledge, insofar as they are relevant to the education of any person, rather than to the education of the specialist alone. This aim presupposes that each of the fundamental disciplines, no matter how technical it may be at the advanced levels, is pertinent to every person as a person, and therefore that it is possible to present its humanly significant leading ideas for general educational use. The teacher's task as a mediator of knowledge is to humanize the disciplines, by showing that knowledge in each of its various kinds has meaning for all rather than for an exclusive group of professionals.

Each discipline examined in the chapters of Part Two will be analyzed along four main lines. First, the *general logical character* of the field will be examined with respect to the patterns of meaning characteristic of the realm to which it belongs. This analysis will afford a justification for the classification of disciplines according to the sixfold scheme adopted in this work.

Second, the distinctive *subject matter* of the discipline will be described, in answer to such questions as these: What is the object of knowledge in language, in physical science, in the dance, in ethics, and in history? What kinds or aspects of things, actions, or attitudes are typical of the discipline in question? What is knowledge in the discipline *of* or *about?*

The third line of analysis will be to indicate the *representative ideas* of each discipline. These are the ideas that best express the essential character of the discipline. They are the conceptual tools used for pursuing inquiries in it. They comprise the scheme of categories by which the meanings in the discipline are symbolized, making it possible to interpret the significance of the field within the total framework of meanings. (Certain of the more important representative ideas are indicated in the text by means of italics.)

The fourth element in the exposition will be the *methods of inquiry* used in the disciplines, both for creating new knowledge and for validating claims to knowledge. Questions like these will be considered: How does the investigator go about making discoveries in mathematics, in biology, in personal understanding, or in religion? How can one test affirmations made in these disciplines?

The characteristic ideas and methods of a discipline are not all of equal importance. Some apply to the whole subject, while others apply only to certain aspects or divisions of it. Some yield profound insight into the nature of the discipline, while others are of less significance. Knowing the *structure* of a discipline means in part being able to order its ideas according to their relative range of application and degree of depth. The analyses to follow are intended to give some sense of the relative precedence of organizing ideas within each discipline.

This structural-methodological-conceptual analysis of the disciplines is designed to illustrate and give substance to the philosophy of curriculum foreshadowed in Part One and developed in greater detail in Part Three. Part Two should be read with this purpose in mind. Its justification is chiefly to point to the kinds of material required for the program of effective teaching and learning advocated in this book.

What is intended by the expositions in Part Two can be made even clearer by the following recital of contrasts.

First, these chapters do not constitute a concise outline of modern knowledge! They are, rather, intended as analytic interpretations of typical patterns of knowledge for the guidance of pedagogy.

Second, the aim in this part is not to provide popularizations of technical materials. Rather, the goal is to give some sense of the ways of thinking actually used by professionals in the disciplines, but for purposes of the mediation and humanization of knowledge.

Third, these chapters are not introductions to knowledge in the various disciplines considered. A person knowing nothing about a particular discipline could learn little about it by reading the appropriate chapter below. The discussions in this book presuppose that the reader already has some knowledge of the subjects discussed. The analyses are meant to give perspective on prior knowledge, highlighting certain features and showing relationships and characteristic patterns that might not have been discerned in the ordinary course of piecemeal learning.

Fourth, the discussions are not statements of what everyone ought to know in the various disciplines. They do not set forth the lowest common denominators of understanding—the minimum that anyone who claims any acquaintance with the disciplines should have mastered. The expositions are not intended to be taken quantitatively, to increase information, but qualitatively, to show how inquiry proceeds in the fundamental disciplines of learning.

Fifth, the chapters are not summaries of what is known in the disciplines discussed. To try to summarize any of the disciplines within the compass of a few pages would be futile and confusing. Rather, the aim is to epitomize the disciplines, indicating by judicious choice of ideas those features that yield insight into important modes of thought.

Sixth, the intention here is not even primarily to indicate the recommended content of instruction. The organizing concepts, structures, and methods are guides for the selection of materials, so that what is taught may be as meaningful as possible. If the educator is to choose teaching methods and contents so as to achieve maximum learning effect, he needs such guides to help him distinguish between what goes to the heart of his subject and what is relatively incidental to it.

Seventh, the delineations of the various disciplines are not complete, either with respect to basic concepts or with respect to the range of disciplines discussed. The discussions are only illustrative of outlook and method. Other significant ideas could be added and other disciplines could be described. All that is attempted here is to present the main patterns of a representative group of fundamental subjects of inquiry.

Eighth, the descriptions are in no way final and definitive. Disciplines undergo changes in concepts, methods, and even to some extent in the kinds of knowledge contained in them. What is offered here are provisional statements based on the state of the various disciplines at one time and in one cultural setting.

Finally, the presentations are not to be construed as authoritative. Insofar as authoritative analyses could be obtained at all, considering how much experts differ concerning the main ideas of their disciplines, these statements would have to come from specialists themselves. The following analyses are based on studies by authorities, but these authoritative sources have necessarily been selected and analyzed by the present author, writing from the standpoint of a philosopher of education for the purpose of illustrating a certain theory of the curriculum. The descriptions are therefore interpretations of the various disciplines, in the light of a philosophy centered around the concept of meaning.

To avoid misunderstandings and to assure the most effective application of these ideas to educational practice, the foregoing considerations should be kept in mind while reading the following chapters on the fundamental patterns of meaning.

THE FIRST REALM: *Symbolics*

5

ORDINARY LANGUAGE

The realm designated "symbolics" is characterized by arbitrary symbolic structures exhibiting certain customary rules of construction and interpretation. There are three main subdivisions within this realm, namely, ordinary language, mathematics, and nondiscursive symbolic forms. This chapter deals with the first of the subdivisions. The other two are treated in the next two chapters.

By the term "ordinary language" is meant the forms of discourse employed in everyday speech and writing. Technical languages, deliberately created for special purposes and not following the generally recognized conventions of speech, are not included. Examples of such excluded languages are the codes designed to conceal information from unauthorized persons and those symbol systems (as used in the sciences and professions) that are unintelligible except to initiates of a particular group of specialists.

There are, of course, many ordinary languages. The variegated peoples of the world can be classified into language groups, membership in which is defined by the ability to communicate intelligibly with the other members of the group. The ordinary languages of mankind include English, French, German, Spanish, Hebrew, Greek, Russian, Chinese, Japanese, Hindi, Sanskrit,

Arabic, and Swahili (to name only some of the widely used modern languages), and a multitude of languages and dialects used by smaller localized groups. The scientific study of these many languages belongs to the disciplines of linguistics, philology, and anthropology. It is the task of a philosophy of language in education to give a general account of what it means to know any language and of the major methods and concepts useful in the teaching and learning of any language.

What does it mean to say that a person knows a language? It means that he is able to use meaningful symbols for communication. Accordingly, knowledge of a language comprises four elements: *use, meaning, symbol,* and *communication,* each of which deserves careful attention.

The test of a person's knowledge of a language is whether or not he can use it. Though he may be able to speak words and recite grammatical rules, if he cannot actually organize the words into intelligible discourse, he does not really understand the language. Language is a form of human behavior, and language teaching is a mode of modifying human behavior. The sovereign rule in teaching it is to demonstrate language in use and to develop correct habits of speech by reinforcing desirable speech behavior. One can learn a language only by *speaking* it, never by simply talking *about* it. Therefore, carefully guided practice and sustained confrontation with situations in which the learner needs to use the language are essential to good language instruction.

The objective of using language is *communication.* Language is a binding force in society. It is a means of establishing human relationships. Through language, communities are created and sustained. The strongest motive for learning language is the primordial urge to belong to a community. Perhaps the deepest of all human needs is to be understood and accepted by others. Such relationships are also the very ground of a person's own selfhood. A language is best learned through participation in a community whose basis of association is that language. Hence, it is important to provide the language student with opportunities to participate actively in the life of groups who use only the language he seeks to learn.

Language behavior and the language community are, so to

speak, the outer face of language. The inner face is *meaning*. The unique mark of being human, as pointed out in earlier chapters, is the capacity for experiencing meanings. Language is not merely a system of signals to which a properly conditioned organism automatically responds. It contains meanings. Ideation intervenes between word and act. Speech is therefore not primarily a stimulus to direct action. Its content is an inner experience of meanings to which the person's deeds are related. It follows that a person knows a language only if he understands its meanings, and not if he merely responds automatically to verbal signals. Human beings are not parrots, and any language teaching that is simply devised to train the students to exhibit approved language behavior without benefit of reflective understanding misses the mark. Speech is an intellectual, not a mechanical, activity. It is not a skill to be learned as one would master a manual technique. For this reason, verbal dexterity should never be cultivated as an independent and self-justifying skill, but always with a view to increasing understanding and facilitating activity based on reflection.

The meaning-content of language is expressed by *symbols,* which comprise another of the outer faces of language. These symbols are spoken sounds or written marks that convey the meanings to be communicated. They are physical entities serving as tokens of intellectual signification. The symbols of a language in relation to the meanings to be expressed constitute its *vocabulary.*

The meaning-contents and the symbol-expressions of each language have certain characteristic *structures.* Knowledge of a language means having a working familiarity with these patterns of symbol and meaning. Language study is primarily a formal discipline in which the typical patterns of discourse are mastered. Because language has this orderliness, it is possible to explain and predict speech behavior and to engage in the activity of communication with a high degree of security and confidence of success.

The subject matter of language is, then, *the formal structures of symbols by which meanings are expressed.* The forms employed are not given in nature, but are cultural constructs. Different languages reflect different ways of organizing experience, and these differences have their bases in the varying histories, environmental settings, and genetic equipments of the populations among whom

the languages develop. That is to say, different life-situations make
for different kinds of communities and hence for different symbol-
systems for communicating meanings.

Ordinary languages are "natural" in contrast to the "artificial" languages of some technical fields, in the sense that they are
products of the natural history of groups of people. They are not
"natural" in the same way as rocks and trees are, because languages
are human inventions. In this sense language is essentially *arbitrary*. Its forms are matters of social convention, and its patterns
accordingly vary from one community of discourse to another.

Despite the infinite variety of possible symbolic systems,
there is another sense in which language is not completely arbitrary. Language is an instrument for communicating meanings
within a common real world, which is given, not simply invented.
Symbols must therefore be devised so as to be adequate to the
needs and purposes of communities in this real world. It follows
that all successful ordinary languages must in some degree correspond to the given realities of the world and of common experience. They are not purely arbitrary creations of human imagination. They are social conventions developed for the purpose of
effectively sharing life within the world as it actually is and for
projecting common activity toward what is possible.

While ordinary language thus presupposes a fund of common
understandings about the world and a body of shareable experiences, the distinctive feature of language as such is not the structure of these understandings and experiences, which belong to the
other realms of meaning to be discussed, but the structure of the
conventional symbolic systems devised to express all meanings that
can be communicated discursively.

Having given an answer to the question of subject matter in
language study, we may add a word about the characteristic
methods of gaining knowledge of language. From our description
of what language is, it is evident that the chief method of acquiring
knowledge of a language is to observe its use in the daily life of the
speaking community and to acquire skill in using it through actual
participation in the common life. But such learning through observation and participation may be facilitated by the analysis of
the patterns of language. Such analysis requires the use of a

number of key concepts for directing and interpreting the observation and participant activity of the learner. In the science of linguistics these concepts are given technical names and are systematically treated in a manner that is quite unnecessary for the ordinary student of language. Nevertheless, efficient mastery of a language follows from attention to these leading ideas, even though they may not be explicitly articulated as a trained linguist would do.

Any language can be analyzed into a series of distinct sound-elements called "phonemes." Actually each phoneme is a limited class of similar sounds distributed according to certain patterns characteristic of the language or dialect in question. By careful study of actual speech behavior, the scientific linguist is able to discover which sounds function in the sound-system of the language in the same way, and these classes of similar sounds constitute the phonemes. The phonemes include stress, intonation, transition, and terminal indicators as well as consonant and vowel sounds. One linguist, H. A. Gleason, Jr., identifies forty-six phonemes in spoken English. [1] An understanding (preferably conscious and deliberate) of the phonemic pattern is essential to the mastery of a language.

The elemental sound-system differs from language to language. One cannot simply apply the phonemes of one language to another tongue. When such an attempt is made, the new language is not spoken correctly, but with a "foreign accent." The point to be stressed is that the sounds of a language are not isolated and separable units; they are components of an entire pattern of sounds characteristic of that one language and incommensurable with the sound-system of any other language. Hence, one cannot learn a new language properly by redeploying the sounds of another language. Each language must be studied on its own terms as an integral, self-contained structure.

Written language has its own special set of visual elements called "graphemes." Graphemes are classes of similar marks, each of which functions in an identical way in the language. Written language is to some extent independent of spoken language, de-

[1] *An Introduction to Descriptive Linguistics,* rev. ed., Holt, Rinehart and Winston, Inc., New York, 1955, chaps. 2–4.

spite the important structural similarities between what are generally referred to as the written and spoken forms of the same language. An important phase of language learning is to gain an understanding of the relation of the spoken to the written version of a language, with due recognition of the inability of the customary graphic forms to do full justice to the richness of the spoken tongue.

Another way of analyzing the structure of a language is by a study of the elemental units of meaning. The name given by linguists to a unit of meaning is "morpheme." As in the case of phonemes and graphemes, morphemes are classes of variant expressions that perform the same meaning function. For example, the three different suffix sounds in the words "dogs," "ducks," and "ditches" all function in the same way, namely, as means of expressing plurality, and thus belong to the same morpheme class. Morphemes, like phonemes, are patterned in characteristic fashion for each language, but unlike phonemes, the number of morphemes in each language is indefinitely large—as numerous as are the distinct meanings to be expressed.

The principal types of morphemes in all languages are *roots* and *affixes* (mainly prefixes and suffixes). Thus, "play," "run," and "send" are one class of roots, and "boy," "ball," and "world" are another class of roots. "-s," "-ed," and "-ing," on the other hand, are suffixes, and "re-," "pre-," and "in-" are prefixes. Roots are the most fundamental units of meaning, being modified by affixes to build up more complex expressions.

Important as the elements of sound and meaning are, they do not constitute the essence of speech. That essence consists in the regular patterns into which the elements of sound and meaning are organized. The study of the meaningful forms of speech is called "grammar," and this study may be divided into (1) "morphology," which deals chiefly with the more intimate combinations of morphemes, designated as "words," and (2) "syntax," which concerns the larger combinations, such as phrases, clauses, and sentences.

In traditional morphology words have generally been classified on the basis of their *meaning* into "parts of speech." This approach has the disadvantage that the lines between the various parts of speech so defined—nouns, verbs, adjectives, adverbs, and so on—cannot be clearly drawn. As Edward Sapir points out, [2] these conventional classes of words are only a vague approximation of the way experience is actually organized. Furthermore, since any scheme for parts of speech turns out to be different from language to language, these concepts are not characteristic of language as such.

Following the principle that the essence of language is structure, modern linguists are abandoning meaning as the basis of word classification and are using structural relationships instead. The ultimate goal of language study is, of course, the understanding of meaning. What is now becoming clear is that meanings depend on structure rather than structures on meaning, and therefore that meaning is best served by concentrating attention on grammatical structure.

A structural definition of English parts of speech, instead of using meaning-classes like "nouns for things," "verbs for actions," "adjectives for qualities," and so on, divides words into *paradigmatic classes* and *syntactic classes*. There are four paradigm classes defined by four typical morphological patterns: *nouns* comprise words with two distinct forms-in-use, e.g., (man, men), (boy, boys); *personal pronouns* comprise words with four forms-in-use, e.g., (I, me, my, mine), (he, him, his, his); *verbs* comprise words with five forms-in-use, e.g., (do, does, did, done, doing), (play, plays, played, played, playing); *adjectives* comprise words with three forms-in-use, e.g., (good, better, best), (red, redder, reddest). The other English parts of speech, such as adverbs, prepositions, and conjunctions, differ from the paradigmatic classes in not undergoing inflection. They are defined by means of syntactic classes, each of which is comprised of all words which play comparable roles in the organization of the larger syntactic structures (phrases, sentences, etc.).

It should be emphasized that paradigmatic classes differ from language to language in the types and numbers of inflections and in the combination rules by which morphemes are organized into larger patterns. Much harm has been done in the academic study

---

[2] *Language,* Harcourt, Brace & World, Inc., New York, 1921, pp. 116–119.

of English by the attempt to force English grammar into the Latin grammatical mold. Such mistakes can be avoided if the structural uniqueness and integrity of each language are duly recognized.

Syntax, like morphology, is concerned with functional classes, that is, with typical conventional patterns for the expression of meaning. The analysis of sentences and their component parts may be accomplished by developing a hierarchy of *constituent classes* (with subclasses and sub-subclasses) based upon characteristic construction patterns. Constituent classes are composed of members which differ in content but whose formal relationships are alike. Two constituents belong to the same class if one can be substituted for the other in any utterance without making the utterance either nonsensical or different in kind. That is to say, syntactical analysis is a matter of discovering the various rules for combining expressive elements into structures of successively higher orders of complexity.

In syntax, as in morphology, the primacy of structure in the expression of meaning is evident. Dictionary definitions are by no means the sole clues to meaning. Meanings are also communicated by the grammatical structure. In many cases the meaning of a word can be better understood by reference to the context in which it is used than by consulting a dictionary. Words have different meanings in different contexts. It follows that the meaning of a whole utterance is not simply the sum of the meanings of its component elements. The meaning is in the complete utterance, and the meanings of the several elements in the composite are dependent on their relation to the whole.

Every language has its own special devices for indicating grammatical structure. In addition to word order and constituent class membership, which apply to all languages and are by far the most important syntactic markers, other related devices are used, including *function words* (e.g., articles and prepositions in English), *government* (e.g., cases for nouns), *concord* (e.g., agreement between noun and adjective or between subject and verb), and *stress* and *intonation indicators* (e.g., rising terminal inflection for a question, falling inflection to conclude a statement).

Our chief purpose here is not to describe the actual grammatical structures of any particular language or languages. That is the subject of the large, complex, and technical subject of descriptive linguistics. The purpose of the present brief analysis of language is to draw attention to the *kind* of understanding a person has when he knows a language. That is to say, we are interested in the logical status of language as a realm of meaning.

Analysis shows that every language includes the following three components: (1) basic sound or visual elements; (2) elements of meaning [including (*a*) concrete concepts referring to objects, actions, and qualities, usually expressed by roots; (*b*) abstract relational concepts, expressed by affixes, inner modification of roots, independent words, or position; and (*c*) a range of concepts intermediate between the purely concrete and the purely abstract relational types] [3]; and (3) characteristic structural devices for organizing the meaning-elements into complex expressive patterns. To "know" a language is to have a working understanding of all three components: sound pattern, conceptual elements, and structural principles. By "working understanding" is meant the ability to use sounds (or visual symbols), concepts, and grammatical devices in accordance with the accepted customs of the particular language community.

As noted earlier, "knowing a language" is not the same as "knowing about language." The former is practical, the latter theoretical. Linguistic theory may be helpful in learning a language, and every teacher of language should certainly be familiar with the fundamentals of linguistic science. Still, a person can know a language very well without the slightest knowledge of linguistics. His theoretical ignorance does not, however, mean that he lacks understanding of the sounds (or visual symbols), the concepts, and the grammatical structures of the language. It is in his intimate and practical comprehension of these components, *in use*, that his knowledge of the language consists.

Knowledge of language is knowledge of *particulars* with respect to the specific sounds, concepts (root and relational), and grammatical patterns that are unique to the given language. On the other hand, the knowledge is *general* in the sense that the sounds, meanings, and grammatical forms are all *classes* of similar

[3] *Ibid.*, chap. 5.

particulars. The adept in the language knows when any particular sound falls within the sound classes proper to the language. He knows the acceptable ways of categorizing experience in the language (both as to basic meaning-elements and as to inflectional modifications, e.g., number, gender, person, tense, mood, voice). He also knows the general patterns—the *kinds* of structures—into which sounds and concepts are supposed to be organized in that language.

A person can be said to know a language only to the extent that he has practical competence in both the particular and the general aspects mentioned above. It is not possible to know language in general. Language knowledge is always knowledge of particular languages (about which the linguist can make generalizations, laws, and theories). At the same time, knowledge of any particular language is not simply a collection of particular sounds and impressions. It is practical understanding of general patterns of sound, concept formation, and structural arrangement. These patterns are generalizations, laws, or rules that define the particular language. Other languages have different sets of such defining principles.

For an elementary philosophy of language, the heart of the matter is that ordinary language consists of *formal conventions,* not given in physical or biological nature, but created in the laboratory of culture in the course of the natural history of particular language communities. To learn a language is to master the formal symbolic systems by which the meanings of the particular community of discourse are expressed.

If it be objected that the foregoing account submerges the relation between language and experience in the real world in favor of an abstract formalism, it must be answered that the distinctive logic of language is in this very abstraction and that the forms of language are necessarily applied to the real world of experience. The abstractness of language is the source of its power to express an infinite variety of experiences and to represent the real world in all its depth and complexity. By this miracle of language the boundless world is opened to shared understanding.

6

MATHEMATICS

In the realms of meaning, mathematics keeps company with the languages. The reason for this classification is that mathematics, like the ordinary languages, is a collection of arbitrary symbolic systems. It will be a main goal of this chapter to elaborate and explain this assertion.

It was stated in the previous chapter that knowledge of ordinary language consists in the ability to use symbols to communicate meanings. While the same statement also holds for mathematics, there are significant differences in emphasis in the two cases. The uses of ordinary language are largely practical. Its symbolic systems exist for the most part to serve the everyday needs of communication. Mathematics is not primarily practical, nor is it created as a major basis for social cohesion. To be sure, mathematics has many uses, as its wide applications in science and technology demonstrate. But these practical uses are not of the essence of mathematics, as the social uses of ordinary discourse are. Mathematical symbolisms are essentially *theoretical*. They constitute a purely intellectual discipline, the forms of which are not determined by the exigencies of adjustment to nature and society.

Many students and teachers of mathematics never really understand the subject because they identify it with calculation for practical ends. Ordinary language is chiefly concerned with the community's adaptation to the actual world of things and people. Mathematics, on the other hand, has no such relation to tangible actuality. Mathematical symbolisms occupy an independent, self-contained world of thought. They need not stand for actual things or classes of actual things, as the symbols of ordinary language do. Mathematics occupies a world of its own. Its realm is that of "pure" symbolic forms, the applications of which, no matter how useful, are secondary and incidental to the essential symbolic meanings.

Another way of expressing the essence of mathematics is to say that it is a language of *complete abstraction*. Ordinary language is abstract, too, in the sense that its concepts refer to classes or kinds of things and that its conventional patterns are types of expression. But ordinary language is less abstract in the sense that it refers back to actual things, events, persons, and relations. Mathematics, having no necessary reference to actuality, is fully abstract. It is purely formal, without any necessary anchorage in the actual world. Interestingly, it is just this complete abstractness that makes possible the elaborate developments of mathematical systems, yielding in the long run the most practical applications.

Mathematics further differs from ordinary language in the usual nature of its symbolisms. The symbol-patterns of common discourse grow naturally out of the experience of the speaking community; for the most part they are not deliberately invented. Mathematical symbolisms, on the other hand, normally are *artificial,* in that they are freely and consciously adopted, constituting deliberate inventions or constructions. Any person may adopt arbitrarily and without reference to previous customary usage any symbolism that serves his formal purposes. It is only incumbent on any such innovator, if he wishes to be understood, that he indicate clearly the terms in which his symbolism is defined.

It follows that mathematical meanings are communicated effectively only to those who choose to become familiar with the symbolic constructions within particular mathematical systems. Mathematical communities thus tend to be specialized and limited rather than inclusive, like the major ordinary language communities. Mathematical languages are, so to speak, artificial dialects understood only by the members of special communities of voluntary initiates. Moreover, the natural ordinary languages are meant to express the whole range of common experiences, while the particular artificial symbolisms of mathematics express special and strictly limited conceptual relationships.

The symbolic systems of mathematics are designed to achieve complete *precision* in meaning and *rigor* in reasoning. Ordinary language, by contrast, growing informally out of the complex experiences of many persons and groups over long periods of time, is relatively vague and ambiguous, and ordinary reasoning is usually full of unexamined commonsense assumptions and inconsistencies. In fact, one of the two main purposes of using special symbols in mathematics is to avoid the imprecision of common speech. The other purpose is to provide symbols which can be more readily manipulated in reasoning processes than is possible using the symbols of common language. On the other hand, since mathematics *could* be done entirely with the symbols of ordinary discourse, with meticulous care in definition of terms, the usual artificial symbolism of mathematics is a convenient expedient and not a necessary feature of the discipline.

It was pointed out earlier that knowing ordinary language does not depend on knowing *about* it. The same does not hold for mathematics. In mathematics one really knows the subject only if he knows about the subject, that is, if he does his mathematics with self-conscious awareness, examining and justifying each step in his reasoning in the light of the canons of rigorous proof. This is why it is not enough to teach students of mathematics how to make calculations and demonstrations skillfully and automatically. Yet, facility in speaking is properly the primary purpose of ordinary language instruction. The student of mathematics can be said to know mathematically only if he understands and can articulate his reasons for each assertion he makes.

In one crucial respect mathematics is other and more than what is usually designated a language. Customarily the term "language" refers to a means of expression and communication using written or spoken symbols. Mathematics includes much more than this, namely, chains of logical reasoning. The subject matter of mathematics includes far more than the formal symbol-patterns. It is chiefly concerned with the transformation of the symbols in accordance with certain rules included in the definition of each particular system. The sovereign principle of all mathematical reasoning is *logical consistency*. By this is meant that the only admissible rules of transformation for mathematical symbols are those that do not entail contradictory propositions within any given system.

The subject matter of mathematics is, then, *formal (abstract) symbolic systems within which all possible propositions are consistent with each other*. Mathematical reasoning consists in the demonstration of relationships among the symbols of the system by means of *necessary inference:* in which each proposition (affirming some relation between symbols) must be shown to be logically entailed by one or more other propositions within the system. Mathematics is more than a language in that it adds to the patterns of symbolic expression the methods of deductive inference by which logically consistent relationships can be systematically elaborated.

Though mathematics is more than language in containing deductive reasoning, it is like language in respect to the indefinite plurality of its admissible symbolic systems. Contrary to what was once universally believed and is still a common misconception, mathematics is not a single system of ideas containing the "truths" of ordinary arithmetic, algebra, Euclidean geometry, the differential and integral calculus, and other subdivisions of the traditional mathematics curriculum. Just as there are many ordinary languages, each with its own patterns for conceptualizing experience and its characteristic ways of combining expressive elements into the larger structures of discourse, so any number of different mathematical systems can be constructed, each with its own pattern of basic elements and characteristic rules of transformation and each consistent within itself but independent of every other mathematical system. Accordingly, mathematics does not express "true" propositions in any absolute or empirical sense, as a statement of the way things really are, or of what is actually so. It does no more than reveal the consistency of propositions within any particular symbolic system. Mathematics does not yield knowledge of facts, which have to do with the contingent actualities of the world as it is, but only conclusions that follow by logical necessity from the premises defining each system.

Any number of self-consistent mathematical patterns can be defined and deductively elaborated. Thus, there are many geometries besides that of Euclid. In fact, the discovery of consistent geometries, such as those of Riemann and Lobachevsky, in which through any point outside a given straight line there are, respectively, no parallels or an infinity of parallels to the line, was a major step in the development of the modern understanding about the plurality of mathematical systems generally. Lest it be thought that such geometries are merely mathematical oddities without practical importance, it should be noted that the theory of relativity, which has played such an important role in the revolutionizing of modern physics and astronomy, shows that physical space-time and the laws of motion require non-Euclidean geometry for their formulation. Similarly, there are many algebras besides ordinary algebra. For example, it is possible to define consistent algebraic systems in which the relation $a \cdot b = b \cdot a$ does not always hold. Some such "noncommutative" algebras also are of great importance in their scientific applications.

The method of mathematics is essentially *postulational*. This means that certain postulates, or *axioms,* are arbitrarily chosen as part of the foundation of a given mathematical system. These postulates are not "self-evident truths," as, for example, the axioms of Euclidean geometry were formerly thought to be. They are assumptions taken as a starting point for the development of a chain of deductive inferences. All mathematical reasoning is of the form "if . . . then," where the "if" is followed by a postulate (or some necessary inference therefrom) and the "then" is followed by a conclusion, or a *theorem.* Neither the postulates nor the theorems deduced from them are either true or false. All that can be said of them is that if the mathematical reasoning has been done correctly, they are related in the manner of necessary implication.

Every mathematical system requires some *basis* of *undefined terms.* This basis, together with the postulates, constitutes what is called the "foundation" of the system. In any language undefined terms are necessary as a basis for defining other terms because the process of definition by reference to other terms cannot proceed indefinitely; somewhere it must come to rest in certain primitive terms that are not themselves defined. From the basis and the postulates theorems are deduced. The entire body of undefined terms, definitions, postulates, and theorems comprises a particular symbolic system, or a *theory*. Thus, from various bases and axioms various theories may be developed, such as *theory of groups, theory of numbers, theory of continuous functions, theory of infinite sets,* and *theory of complex variables,* to name only a few.

The meaning of "theory" in mathematics differs somewhat from its meaning in the empirical sciences, as the analysis in following chapters will show. In the sciences a theory usually refers to a general explanation for a group of related facts and generalizations. For example, in physics the behavior of gases is explained by the kinetic theory, and the facts of paleontology and comparative anatomy may be explained by the theory of evolution. In mathematics, on the other hand, theory is the whole body of symbolic content of a given postulational system.

Any mathematical theory can be defined by means of *sets*. A "set" is simply a class, family, or aggregate of abstract conceptual entities (*elements*) all of which have some common property or properties specified by the axioms upon which the theory is founded. Two sets, A and B, are said to be *equal* if they contain the same elements. A set B is called a "subset" of a set A if all of the elements of B are elements of A. The *sum* $(A + B)$ of two sets A and B is defined as the set containing all elements that are *either* in A *or* in B. The *product* $(A \cdot B)$ of two sets A and B is defined as the set containing all elements that are in *both* A *and* B. The *difference* $(A - B)$ of A and B is defined as the set consisting of all elements in A *and not* in B. The *Cartesian product* $(A \times B)$ of A and B is defined as the set of all *ordered pairs* of elements in A and B, that is, a set each of whose elements consists of a pair of elements one of which is an element of A and the other an element of B.

These ideas of elements, sets, equality, sum, product, and difference comprise basic terms from which all other mathematical concepts can be developed, provided certain basic logical concepts are also presupposed. These essential logical concepts include the following: "is a member of," "not," "all, or every," "such that," "there exists, or there is," "if . . . then," "or," and "and." The primitive materials (elements, sets, and their rules of combination) together with the elemental logical concepts constitute the basis for any mathematical theory.

Another concept of far-reaching importance in mathematics is that of *relation*. A "relation" is defined simply as a subset of the Cartesian product of two sets. It is a means of separating out certain pairs of elements from others. For example, if two sets A and B have elements (a_1, a_2, a_3) and (b_1, b_2, b_3) respectively, the Cartesian product is the set $A \times B$ with elements $[(a_1, b_1), (a_1, b_2), (a_1, b_3), (a_2, b_1), (a_2, b_2), \ldots, (b_1, a_1), (b_1, a_2) \ldots]$ covering all possible pair combinations. Any subset of $A \times B$, such as the set containing only the two elements $[(a_1, b_2), (a_3, b_1)]$, is then a particular relation on $A \times B$. The three-element subset $[(a_1, b_1), (a_2, b_2), (a_3, b_3)]$ is another and different relation.

A special case of a relation is a *function*, which is another concept of great importance in mathematics. A "function" is defined as a relation in which one and only one element in one set corresponds to any element in another set. For example, in the above illustration the first of the relations cited is not a function because no element of B is paired with a_2. The second relation is a function because a_1, a_2, and a_3 are each uniquely paired with an element of B. On the other hand, the relation $[(a_1, b_2), (a_1, b_3), (a_2, b_2), (a_3, b_1)]$ is not a function because a_1 is paired with two different elements of B. When the functional relation works both ways, so that to each element of A a unique element of B corresponds and vice versa, the relation is called "one-to-one correspondence."

Finally, the concept of *binary operation* on B by A to C is defined by the requirement that to each pair of elements in the Cartesian product of A and B a unique element of C corresponds (i.e., that C is a function of $A \times B$).

Returning to the similarity of mathematics to a language, or better, to a collection of languages, one can compare the undefined terms to the elements of sound and meaning upon which any given language is based, and the various rules of combination (sum, difference, product, relation, function, one-to-one correspondence, and binary operation) to the morphological and syntactic rules by which ordinary discourse is organized into an ordered hierarchy of expressions. The above fundamental combinatorial concepts are the grammar of mathematics. They designate the patterns according to which the deductive elaboration of any mathematical system (i.e., the drawing of successive inferences from primitive terms, definitions, and axioms) must proceed. [1]

The reason why the concept of *set* is so central in mathematics is that it embodies the principle of abstraction, which is the essence of mathematical thinking. A set is specified completely by the properties of the elements composing it. Those properties are abstractions since they define elements in these terms: "any entity such that. . . is an element of the set." The idea of *any such that* entails that particular things are not under consideration, but only *kinds* or *classes* of things. By means of this idea of abstraction the key mathematical concept of *variable* may be understood. A variable does not refer to something that moves or changes, as it would in ordinary speech. In mathematics a variable, designated, say, by the symbol x, is such that x stands for, or in the place of, any element of a specified set. Variables are simply ways of representing the general idea of *any* or *some* as contrasted with particular elements. For example, if the variable x belongs to the set of rational numbers (fractions) between 0 and 1, it represents the idea of *any or some rational number between 0 and 1.*

It will have been noted that such ideas as number, point, line, distance, and quantity, which in everyday thought are considered typically mathematical, have hardly been mentioned in the preceding account of mathematical knowledge. The reason is that such concepts (with the possible exception of number, which in some formulations is taken as primitive) are special and derivative in comparison with the very general and primary concepts used in the above analysis. The integers and the counting process, for example, can be defined by means of the theory of finite sets, and the rational and real numbers by the theory of infinite sets. Furthermore, Euclidean geometry and common algebra can be shown to be alternative interpretations of an identi-

---

[1] The above outline of the basic concepts in any mathematical theory largely follows the treatment given by R. B. Kershner and L. R. Wilcox, *The Anatomy of Mathematics,* The Ronald Press Company, New York, 1950 esp. chaps. 4–5.

cal theory of sets of real numbers (R). Thus, a "point" may be defined as an ordered pair of real numbers, and a "line" as a relation on (i.e., a subset of) the Cartesian product $(R \times R)$ of two real number sets. Similarly, the calculus and the theory of functions can be shown to follow directly from a general study of relations on $R \times R$, and the theory of complex numbers can be shown to result from the study of ordered pairs, combined according to the following rules: $(a, b) + (c, d) = [(a + b), (c + d)]$ and $(a, b) \cdot (c, d) = [(a \cdot c - b \cdot d), (a \cdot d + b \cdot c)]$.

Alfred North Whitehead called *form, variable,* and *generality* "a sort of mathematical trinity which preside over the whole subject," and he added that "they all really spring from the same root, namely from the abstract nature of the science." [2] We have already dwelt on the formal nature of mathematical systems and on the concept of variable. Some discussion is now needed about generality. The development of mathematical ideas is marked by a progressive increase in generality. The concept of number, for example, beginning with the positive integers, may be successively generalized to include zero and the negative integers, rational numbers (fractions), irrational numbers (like $\sqrt{2}$), real numbers (having a one-to-one correspondence with all the points on a line), complex numbers, vectors (directed magnitudes), and infinite (or transfinite) numbers.

In geometry the study of two-dimensional manifolds (defined by ordered pairs of numbers) can be generalized to three, four, or any higher number of dimensions by using ordered triples, quadruples, or generally, n-tuples (where n is any integer). Though such hyperspace geometries cannot be visualized, in the way that two- and three-dimensional configurations can be, they are nonetheless valid systems of geometry, which, incidentally, prove to have important applications in the sciences.

One of the ways in which generalization takes place in mathematics is in connection with the *transformation* of one set into another through what was earlier defined as a binary operation. In any such transformation certain relations remain unchanged,

---

[2] *An Introduction to Mathematics,* American rev. ed., Oxford University Press, Fair Lawn, N.J., 1948, p. 57.

or *invariant*. For example, Euclidean geometry is concerned with transformations that leave intervals and angles invariant, i.e., in which figures may be translated or rotated but not distorted. A more general geometry (*projective geometry*) is concerned with transformations (projections) that may alter intervals and angles but leave unchanged a quantity known as the "cross ratio." The most general geometry (*topology*) deals with transformations where the connectivity pattern of the subspaces is not changed (e.g., in three-dimensional space, where surfaces may be distorted but not cut or punctured).

To sum up, mathematics is a discipline in which formal symbolic systems are constructed by positing certain undefined terms (elements, sets, rules of combination), elaborating further concepts by definitions (conventions), adopting certain postulates (concerning both the undefined and the defined terms), and then, using the principles of logic, drawing necessary deductive inferences, resulting in an aggregate of propositions called "theorems." The propositions of mathematics are formal and abstract in that they do not necessarily refer to the structure of the actual world but comprise a series of purely abstract formalisms all having in common the one rule of logical consistency.

It is well known that mathematics is of great practical value in science and technology. However, the nature of the subject is misconstrued if it is regarded primarily as a "tool" subject. Technical skill in computation and the ability to use mathematics in scientific investigation, valuable as they may be, are not evidence of mathematical understanding. Such understanding consists in comprehending the method of complete logical abstraction and of drawing necessary conclusions from basic formal premises.

7

NONDISCURSIVE
SYMBOLIC FORMS

We come now to a third type of symbolisms that differ in function, and to a large extent in content, from ordinary languages and mathematics. While they vary among themselves more than do the two kinds of symbolism previously discussed, common to all of this third type is their use in what are called "nondiscursive" modes of expression. The symbolisms employed in such expressions may then be referred to as "nondiscursive symbolic forms."

To say that ordinary languages are "discursive" means that they are used in customary speech for communicating ideas in a consecutive, connected fashion, following the principles of common logic. Such discourse is appropriate for assertions of fact and other utterances meant to be understood literally. It is intended as a means of effective cohesion and practical action within the community. Similarly, mathematics is discursive because it is based on logical deduction, with arguments moving from premises to conclusions by consecutive steps. Both kinds of discursive forms are used for factual statements in the sciences, where rational order is of the essence.

The nondiscursive symbolic forms are used in all the arts and for the expression of feelings, values, commitments, and insights in the domains of personal knowledge, metaphysics, and religion. In these fields the aim is not literal statement, but figurative expression. The appeal is principally to the imagination rather than to consecutive argument. In the discursive domains language is used for common understanding of objective conditions; in the nondiscursive domains language is used to express personal subjectivity. The former is outwardly oriented, the latter inwardly.

Alfred North Whitehead and Susanne Langer have defined the contrast between the discursive and nondiscursive by means of the concept of *presentational immediacy*. In the discursive forms meanings unfold in sequential argument. In the nondiscursive forms meanings are presented in a unitary vision, i.e., in direct or immediate insight. In the former, meaning is attained at the end of a demonstration (whether explicit or implicit), while in the latter, meaning is grasped all at once, as an immediate presentation.

It was said above that in discursive language the ideas are organized according to the principles of ordinary logic. It is not to be inferred from this that the nondiscursive forms have no logic. They have their own kind of logic, meaning their distinctive patterns and characteristic orders and relationships. They are not haphazard or disorganized. It is simply that their organization does not follow the lines of literal rationality. In this sense they are the modes of expression suited to nonrational (though not necessarily irrational) kinds of experience.

While the nondiscursive symbolisms are chiefly used to express meanings in the realms of esthetic experience, personal knowledge, and synoptic insight, they are sometimes used in practical affairs and ordinary social life, as in the case of signals, manners, and gestures (to be discussed below). This indicates that the essential distinction between the two types of symbolism is not in the fields of application, but in the contrast between discursive and nondiscursive. Nondiscursive forms are appropriate even in ordinary practical affairs when the purposes of communication are best served by direct presentation of a form instead of by reasoning to a conclusion.

Perhaps nondiscursive symbolic forms may best be characterized as particular sensory objectifications of subjective states. Subjective meanings are thus contained in unified patterns of sense perception.

This general description of nondiscursive symbolisms may attain greater clarity and point, and the differences among the various forms may become evident, from the following brief analysis of the principal types of nondiscursive forms.

Signals are codes for communicating action-cues. Strictly speaking, they are not nondiscursive, because they are to be understood literally and logically, nor are they even really symbols, because they are ideally used as stimuli to automatic action and not as bearers of reflective meaning. However, since they are a kind of language, with regular patterns, and since they are capable of being reflectively understood, they are at least analogous to nondiscursive symbols.

Every person must master a large vocabulary of conventional signals if he is to adapt safely and efficiently to his environment. In a modern city he has to know what a host of light signals and sound signals mean if he is to travel securely. An employee in an office or factory must understand the meaning of bells, whistles, dials, and colored lights if he is to do his job. With the increasing mechanization of industrial civilization, more and more such regulatory signals are necessary and the mastery of the signal language occupies an ever larger place in each person's education.

Some signals are natural rather than conventional. For example, the barking of a dog or the hissing of a snake may be a signal of danger. A black sky, lightning, and thunder may indicate coming rain. These stimuli to action are not properly part of language, which is generally limited to communication between human beings. However, natural signals are sometimes metaphorically referred to by such terms as "the language of the animals" or "the language of the elements." In any case, it is part of everyone's education to learn to "read" the meanings communicated by natural events and to act accordingly.

Bodily gestures have several different communicative functions. They are sometimes signals, as in the case of a policeman directing traffic or a person in a meeting raising his hand for recognition by the chairman. In other circumstances they may be symptoms, as when a person is convulsed with pain, recoils in terror, or leaps with joy or excitement. Symptomatic gestures are natural rather than conventional signs, except that their forms may be modified by cultural expectations. Bodily gestures may also be truly symbolic, as when one opens his arms to welcome or comfort another or clenches his fists in threat or defiance. While such symbols are also cues to action and to some extent symptoms of inner conditions, they are predominantly means of expressing ideated meanings, in which the distinctively human powers of imagination, self-consciousness, and rational deliberation are interfused. Moreover, the mode of expression is a visible act, communicating the meaning by direct presentation.

The same remarks apply to *facial expressions* as to bodily gestures. They may likewise be signals, as when a frown means "it is time to leave," or symptoms, as when a smile indicates satisfaction or pleasure, or symbols, as when a puzzled expression is used to convey the idea of doubt or uncertainty.

Bodily gestures and facial expressions are not only in themselves expressive forms, they are also important accessories to ordinary language. Some people speak with their hands as much as with their lips. Indeed, deaf-mutes may have to depend wholly on gesture-language. In this event gesture becomes discursive and is not essentially different from ordinary spoken or written discourse; it only employs a different symbol-system. However, much bodily expression is not used as a vehicle for discursive meanings, but serves a presentational function. Everyone knows the qualitative difference between the meanings imparted by only reading or hearing and by both hearing and seeing the speaker. It is a commonplace among teachers of speech that communication is a function of the person as a whole, including gestures, facial expressions, and bodily posture. It follows that the proper mastery of language includes far more than the acquisition of vocabulary and understanding and skill in grammatical construction. Practice in the varied and subtle arts of bodily expression is also needed if a person is to be able to articulate nondiscursive as well as discursive meanings.

The whole human body is an instrument for communication, and the symbols of bodily movement have their characteristic elements and grammatical relationships, which are an integral part of the subject matter of language instruction. From such a holistic standpoint, the student is not taught to read words and sentences as self-subsistent verbal forms. He is taught to read the complete and interconnected symbolic patterns of the communicating person by attending to all of the visual and auditory stimuli that emanate from him.

By elaboration of bodily expression-symbols the more complex languages of *manners* and *customs* are constructed. Like speech, conventional behavior patterns are important for social cohesion and harmony. Actions may speak more plainly and eloquently than words. The myriad forms of social usage do much to set the tone of life of a people, providing means of expression which extend, complement, and enrich the meanings carried by ordinary language. Cultural anthropologists have done much to demonstrate the significance of customs in the life of mankind. They have shown that customary behavior, like ordinary language, is not a mere aggregate of separate elements, but is patterned into an interconnected whole. For example, relationships between parents and children are regulated by a great many mutually reinforcing acts symbolizing respect, authority and freedom, dependence and independence, responsibility, and other aspects of status and expectation. Not only is the language of custom a structured whole, but there are as many such languages as there are different cultures. Moreover, the languages of custom are relatively independent of the ordinary languages, as shown by the fact that people within the same broad culture group may speak different tongues and that peoples with widely different cultural patterns may be found within any one language group.

Modern anthropologists have demonstrated in their study of cultures how to go about learning the vocabulary, morphology, and syntax of the language of custom. [1] The first requirement is an attitude of interest in, respect for, and attentiveness to other peoples and their ways. The second rule is to discover the characteristic *patterns* of meaning, so that isolated acts may be interpreted within the context of the culture as an intricately balanced

[1] See particularly Edward T. Hall, *The Silent Language,* Doubleday & Company, Inc., Garden City, N.Y., 1959, for a vivid discussion of cultural forms as a kind of language.

and articulated whole. This same approach holds, *mutatis mutandis,* for the study of other tongues.

The centrality of manners and customs in the life of mankind is delightfully portrayed by Harold Nicholson in his book, *Good Behaviour: A Study of Certain Types of Civility,*[2] in which he presents sketches of twelve civilizations, from ancient China, Greece, and Rome, through the Middle Ages and the Renaissance, to nineteenth-century Germany and England. What stands out from this survey are the substantial differences in patterns of culture and the fact that the quality and tone of a civilization are mainly expressed in the system of manners. Furthermore, one is impressed at how largely the educational effort of each society is directed toward the perpetuation of the customary behavior patterns. Parents and teachers today would do well to recognize how much of their own instruction is either directly or indirectly aimed at the inculcation of social conventions and to become aware of the meanings communicated by these symbolisms of the act.

Closely related to gestures, manners, and customs are the languages of *ritual.* Ritual tends to be more stylized and less individual than gesture and less concerned with ordinary social amenities than manners. Ritual is intended to express through symbolic acts meanings at a somewhat deeper level than those arising out of everyday experience. Some rituals are individual and private, and are concerned with objectively trivial matters (e.g., routines of eating or washing). Such personal rituals are usually regarded as pathological, reflecting neurotic compulsions growing out of deep-seated emotional disorders. Most rituals are communal and have to do with matters of large human import. For example, every momentous event in a person's life—birth, graduation, marriage, death—has its ceremonial accompaniments. The meaning of a nation's life is symbolized in patriotic rites, and the ultimate values and purposes of existence are expressed in the many varieties of religious ritual.

It is a common error of literal-minded moderns to assume that rituals are useless superstitions carried over from a pre-

[2] Beacon Press, Boston, 1960.

scientific age. Implicit in this attitude is the assumption that all meanings are of the discursive logical type. As we have already seen, there are many meanings not expressible in discursive form. Included among them are those symbolized in ritual. Mankind's highest hopes, deepest anxieties, and firmest commitments have always found articulation in the vivid presentational forms of ritual activity, in which the participant acts out, or dramatizes, the meanings instead of merely voicing them. The language of ritual is learned both by participation and by observation, and its meanings are enriched by interpretations using ordinary language (even though such explications can never fully interpret the meanings conveyed by the rituals themselves). Modern educators, who tend to overemphasize the literal and verbal modes of communication, would do well to devote more attention to the abiding importance of ritual symbols in the nurture of human personality and in the conservation and enrichment of cultural values.

In addition to symbolic acts, *graphic* or *object-symbols* are used to express the more profound meanings in human existence. Unlike signals, these visual symbols are not merely cues to action. They are bearers of meanings that exceed the bounds of ordinary logic. Examples of such symbols are flags, which focus patriotic sentiments, stars, crescents, and crosses, which carry religious meanings, and astronomical and astrological signs (like the signs of the zodiac). [3] Some of these symbols are purely conventional (e.g., many flags) while others are "natural," in the sense that the forms of the symbols are in certain essential respects congruent with the meanings symbolized. For example, the Christian symbol of the cross visually represents the ideas of contradiction or conflict and of the meeting of the human and the divine (the horizontal and the vertical bars, respectively). The swastika, an ancient Indian symbol, later adopted by the Nazis and derived originally from the sun wheel, represents the ideas of a primal source of light and life, of universality (the four arms), and of energy or power (the sense of movement conveyed by the jointed arms). Similarly, the ancient Chinese symbol is taken as represent-

[3] See Rudolph Koch, *The Book of Signs,* Dover Publications, Inc., New York, n.d., for a description of 493 symbols used by primitive and ancient peoples.

ing the dynamic contrast and interfusion of the two cosmic principles of *yin* and *yang*, the union of opposites (e.g., male and female, light and dark, heat and cold) that is the ultimate mystery of all being and becoming.

Dreams are a uniquely significant class of symbols that are once more a subject of lively interest, after a period of neglect and discrediting. From ancient times many have thought that dreams have meanings other than their obvious pictorial significance. It has been assumed that hidden behind and within the images are messages of importance to the dreamer, perhaps in the nature of portents, warnings, or directions for action. Among the skeptical, rationalistic, and literal-minded, especially since the Enlightenment, dreams have been dismissed as insignificant consequences of bodily disturbances or as the meaningless vagaries of a wandering imagination. Since the work of Sigmund Freud, dreams have once more become a subject of serious inquiry, and the art of dream interpretation has been reestablished on more secure foundations. According to psychoanalytic views, dreams are an important clue to the dreamer's emotional life, the true nature of which to a large extent lies buried in the unconscious and which leads him to behave in ways neither he nor others may understand, approve, or be able to control. It is further believed that the language of dreams can be mastered and that, once the meanings communicated by them are understood, progress can be made toward emotional health. The language of dreams is thus regarded as a secret code, which it is the task of the analyst to help decipher. When the secrets are discovered, self-understanding replaces self-ignorance, and confusion and meaninglessness give way to insight and clarity of purpose.

There are many different schools of thought concerning dream interpretation. Erich Fromm, in an illuminating treatment of the subject in *The Forgotten Language: An Introduction to the Understanding of Dreams, Fairy Tales, and Myths,* [4] discusses the history of dream interpretation, giving particular attention to Freud's view that dreams represent irrational and asocial wishes, to Jung's view that dreams are revelations of archetypal

[4] Grove Press, Inc., New York, 1951.

forms of wisdom from the "collective unconscious," and to his own position that dreams express many kinds of mental activity, both irrational and rational, moral and nonmoral. Fromm contends that the symbols of the inner life that appear in dreams are not conventional, but either "accidental" or "universal," the former referring to images which arise out of chance associations that have proved to be personally important, the latter representing types of experience that are inherent in the human condition. In the case of universal symbols there is an intrinsic relation between the inner feelings and their sensory representation. For example, the symbol "fire" represents the feeling of life and energy (or of fear and destructive power, depending on the context), and "valley" represents feelings of security (or of imprisonment, in other situations).

The main point for a philosophy of the curriculum is that the symbolism of dreams is a significant language that can be learned with great benefit to the learner. Fromm believes

that symbolic language is the one foreign language that each of us must learn. . . . It helps us to understand a level of experience that is specifically human because it is that level which is common to all humanity, in content as well as in style. . . . Both dreams and myths are important communications from ourselves to ourselves. If we do not understand the language in which they are written, we miss a great deal of what we know and tell ourselves in those hours when we are not busy manipulating the outside world. [5]

As suggested in the above quotation, *myths* are another kind of nondiscursive symbolism. Unlike any of the other nondiscursive forms previously mentioned, myths are expressed in ordinary language rather than in pictorial form or in act. The same is true of a number of other kinds of symbols, including *allegories, parables,* and *fairy tales*. While these are not in themselves languages, they use ordinary language so as to communicate nondiscursive meanings. This is accomplished by employing ordinary language in an extraordinary way, so as to impart the *figurative* or *metaphorical* sense rather than the literal sense of ordinary discourse. The meanings of whole myths, allegories, parables, and

[5] *Ibid.,* p. 10. Reprinted by permission of the publisher.

fairy tales properly belong to the domain of literature (see Chapter 15) rather than to symbolics as such. In fact, the line between the meanings of literature and of the metaphorical language of literature cannot be sharply drawn, for to a considerable degree the meaning of literature is in the language itself, and, conversely, the meaning of the language is discernible only through its use within the concrete literary creation.

Symbol interpretation was once a thriving art. Medieval scholars, notably Hugo of St. Victor, wrote systematic accounts of symbolism, showing the various levels of possible interpretation, including the literal, allegorical, mythological, moral, and spiritual. Dante's *Divine Comedy,* one of the greatest works in all literature, is an outstanding example of verbal symbolic forms used to present nondiscursive meanings on several levels, of cosmic scope and universal human significance. In the present scientific age metaphorical usage has lost the place of honor in favor of literal modes of discourse. It is now becoming clear to many students of language that the earlier interest in metaphorical language was not unjustified, and a new appreciation is arising for the study of meanings that cannot be expressed by literal utterances.

A final group of symbol-systems to be mentioned are the forms in which other arts besides literature are expressed. In music various sets of tonal, harmonic, and rhythmic conventions are adopted as a vehicle for musical expression. For example, scales provide ordered series of standard tones to be used in constructing musical patterns. Similarly, the visual arts consist of colors, textures, and movements organized according to certain conventions, and these elements and their principles of organization are, like musical elements and forms, analogous to the materials and structures of ordinary language.

However, the study of the expressive patterns of the arts belongs to the realm of esthetic meaning and not properly to the study of symbolisms as such, for, unlike the case of ordinary language, the forms of music, painting, sculpture, architecture, and dance cannot be separated from their substance. Hence, any further discussion of the "language of art" will be reserved for the chapters to follow on meaning in the arts (Chapters 12 to 15).

This completes our summary of the various major types of

nondiscursive forms comprising the last of the three subrealms of symbolics. The nondiscursive forms are not widely recognized as being comparable to languages, nor are materials generally available for studying and teaching them, as are materials for ordinary language and mathematics. One reason for this is that there are many different kinds of nondiscursive forms, making any common measure more difficult than for ordinary languages and mathematical systems. Another reason is the previously mentioned fact that these symbolisms cannot always be treated as autonomous disciplines independent of the fields of meaning in which they are used (e.g., in the esthetic and synnoetic realms).

Nevertheless, one feature distinguishes all three subrealms, making it appropriate to include them all within one realm and to bear a common name. It is characteristic of all three that they are humanly constructed symbolic formalisms. They are instruments for the expression of meaning. The emphasis in learning any symbolism is not on the content of the meanings expressed, but on the conventional expressive forms used to objectify and communicate meanings. The content of the meanings to be expressed is the subject of the other realms of meaning, to which we now turn.

THE SECOND REALM: *Empirics*

8

PHYSICAL SCIENCE

The essence of symbolisms is formal expressive patterns created for purposes of communication. Empirical meanings require ordinary language and mathematics for their expression, but the formalisms thus used do not constitute empirical knowledge itself. *Science,* or systematic empirical inquiry, is concerned with *matters of fact,* not with symbolic conventions. Knowledge in language is of formal properties and relations within a symbolic design. Knowledge in science is of the actual world, or better, of the world as it appears to be in sense experience and as it is inferred to be on the basis of this experience. In short, while language knowledge is purely formal, scientific knowledge is factual.

The contrast between symbolics and empirics can further be stated as that between symbolic prescription and factual description. To know a language is to be skillful in the use of the rules prescribed for discourse within the particular language community. To know a science is to be able to formulate valid general descriptions of matters of fact.

Because language is prescriptive, knowledge of it does not yield truth, but only the power of intelligible expression. On the other hand, the scientific enterprise is aimed at the discovery of truth. Conventions are never true or false; they are only more or less convenient or appropriate to specified purposes. The *forms* of descriptions in science are likewise more or less convenient, but what is asserted is either true or false (or probable).

Science is characterized by descriptions which are essentially *abstract*. It does not deal with the actual world in the fullness of its qualitative meanings. Rather, certain carefully defined aspects of the experienced world are selected as the basis for scientific descriptions. Different sciences deal with different aspects of the experienced world, using different schemes of abstraction. In the present chapter we shall deal with those aspects of the world that are the subject matter of *physical science*.

Physical science provides descriptions of the world as experienced through the activity of *physical measurement*. By "physical measurement" is meant the quantitative assessment of material objects by reference to agreed upon standards of *mass, length,* and *time.* That is to say, the world described in physical science is the world revealed through measurements made by standard balances, rulers, and clocks, or equivalent instruments. Anything whatever is an appropriate object of physical description, including stars, rocks, liquids, gases, plants, animals, and people. The only requirement is that the things described be accessible to physical measurement.

Because of the severe limitations imposed by the requirements of physical measurement, it is clear that physical science provides only a limited description of the experienced world. That is to say, it affords only knowledge of certain selected aspects of things. It does not express the whole truth about the world. It deals with the world as apprehended or inferred from certain narrowly specified classes of sense experience, namely, the reading of scales on instruments that directly or indirectly measure mass, length, and time.

There are two reasons for using the process of physical measurement. The first is that such measurements are capable of yielding universal agreement. The reading of measuring instruments is in principle the most simple and certain of operations. It requires only the ability to perceive the position of a pointer on a scale. Being exactly defined and demanding only the most elemental sensory capacities, physical measurements yield data on which agreement by all observers is possible, subject only to errors of measurement that can be progressively reduced by refinement of instruments and repeated observations.

The second value of physical measurement is the opportunity it affords for mathematical formulation. Physical science is completely quantitative. It takes no account of qualities of things that are not expressible in numbers. For example, colors as directly perceived qualities have no place in physical science. Colors enter only in the form of measurable wavelengths of light, which are expressible numerically. This quantification of the data of physical observation makes available to the scientist the rich resources of the field of mathematics, facilitating the process of inference and providing powerful and precise formulations of scientific ideas. The ideal of knowledge in physical science is the expression of its propositions in mathematical form.

Physical measurement provides the data that are the basis of knowledge in physical science. The measurements are in themselves of no scientific value. They yield scientific knowledge only when they are used to establish *generalizations, laws,* and *theories.* The goal of scientific investigation is not the accumulation of particular observations, but the formulation and testing of general laws. To understand the methods of scientific inquiry, it is necessary to be clear as to how generalizations are obtained from the data of observation. The process is essentially indirect. Generalizations are not directly derived from the particulars of observation by a chain of logical inference. It is truer to say that generalization comes first, as an imaginative construction, and that the data of observation are then used to validate the generalization. In teaching science the importance of this priority can hardly be exaggerated. The student completely misunderstands science if he thinks that observations somehow speak for themselves, yielding laws and theories by some straightforward process of reasoning from the data of sense to the general propositions of science.

In fact, the priority of generalization to observation is even more thoroughgoing than just indicated, for observation itself is guided by reference to what is to be established. The investigator cannot learn anything by taking measurements at random. He must carefully arrange his observations and experiments with the aim of verifying some generalization he already has in mind. Therefore, in science the observations follow from the generalizations; the generalizations do not (as commonly assumed) follow from the observations.

Generalizations thus introduced in scientific investigation are called "hypotheses." From the hypothesis a plan of *experiment* and *observation* is laid out. If the hypothesis is true, it is argued, then such and such observations could be made and such and such measures obtained. When the indicated measurements are taken, the hypothesis is either confirmed or not confirmed. If the observations do not check with what is expected from the hypothesis, the hypothesis is not necessarily rejected. What may be required is a restriction of the conditions within which the hypothesis holds.

For example, from the hypothesis that the formula relating distances to time for freely falling bodies is $s = \frac{1}{2}gt^2$ one can predict a series of measurable length and time correspondences that can be checked against actual observation. If observations do not agree with predictions, the hypothesis is not at once rejected. It may be argued instead that the formula holds true, but only on the condition that there is no air friction. The validity of this condition may be checked by further experiments using evacuated vessels.

Stephen Toulmin in *The Philosophy of Science: An Introduction* [1] provides an illuminating illustration of method in physical science by a discussion of optical phenomena. Geometrical optics is based on the principle of the rectilinear propagation of light. What is the logical status of this principle, that light travels in straight lines? The principle is not the consequence of any direct observation. Rather, it is a deliberately chosen way of representing optical phenomena, and it is justified by the fact that expected results, such as the casting of shadows of specified positions and dimensions, are actually observed. When in other experiments the principle appears not to hold, as, for example, in the passage of light from one medium to another of different density,

[1] Harper & Row, Publishers, Incorporated, New York, 1960.

the principle is not simply rejected. Instead, it is accepted as applying under the limiting conditions of homogeneity in the medium of transmission, and for this refracted light a new principle may be adopted, taking account of the change in direction that occurs on passage to a new medium (quantitatively expressed in Snell's law).

The phenomenon of refraction requires for its explanation new principles, from physical optics, in which light is regarded as a series of wave fronts. This is another way of representing light, justified by agreements of predictions with observations in experiments with refraction as well as other phenomena, such as diffraction and interference.

The wave principle also proves to have limitations. The wave representation turns out to be incapable of explaining certain other phenomena, notably those of photoelectricity. Here a new representation is introduced to the effect that light is made up of photons, or discrete packages of energy. The photon principle permits further quantitative predictions which can be tested by a variety of experiments and observations.

The essential points to be established are these: first, that *principles, generalizations, and laws are not directly inferred from the data of observation,* and second, that *observations do not test the truth or falsity of hypotheses, but rather their scope and limitations.*

While no sharp lines can be drawn between *facts, hypotheses, principles, generalizations, laws,* and *theories,* the distinctions implied by these different terms are useful. "Facts" usually refer to particular data of observation. As we have seen, the determination of which facts are relevant and the methods of formulating observations and experiments depend on the prior construction of hypotheses. "Hypotheses" are generalizations in need of testing by further observations. "Principles" are fundamental ways of representing physical processes, suggesting further consequences to be tested by experiments and observations. "Generalizations" are hypotheses whose scope of application has been well tested. "Laws" usually refer to generalizations that have been firmly established and precisely formulated. "Theories" are conceptual structures that provide explanations for laws.

For example, the study of the behavior of gases yields certain observable *facts* about pressure, volume, and temperature. Experiments can be performed to test the *hypothesis* that under constant temperature, when the pressure of a given mass of gas is increased, its volume will decrease. This hypothesis, when confirmed by experiment, becomes a valid *generalization*. When quantitatively expressed by the mathematical relation $PV = $ constant, it qualifies as a *law* (Boyle's law). The *principle* implicit in this investigation is that gases may be treated as homogeneous compressible substances with such measurable properties as pressure, volume, and temperature (each specified by experimental operations). The explanation for Boyle's law (and others, including Gay-Lussac's law and Charles' law) is provided by a *theory* (the kinetic theory of gases), according to which a gas is regarded as a collection of perfectly elastic molecules in random motion.

In the formulation of theories in science, use is made of *models*. A "model" is any kind of pattern or structure that provides a satisfactory basis for theory construction. For example, the kinetic theory of gases makes use of the model of mechanical interaction of colliding hard bodies, even though gas molecules themselves are not regarded as actually being such entities. The model is useful because when gas molecules are treated *as if* they were colliding elastic bodies, the resulting predictions are largely verified by experiments. Similarly, the Bohr model of the atom, in which the electrons are represented as miniature planets revolving in elliptical orbits around a nuclear sun, is not regarded as literally true, but only as a useful representation for atomic theory, giving a basis for explaining (among other things) the observed frequencies of light revealed in spectrum analysis.

Not all models are mechanical or pictorial, as in the two cases cited above. More common are *mathematical models*—formal symbolic patterns that fit the data of observation reasonably well. For example, a set of partial differential equations provides the model in the Schrödinger theory of the atom, producing predictions as good as or better than those of the Bohr model, and with more predictive power, flexibility, and elegance.

Models and the theories constructed from them may perhaps

best be understood after the analogy of *maps*. A "map" is a formal representation of an area, chosen for the purpose of directing travel in that region. Its usefulness derives from the fact that the relationships among the elements on the map are congruent with the relationships between places and things in the area mapped. So, a theory or model (whether visual or mathematical) provides an abstract pattern whose structure in relevant respects is congruent with the structure of the physical world, as demonstrated by the agreement between observations and predictions made from the theory or model.

It should be added that, as in the case of principles, generalizations, and laws, any particular model or theory is not so much to be accounted true or false as more or less successful in the guidance of observation and experimentation. Models and theories are thus mainly judged as to scope of application and degree of relevance to the physical systems studied.

We return again to the point that the ultimate goal of science is theoretical understanding. Individual facts are not in themselves important scientifically. They are significant only as they contribute to generalizations, laws, and finally to theories that explain all the lower levels in the hierarchy of scientific propositions. It is in this theoretical manner that physical science is concerned with descriptions of the metrical features of material things. The descriptions sought are not of particular things, but of regular patterns of change in the measurable aspects of material bodies.

In the above discussion of scientific methods the primacy of the general and theoretical has been stressed, but no indication has really been given as to the basis for selecting the hypotheses, principles, and models to be tested experimentally. For the most part the choice is made by noting similarities between new phenomena and more familiar ones and adapting to the new situation conceptual schemes that have previously proved successful. However, there is no routine or foolproof system of hypothesis formation. The construction of fruitful conceptual patterns to be tested by observation is essentially a work of the creative imagination, which actively projects possibilities and reflectively sifts them by well-informed thought-experiments before undertaking any actual physical tests.

The methods of theoretical science are remarkably similar to those of mathematics in that imaginative construction of conceptual schemes with deductive elaboration occurs in both fields. The one decisive difference is that in empirical science the deductions must finally be checked against sense observations. In mathematics the only requirement is internal consistency within any given theory. In empirical science the chain of propositions must also be consistent with the results of actual physical measurements.

Because future observations might at any time fail to agree with predictions made on the basis of earlier verified hypotheses, no generalization, law, or theory in science may be regarded as finally and fully proved, no matter how accurate previous predictions have been. All empirical propositions are provisional, holding good only within the limits established by prior tests and always subject to revision in the light of new evidence.

Much of the above treatment of methods in scientific investigation applies to all branches of science and not only to physical science. The high degree of precision and quantification possible in the physical sciences makes them the ideal toward which the other sciences aim. Nevertheless, there are representative ideas that belong specifically to physical science. These will be considered in the remainder of this chapter.

The basic concepts of physical science derive from the definition of physical measurement by means of rulers, clocks, and balances, or their equivalents. All physical sciences deal with patterns of matter (or energy) in motion under the influence of forces of interaction. Rulers measure space intervals and therefore material configurations. Clocks measure time intervals, which, in conjunction with spatial measurements, yield information about motion. Balances measure the forces of interaction that effect changes in motion.

The fundamental model for analyzing any event in the physical world is that of *particles* moving in *fields of force,* the fields being themselves determined by the character and configuration of the interacting particles. The material world is built up in a hierarchy of successively complex configurations, beginning with certain *elementary particles,* including electrons, neutrons, and protons, and more than two dozen other particles which play important roles in establishing stable patterns of interaction. The strongest interactions occur within the most intimate material configurations, the atomic nuclei. The weakest known interactions between elementary particles are those of gravity. Intermediate in strength are the interactions in electromagnetic fields and in the process of nuclear decay.

The elementary particles are organized into more or less stable energy distributions called "atoms," each consisting of a nucleus of given mass and charge surrounded by one or more layers of orbiting electrons. The structural patterns of the various kinds of atoms are the basis for understanding the physical and chemical properties of all material bodies whatsoever. Each distinct atomic pattern belongs to one *element* (e.g., hydrogen, sodium, carbon), and these elements may be arranged in cycles according to the *Periodic Table of the Elements,* certain physical and chemical similarities among elements belonging to the same cycle being explainable by their corresponding patterns of orbital electrons.

Atoms interact to form still more complex structures called "molecules," the combination possibilities of which depend upon the patterns of interaction between the electron systems of the constituent elements. The study of these structures and processes belongs to the field of chemistry.

The study of the modes of atomic and molecular patterning occurring in crystals and metals is usually designated as the field of *solid state* physics. More random types of particle distributions are studied in the theory of liquid flow (*hydrodynamics*) and in the *theory of gases.* The statistical analysis of random molecular motions is the key to all the phenomena connected with heat and forms the substance of *thermodynamics.*

Electromagnetic theory deals with particles bearing electric charges and with the fields of force resulting from these charges and their movements. Within this theory are comprehended not only the phenomena of electricity and magnetism in their ordinary sense, but also those of light and of radio waves, infrared rays, X rays, gamma rays, and cosmic rays. In modern physics it has further been shown that the field theory of these various forms of electromagnetic radiation must be complemented by a particle theory, since the energy in such fields is not continuous, but "quantized," i.e., comes in discrete units or packets (*quanta*). Thus, the particle-field model is appropriate not only to the domains of atomic and molecular interactions, but also to the study of energy distributions themselves. This is to be expected in view of the known equivalence of mass and energy.

Gravitational interactions, which become important with large aggregations of matter, are most thoroughly analyzed in the study of *celestial mechanics*. In this study planets, stars, and satellites at great distances from one another can be treated as interacting particles in gravitational fields of force, using models similar to those applicable to the motion of charged particles in electromagnetic fields.

The same fundamental ideas apply in every other branch of physical science. *Geology*, for example, is concerned with the structures and transformations of the material aggregates forming the crust of the earth. This study requires the use of the same conceptual tools as in physics and chemistry for the analysis of the hierarchies of material configurations, movements, and forces which effect changes.

In the most general terms, scientific inquiry is aimed at bringing some order and intelligibility out of what appears to be a miscellaneous and unrelated profusion of phenomena. A principle is a way of ordering sense perceptions according to some rational scheme. A law reveals a pattern common to many particular happenings. Theories bring many apparently diverse events within a single conceptual scheme. The search for principles, generalizations, laws, and theories is aimed at discovering similarities among different things and constancies among changing things. For example, the general gas equation, $PV = RT$, shows that when a given body of gas undergoes changes due to heating or cooling, expansion or contraction, increase or decrease of pressure, something remains constant, namely, the quantity PV/T.

Every law expresses relationships that remain invariant despite changes in variable factors. Laws of motion are constant patterns that changing things exhibit. Thus, while the planets move around the sun, constantly changing their positions and velocities, Kepler's laws of planetary motion express the fact that certain relations among these changing factors remain unchanged. The theory of relativity, beginning with the premise that physical measurements are definable only in relation to arbitrarily designated frames of reference, culminates in the formulation of laws that are invariant under changes in frames of reference and in the discovery of an important metric invariant, namely, the speed of light in a vacuum.

The idea of constancy amid change is particularly well illustrated in the various laws (or principles) of *conservation* in physical science. For instance, according to the law of conservation of energy, in any closed or isolated system, while energy may change from one form to another (e.g., from energy of position to kinetic energy to heat energy), the total amount of energy in the system remains unchanged. Similarly, according to the law of conservation of mass, when a given body of material undergoes physical and chemical transformations, the total mass of the material remains unchanged. While it is now known that this principle does not hold except for closed systems and with the understanding that mass and energy are interchangeable, it is still of great value in scientific investigation, as in the study of chemical reactions. These and other conservation principles, including the conservation of momentum and the conservation of parity—a recent discovery in nuclear physics—are powerful concepts for exploring unchanging properties and relations of changing things, thus contributing to the rational ordering of physical phenomena.

In sum, the essence of physical science is the discovery and formulation of general patterns among quantities derived from the process of physical measurement. These patterns express constancies that hold, within specified limits and under stated conditions, throughout the changes occurring in the interaction of material entities within given fields of force.

9

BIOLOGY

Meanings in biology are of the same general logical type as meanings in physical science. They are empirical descriptions of matters of fact, ideally formulated in terms of exact laws and explanatory theories of great generality.

The difference between the life sciences and the sciences of physical nature consists in the scope of their subject matter. Physical science is concerned with all matter-energy systems whatever, while biology deals only with some of these systems, specifically, those that are *alive*. As it turns out, the precise delimitation of the class of living things is not an easy task. One of the most difficult problems in biology is the construction of a satisfactory definition of exactly what distinguishes the animate from the inanimate. At issue in such a definition is the nature of life science as an intelligible field of study.

Briefly, a thing is said to be alive if it sustains itself through dynamic interaction with its environment, utilizing matter and energy from without in such a way as to preserve its own integrity and to reproduce its own kind. The study of matter-energy systems having these extraordinary properties is the province of biology. It clearly occupies a more limited domain than that of physical science. Moreover, it is an autonomous science, having its own characteristic categories appropriate to its distinctive subject matter. While living things have physical properties and are thus included within the domain of physical science, the study of the particular properties that make the adjective "alive" appropriate to these things is the special office of biology.

As in all science, biological descriptions are abstractions from the concrete actuality of the things investigated. No attempt is made to give a full qualitative account of living things. Instead, certain carefully defined aspects of these things are separated out for special attention in such a way as to render the resulting descriptions capable of being verified by any observer. In this fashion biology qualifies as an objective science.

The obvious starting point in biological investigation is observation of the world of living things. The attempt to render that world intelligible results in the creation of descriptive categories by which observed similarities and differences may be noted and living things assigned to specified classes. The process of classification is, of course, implicit in all rational activity. As pointed out in the discussion of language, the symbols of discourse refer to classes of entities. For example, "run" refers to a class of actions, and "book" to a class of objects. In mathematics, the idea of *set* or *class* was likewise shown to lie at the basis of the subject. Similarly, the systematic study of living things naturally begins with the attempt to order and simplify the enormously variegated and confusing world of life by the use of descriptive classifications. This process of classification is known as "taxonomy."

The fundamental taxonomic unit in biology is the *species,* consisting of all organisms which interbreed. Similar species are grouped together to form a *genus.* Genera in turn are combined by more far-reaching similarities into *families,* families into *orders,* orders into *classes,* classes into *phyla,* and phyla into *kingdoms* (plant and animal, respectively, the most general groupings). For example, human beings belong to the species Homo sapiens, the genus Homo, the family Hominidae, the order Primates, the class Mammalia, the phylum Chordata, and the kingdom Animalia. These taxonomic distinctions and other intermediate levels (such as subphyla, e.g., Vertebrata, and superclasses, e.g., Tetrapoda) are based upon somewhat arbitrary judgments of similarity in structure, function, and development, which are generally agreed upon by most qualified biologists.

The process of classifying natural objects is part of the descriptive task of any science. It is the aspect of science that is closest to common sense. By the same token, it is least prominent in those sciences that have achieved the highest degree of theoretical elaboration. In physics, for example, classification now plays almost no part, as it did in the early days of the science when names were assigned to different kinds of motion. While astronomy still includes classification of celestial bodies, the center of interest in this discipline now lies in the general laws and principles that make the observed phenomena intelligible. Similarly, chemistry, which was once largely a taxonomic discipline, arranging various material substances in kinds according to qualitative properties, has finally become a precise theoretical discipline using substantially the same methods and concepts as physics. Even geology, in which the taxonomy of substances and processes constituting the earth still comprises a major part of the standard content of the field, is steadily moving closer in concept and procedure to the exact theoretical models of physics and chemistry.

This progressive subordination of taxonomy to theoretical analysis is particularly evident in biology. Linnaeus, the great eighteenth-century Swedish botanist, developed the art of classification of living things to a high level, establishing biology as the taxonomic discipline par excellence. While the student of modern biology also must know the kinds of living things and the names assigned to them, this ordering of types is now considered only the beginning of the science. Far from being the explanation of the world of life, it is only the statement of the problem that theoretical biology has to solve. Accordingly, in contemporary biology the refinement of common sense attained in the description of living things by the process of classification is not a measure of understanding in the subject. Meaning in the life sciences consists primarily in theoretical understanding of how the various orders of living things came into being.

In the search for these meanings biologists use the method of *natural history*. In this respect biological inquiry differs markedly from the physical sciences. In physics and chemistry the origin and development of various kinds of physical systems is of little interest. Time enters symmetrically and on equal terms with length and mass in the formulation of laws of motion. In biology, on the other hand, the temporal factor becomes a separate and prominent consideration. Inquiry is no longer directed primarily at the discovery of invariant relationships among the three metrical elements, but at the question of how each particular kind of organism came to be what it is—of the causes and the processes giving rise to the manifold special patterns of life.

To be sure, natural history does have some relevance in physical science too. Physical cosmogony has to do with the origin and development of the physical world as a whole—the birth and death of stars and planets, the creation and destruction of matter, and the past and future of space itself. Geology also makes large use of natural history in tracing the metamorphosis of the earth. But none of the physical sciences is as directly and centrally concerned with natural history investigation as is biology, where general laws are sought for the sake of understanding the intrinsically interesting and puzzling particular forms of life.

The ruling idea in natural history is the concept of *evolution,* a revolutionary idea distinguishing the thought of the past century and a half from that of all earlier times. It was formerly believed that the orders of nature were immutable and that the various kinds of material bodies and living things had existed as such from the beginning. In the nineteenth century it became widely recognized that the world is a dynamic order rather than a static one and that the myriad sorts of things, both animate and inanimate, comprising the world exist in their present forms as a result of a process of temporal development.

The explanatory basis for the observed and inferred phenomena of natural history in the world of living things is the theory of evolution, with which the name of Charles Darwin is preeminently associated. Three concepts figure prominently in this theory. The first is that of *inheritable variations.* Clearly, if the kinds of living things change over time, variation must occur in individual organisms and be passed on to succeeding generations. These inheritable variations occur either as a result of sexual re-

combinations or by mutations (chance modifications of genetic patterns). The second concept is *adaptation*. Each organism lives in
an environment (both physical and organic) and interacts with it
in such a way as to maintain itself. Adaptation is measured by the
degree to which such self-maintenance succeeds. The third concept is *differential reproduction* or *natural selection*. If inheritable
variations are such that an organism is fertile and well enough
adapted to survive and prosper through the reproductive period,
those variations will be confirmed, while others that lead to ster-
ility or poor adaptation will not. By this process, it is believed,
over long periods of time existing forms of life have come into
being. The theory is confirmed by abundant evidence from paleontology (chiefly the study of fossils) concerning the forms of life
that existed at various stages in the earth's history.

Not only does natural history explain the existence of observed
taxonomic classes, but classifications may also be improved by
reference to developmental factors. Significant groupings of organisms can best be made by analyzing lines of descent, indicating
origins, divergences, and convergences of types. Natural history
analysis thus provides a useful basis for the construction of an
intelligible hierarchy of patterns of living things so organized in
temporal sequence as to provide satisfying explanations for the
observed similarities and differences in kinds of organisms.

The methods of biological investigation are by no means
exhausted by taxonomy and natural history. More general than
these methods and including both are the interrelated methods of
structural and functional analysis. Structural analysis has to do
with the patterns of organization of things, and functional analysis
with processes or modes of activity. The two are intimately connected in that the organism's structures make possible its activities
and the functional demands made upon it give rise to its organized
patterns. In modern biology, however, since the concept of dynamic process is considered more fundamental than that of static
design, functional analysis has theoretical priority over structural
analysis. Taxonomy belongs to structural analysis, and natural
history to functional analysis. This confirms the previously mentioned theoretical priority of the method of natural history in
biology over the method of classification.

In addition to taxonomy, structural analysis includes descriptions of the forms of living things both internally and in their relationships with each other. One of the central concepts of biology is *organization*. Biology is, in fact, the study of the patterns of organization of living things. Concern for organization is not peculiar to biology. It is the condition for intelligibility in any field of inquiry. It was illustrated in our discussion of language patterns and of the structures of matter and energy in the physical world. What is peculiar to biology is the kind of organization exhibited by living things. This distinctive type of organization is the clue to all understanding of the world of life.

A living thing has a particular kind of organization constituting it an *organism*. An "organism" is a patterned whole composed of interdependent coordinated parts. But not all organized wholes are organisms. Atomic nuclei, atoms, molecules, crystals, geological formations, and astronomical systems also have intelligible structures, with parts functioning interdependently. Living things have their own special kinds of organization that are made possible through the unique bonding properties of the element carbon. This element is structured in such a way that compounds of great complexity and virtually boundless variety can be built from it, using other elements, chiefly hydrogen, oxygen, nitrogen, and phosphorus. Especially important for life are the linked carbon compounds. These include glucose, glycerine, fatty acids, amino acids, pyramidines, purines, polysaccharides, fats, proteins, enzymes, nucleotides, nucleic acids, and finally, nucleoproteins, the largest known molecules, having the remarkable and singular property of *self-duplication*.

These highly complex self-duplicating organic compounds comprise the unique substance *protoplasm,* of which all living things consist. This living substance is itself further organized into a variety of structures, most basic of which are the *cells*. Cells, together with other noncellular protoplasmic materials such as fibers and body fluids, are the constituent parts of a vast hierarchy of organic patterns in which each successive level has greater structural complexity, larger size, more energy requirements, and more instability than the lower levels. Aggregates of cells with similar functions comprise *tissues*. Cooperative aggregates of tissues form *organs.* These are in turn coordinated into *organ systems,* and finally into complete *organisms.* Organisms are further organized into *families* and *societies,* with specialization and division of labor as the basis of cooperation, mutual aid, and increased efficiency.

Structure extends even beyond the society level to the formation of *communities.* These are local associations of interdependent organisms of different species, living in a *symbiotic* relationship, with member populations specializing and serving one another either mutually or parasitically in respect to food, reproduction, and protection. Finally, living communities are organized, with the physical environment, into the entire world of living things, forming the total interactive rhythmic pattern of animate existence.

As indicated earlier, organic structures cannot really be explained apart from their functions. Hence, if an understanding of the particular patterns of living things is to be attained, the characteristic activities in which they engage must be described. Every organism has two broad categories of functions: *metabolism* and *self-perpetuation.* "Metabolism" refers to the processes by which the organism draws in, transforms, incorporates, and returns matter and energy from the environment. "Self-perpetuation" includes the activities which enable the organism to persist through time in spite of disorganizing forces both outside and within.

Metabolism comprises three main processes: nutrition, respiration, and synthesis. *Nutrition* is the activity of supplying the organism with the raw materials of life. Some organisms have *autotrophic* nutrition, i.e., they live on inorganic substances from the environment, while others are *heterotrophic,* requiring supplies of organic nutrients. The most important autotrophs are the green plants, which use light to transform water and carbon dioxide into carbohydrates in the process of *photosynthesis.* Animals, on the other hand, are heterotrophic, ultimately depending on plants for their nutriments. Of special interest is the fact that the structures of both plants and animals are in part explainable by these nutritional activities. Plants are structured with roots, leaves, and other parts for direct and continuous association with the inorganic environment. Animals, depending for their food on other living things, require skeletons and muscles for locomotion, together with chemical and neural coordination systems for rapid adjustment to encountered objects. They also need alimentary and circulatory mechanisms for the ingestion, digestion, absorption, and transport of nutrients, and for the ejection of waste products. Animal and plant organization thus reflect different ways of life, involving different means of exploiting the environment to obtain nutriment.

The organism secures energy from the nutrients through the second metabolic process, *respiration*. In most animals and plants energy is released through oxidation. For this function various structures for bringing in oxygen and taking carbon dioxide away are developed. Gas exchange is more direct with plants than with animals, which require breathing and circulation systems to effect gas exchanges for the cells not directly exposed to the atmosphere.

Finally, the energy released in respiration is utilized by the cells for the *synthesis* of new protoplasm by means of complicated enzyme reactions.

While the three metabolic functions are necessary to life, they are neither sufficient nor really distinctive to living organisms. Nonliving systems can also be devised so as to take in, transform, and utilize materials from outside themselves. The characteristic functions of living things are those connected with self-perpetuation, the meaning of which is the key to all biological understanding. Living things are *open systems* exchanging matter and energy with their surroundings in such a way as to perpetuate themselves. Self-perpetuation includes three kinds of functions: steady-state control, reproduction, and adaptation.

Steady-state control is the process of maintaining stability in the organism in the face of changing internal and external conditions. Structures effecting such control are (1) *genes,* which guide protein synthesis in accordance with code patterns reflecting the structure of the entire organism, thus making each cell act in relation to the plan of the whole, (2) *vitamins* and *hormones,* which regulate the cells' metabolic functions, (3) *excretory* and *circulatory systems,* which maintain a suitable environment for cells within the body, and (4) *nervous systems,* which effect the coordination of the whole organism and receive, transmit, transform, and store information from the environment.

Reproduction is possible because of the self-duplicating power of living substances. Under the guidance of the genes new cell structures are reproduced from existing ones, and a process of development occurs in which cells divide and are differentiated according to their function within the whole organism.

Adaptation is the process of adjustment of the organism to its environment, enabling it to survive, prosper, and proliferate. The mechanisms for adaptation are those of evolution, through which new organic forms arise and are perpetuated or not in accordance with their degree of adaptation and therefore of reproductive capacity. As earlier indicated, sexuality is not primarily an instrument of reproduction (though by means of it new organisms of similar kind are generated), but a source of fresh trait combinations in the progeny, which are then subjected to the process of natural selection, resulting in the perpetuation of the best adapted types.

The analysis of adaptation brings us at last to the theoretical basis for the understanding of the taxonomic classes with which biological description begins, and the study of the world of life comes full circle.

Summing up, meanings in biology, as in all other sciences, are empirical, factual, descriptive, and ultimately general and theoretical in orientation. The distinctive features of biological meanings arise from the special subject matter studied, namely, living things. The unique property of living things is their power of self-perpetuation, supported by the processes of metabolism. Corresponding to these basic life-functions are characteristic organic structures, constituting open systems arranged in hierarchies of increasing complexity and interdependence of differentiated parts. Finally, biological ideas express dynamic principles in which individual organisms and kinds of organisms are traced developmentally and in evolutionary perspective, yielding theoretical understanding both of individual living things and of the multitude of kinds of animate creatures inhabiting the earth.

10

PSYCHOLOGY

The relation of psychology to biology is similar to that of biology to physical science. In both cases the first discipline is in one sense dependent on and included in the second, yet at the same time remains autonomous within its own sphere. Since the science of psychology, like biology, deals with living things, it may be regarded as a branch of biology. On the other hand, psychology is concerned with only certain aspects of living things and these determine the distinctive features of psychology.

The subject matter of psychology is *mind,* or the mental (psychic) aspects of living things. Just what the term "mind" means is, however, one of the chief questions in psychology, just as the meaning of the term "life" is a major problem in biology. Some biologists (vitalists) hold that life is a mysterious primal force that cannot be analyzed into anything else. Opponents of this position (mechanists) insist that life is nothing but certain complicated physicochemical reactions. An intermediate (organismic) view (generally the one reflected in the previous chapter) is that life is to be interpreted as a hierarchy of interdependent open systems.

Psychologists show a similar range of positions. On the one extreme, mind may be regarded as an inner psychic reality, directly known to the conscious person and not dependent on anything else. On the other extreme, mind may be considered as nothing but the activity of the brain, which in turn is merely a matter-energy complex in principle wholly explicable by physical science. Mediating psychologists seek to avoid identifying mind either with a substantial soul or with physical mechanisms, by using concepts referring to the characteristic functioning of the organism as a psychophysical whole.

It is more difficult to define psychology than the sciences previously discussed, for the following reason. The ideal of science is objectivity, and the goal is a system of publicly verifiable general propositions. Yet in psychological inquiry, the subject of investigation is mind, which some consider to be essentially subjective, individual, nonobjectifiable, and not open to public scrutiny. It is then argued that any attempt to analyze mind after the manner of the natural sciences can yield no knowledge of mind as it is in itself, but only of certain nonmental correlates of mind.

The scientific psychologist's problem is to do justice to the realities of mental life without giving up the principle of objectivity. The usual solution to this problem is (1) to take as the field of psychological investigation not mind as such, but the observable organized *behavior* of the higher animals (including human beings), and (2) if the various subjective phenomena of the mental life are used at all, to employ them within conceptual schemes to explain the observed behavior patterns. In this fashion psychology may be maintained as an objective scientific discipline, with behavior as its most fundamental concept, and the differences among the various psychological positions may be reduced to differences in the interpretation of observed behavior. The strict reductionists try to avoid all explanatory concepts which are not closely linked to observable body behavior, while the more intuitive, introspective, and existentially oriented psychologists find it necessary to use concepts referring to subjective experience in order to interpret observed behavior adequately.

The more mechanistic types of psychology are constructed as far as possible after the pattern of the physical sciences. Care is taken to use only concepts definable either directly or indirectly in terms of measurement operations, permitting observations to be quantified and generalizations to be formulated mathematically. Psychology so conceived is an experimental natural science in which the categories and methods of physics and biology are regarded as fundamental and sufficient for the explanation of animal behavior. Furthermore, it is assumed that human psychology is not different in kind from the psychology of other animals and that experiments with animals may throw great light on the problems of human behavior.

In all experimental science, including psychology, the quality of the empirical meanings obtained in inquiry depends on the investigator's skill in *experimental design*. Essentially this is a matter of asking significant questions, answers to which are provided by the experiments performed. Good design is primarily achieved by the imaginative construction of shrewd hypotheses, which by their formulation set the terms of the answers to the questions asked of nature.

In every empirical science an important aspect of experimental design is the construction of appropriate *instruments*. Astronomy could never have advanced to its present stage without the telescope, nor physics without the spectrometer and the particle accelerator, nor biology without the microscope. Precise discriminations and accurate measurements are possible only by the use of highly refined tools of investigation. The student of science needs to understand how largely our civilization owes its empirical understandings to the combination of manual skill, engineering technique, and inventive imagination that have produced the ingenious instruments used in experimental science.

The types of instruments employed differ from problem to problem and from one science to another, depending upon the kinds of things studied and the questions being asked. By and large the instruments of the psychologist are less elaborate than those of the experimental physicist, chemist, or even biologist. They may also not be of the mechanical type at all, consisting of questionnaires, pencil and paper tests, and other symbolic patterns designed to evoke certain behavioral reactions in the experimental subjects.

Because of the extreme complexity of the matters investi-

gated in psychology, the mathematical formulations in this field
tend to differ from those of the more exact sciences. Many of the
laws of astronomy, physics, and chemistry are expressible in the
equations of algebra or of one or another calculus. To some extent
in biology and even more in psychology and the social sciences the
formulations are chiefly in *statistical* terms. Statistical methods of
analysis are useful whenever the data of measurement prove incapable of exact mathematical formulation. The essential purpose
of statistics is to organize the facts of observation into intelligible
patterns, thus bringing order out of otherwise incoherent collec-
tions of data.

Something of the character of statistical methods may be indicated by the following discussion of some common types of uses
for statistics.

Statistics are used as a means of *direct quantitative descriptions of groups or populations,* by exhibiting the distribution of
specified measures within these populations. Such descriptive
statistics may be presented in various forms, such as tables, bar
and line graphs, and pie diagrams. The purpose of all such representations is to arrange the data of observation so that the specified
metrical aspects of each group of things investigated may be comprehended in an orderly and unified manner. If a single quantity
is desired for any specified measure, to represent the group (or
population) as a whole, a measure of *central tendency* (e.g., arithmetic mean, geometric mean, median, or mode) may be calculated.
A second representative quantity (e.g., the range or the standard
deviation) may be calculated to indicate the *variability* or degree
of *dispersion* of the measures on either side of the central tendency.
By using the central tendency and dispersion it is possible to make
quantitative comparisons between different groups of things.

Another major use of statistics is in discovering the relationships among different measures of the same groups of things by
the methods of *correlation analysis.* Statistical correlations are
analogous to the invariant relations symbolized by the mathematical equations of exact science. Correlation studies distinguish
between variables which are independent of one another and those
which are in some way interlinked. These relationships may be
exhibited graphically by scatter diagrams, in which the values of

the two measures being studied are plotted as points on a two-dimensional graph, each point representing one element of the collection under investigation. *Coefficients of correlation* may also be calculated, giving numerical values to the degree of interdependence. For instance, the relationship (if any) between age and intelligence could be studied in a group of students by plotting the values of age and intelligence quotient for each student and calculating the correlation coefficient for the series. From many such studies it might be possible to formulate certain generalizations or laws concerning the variation of intelligence with age.

Most of the uses of statistics grow out of the fact that the objects measured do not seem to behave in accordance with fixed rules and precisely defined laws, but exhibit a certain degree of apparently random variation. Hence, descriptions of behavior need to be expressed in *probabilities,* or expected average distributions of randomly varying measures that are not individually predictable. Probability calculations are the basis for the statistical analysis of *samples*. A "sample" is a selection of elements from a *population,* used as a basis for estimating the character of the whole population. For example, a sample of 1,000 high school students might be measured in respect to certain properties, as a method of getting an idea of the probable distribution of measures for a much larger group of high school students from which the sample was drawn. The validity of sampling techniques depends on making selections as free as possible of systematic bias, so that the assumption of random variation on which probability calculations are based may be justified.

Statistical calculations enable the investigator to estimate how accurately a sample of a certain size permits him to generalize to a larger population. Likewise, he can compare different groups of entities so as to ascertain the probability that they are samples drawn from the same population.

An important application of sampling analysis is found in the use of *experimental* and *control* groups. In psychology it is seldom possible to study the effect of a particular factor on an animal by comparing its behavior in experiments with and without the factor present because the first experiment modifies the animal and makes the second experiment not comparable. To overcome this difficulty it is common practice to select at random from a common population (1) control groups, which are tested without the factor being applied, and (2) experimental groups, which are tested with the factor applied. The two kinds of groups can then be statistically analyzed to see whether or not the presence of the factor in question produces any significant difference in behavior, i.e., whether after introducing the factor the two kinds of groups still qualify as random samples of the same population.

One other application of statistics is in the analysis of *errors in measurement*. Limitations in accuracy of instruments and random fluctuations in the entities measured often make it impossible to arrive at exact values of variables. The errors can be reduced by averaging the results of several independent measurement operations, and the probability that such an average deviates by any specified amount from the true value of the variable can be calculated by considering the observed values as a sample of a hypothetical infinite population of observation results.

The objective of inquiry in experimental psychology is to describe and explain the varieties of animal behavior in quantitative terms, using publicly observable measurement procedures. Probably the focal concepts in all such inquiry are the pair *stimulus* and *response*. Animal behavior is regarded as a series of responses to various stimuli. The animal is considered as an organism whose conduct is determined by interaction with a variety of other objects in its environment. Energy is received by the sense receptors, which in turn energize a complex pattern of conducting fibers and activate certain circuits in the central nervous system, which send forth impulses to the effectors that produce the behavioral response.

The stimulus-response concept enables the psychologist to classify behavior in the following four broad classes: (1) *reflex*, where the response is immediate, direct, and unlearned, (2) *conditioned reflex*, where an immediate response occurs, but only after certain prior stimulations have formed new neural connections between sense organs and effectors, (3) behavior under conditions of *set*, where the response may not occur at once, but only after certain body fluid or neural controls have opened the way for it, and (4) *ideated* behavior, controlled wholly or in part by autonomous neural activities without need of immediate sensory stimulus. [1] Ideation, or thought, is here regarded as a *mediating process*, intervening between stimulus and response, delaying and modifying the response in accordance with previous experience recorded in the pattern of neural pathways.

The prime objective of precise behavioral analysis is to explain all forms of conduct by reference to neurophysiological mechanisms and to avoid intuitive, subjective, and animistic concepts. All mental processes are regarded as *inferences from behavior* and not as matters of direct introspection.

Learning is the modification of behavior by experience, and the measure of what has been learned is the change in observable behavior. The major conceptual tool for the investigation of learning is *conditioning*. A conditioning stimulus S produces the desired behavioral response R when R follows S repeatedly and contiguously in time and with *positive reinforcement*. The latter term refers to any event following the response (such as a reward) that tends to encourage its continuation. While it is not yet fully clear just how reinforcement occurs, it is probably connected with drive reduction (e.g., sex or hunger satisfaction, or pain avoidance) and (less clearly) with certain mediating processes (ideation). The learning which occurs at any time is greatly influenced both by what has been learned before (this is the phenomenon of *transfer of learning*) and by the *learning set* or generalized procedures for learning which have been acquired earlier.

Memory is similarly definable in purely objective terms, without reference to inner images of the past, as the demonstrable retention of previous learning. The precise meaning assigned to the term "memory" is determined by the experimental procedures adopted. For instance, memory may be tested by measuring the subject's ability to repeat, to use effectively, or to relearn an activity. Even though such different definitions of memory may be used, they may all be satisfactory from an objective behavioral standpoint.

Motivation is an inferential concept referring to the fact that

[1] See Donald O. Hebb, *A Textbook of Psychology*, W. B. Saunders Company, Philadelphia, 1958, pp. 46–48.

the animal is active rather than inactive and engages in certain kinds of activities rather than others. The organism has certain biological needs for self-maintenance and self-perpetuation which arouse certain drives and direct the animal into activities that will satisfy the needs in question. Closely related to motivations are *emotions,* such as fear, anger, love, and joy, referring to special states of motivation. These states can be studied objectively, though not without difficulty, by observing certain unusual behavioral manifestations, such as avoidance, aggression, and modifications of pulse and breathing patterns.

Much attention has been given by psychologists to the phenomena of *perception,* and great ingenuity has been shown in their efforts to describe it objectively rather than introspectively. Behaviorally, perception is regarded as a theoretical inference, not as a direct datum of experience to be reported by the perceiver. According to Hebb, perception "is a change in connections in the switchboard (neural), transient or lasting, which will modify any of an indefinitely large class of responses to subsequent stimuli. To the extent that the change of connections is lasting, it constitutes knowledge . . . knowledge is a potential modification of a large class of responses." [2] The test of what one perceives and knows as a result of any experience, is, then, the modification of typical responses to specified kinds of stimuli. Most important are tests of discrimination, in which subjects are led to make differential responses among stimuli, indicating judgments of similarity and difference. Analysis of such responses yields reliable objective information on how things are perceived and understood by the subjects tested.

Finally, such higher mental activities as conscious reflection, purposing, speaking, and problem solving are also investigated by inference from observed behavior. These processes are most highly developed in human beings. They are characterized by the dominance of mediating processes over reflex and sense-directed activity. The higher processes (generally referred to as *conscious* ones) determine a great variety of activities and integrate behavior over considerable periods of time, linking past, present, and future

[2] *Ibid.,* p. 198. Reprinted by permission of the publisher.

activities. In *problem-solving* activities the occurrence of *insight* is inferred from sudden success in reaching a goal. *Purpose* is seen in persistent efforts to reach goals, in which methods of attack change as circumstances require, but with constant ends in view. *Linguistic communication* is activity using symbols (words, gestures, marks) for the purpose of influencing the behavior of others.

The foregoing paragraphs are intended to indicate some of the methods and concepts characteristic of the experimentally minded psychologists whose goal is the quantitative description and explanation of observable patterns of behavior, without reference to introspective data and with insistence on the continuity between the behavior of human beings and of the other animals. Other psychologists hold that such a reductive approach to the study of mind is insufficient and that the use of concepts referring to the immediate experiences of mental life is necessary. These investigators take distinctively human psychic experience as their center of reference rather than animal behavior and neurological mechanisms. Concepts such as memory, expectancy, imagination, and purpose, which for the experimental psychologist are inferences from observed behavior, may be regarded by the less mechanistic psychologist as being themselves essential to the understanding of behavior. That is to say, instead of being defined by behavior, what these concepts symbolize in experience is taken as the basis for explaining behavior.

When the phenomena of mind as directly experienced rather than as inferred are taken as appropriate to psychology, the methods of investigation are considerably altered. No longer are measurement, statistical analysis, and operational definition the criteria for approved inquiry. To these methods are added qualitative, intuitive, and dialectical modes of thought. Moreover, psychology is regarded much more as an autonomous field of inquiry with its own characteristic concepts and methods rather than as nothing more than a branch of animal biology. In this relatively autonomous field the mental life of human beings takes priority, animal psychology being regarded as the special limiting case where many of the most interesting and characteristic functions of mind are either absent or rudimentary.

A good example of this broader, qualitative approach to psychology is found in Gordon W. Allport's *Becoming: Basic Considerations for a Psychology of Personality.* [3] Allport contrasts two traditions in psychology, which he designates as the "Lockean" and the "Leibnitzian," respectively. The former refers to the generalized mathematical-natural science approach already discussed, and the latter refers to a psychology of individual personality growing out of reflection on our own experience as persons. He is careful to disavow prescientific animistic conceptions of the substantial self, soul, or "homunculus," but he does not believe it is necessary in avoiding such ideas to retreat into a reductionism that falsifies the essential quality of mental life.

Allport's central concept is the "proprium," a term referring to "all aspects of personality making for inward unity." [4] These aspects include the following: sense of bodily identity, temporal self-identity, self-seeking tendencies, ideals and loyalties, rationality, consciousness of present and desired status and roles, motivation to actualize oneself, and integral self-knowledge. While a person's development is partly a matter of inherited factors and environmental influences and of specialized learnings, the most important factor in personal development is "oriented becoming," which fulfills the central strivings and intentions of the individual, enabling him to realize his own unique human destiny. Such a view requires a new theory of motivation, in which distinctively human activity is seen to stem not from drive reduction (deficit motives), but from creative tensions toward self-fulfillment (growth motives).

In such a psychology of personality certain concepts which played a large part in earlier philosophical psychology and still figure prominently in the humanistic fields are reinstated as essential features. Among these concepts are *conscience,* in the sense of generic self-guidance according to a personally acknowledged system of *values* to which one willingly commits himself, *guilt* and *anxiety* growing out of the acknowledgment of *freedom* and the acceptance of *responsibility* for one's deliberate ac-

[3] Yale University Press, New Haven, Conn., 1955.
[4] *Ibid.,* p. 40.

tions, and the *religious sentiment,* according to which the person feels himself linked meaningfully to the whole of reality.

To sum up: the special province of psychology is the study of mind. The meanings obtained in this field are empirical, descriptive, and theoretical. They are concerned with the facts of mental life and the explanations for those facts. The limitation of subject matter in psychology makes it a special field with its own appropriate concepts and methods. The still unresolved issue in this science is the degree to which the high abstractions and quantifications of the natural sciences can do justice to the facts of mind, particularly in human beings. It would seem wise to continue the effort to study behavior using measurement operations, statistical analysis, and neurophysiology, and at the same time to remain open to the insights coming from the more broadly conceived humanistically oriented approaches to the study of personality.

The meaning of empirical knowledge in psychology and the methods and concepts characteristic of this field are more problematical than in the fields previously discussed. While this situation may cause some uncertainty and confusion, it may also be the basis for gaining an understanding of the inevitable tensions within every living field of inquiry (especially a relatively young one) and for gaining a glimpse of the wide ranges of meaning possible even within the realm of empirical knowledge. [5]

[5] Some reference will be made to the psychoanalytic movement in the discussion of personal knowledge in Chapter 16.

11

SOCIAL SCIENCE

Psychology is a transition field belonging both to the sciences of nature and the sciences of man. This dual membership is evident in the tension between the two main lines of psychological inquiry discussed in the previous chapter. The social sciences, chief among which are social psychology, sociology, anthropology, economics, and political science, are clearly in the domain of the sciences of man. In these disciplines the effort to identify with the concepts of the natural sciences is no longer as evident as in psychology, and the distinctive features of the autonomous study of various types of human behavior come into view.

Geography may also be included among the social sciences. It is a descriptive discipline concerned with facts about the earth as man's habitation. However, it differs from the sciences in one major respect, namely, that the ideal of geographic knowledge is not generalizations and laws, but full understanding of particular peoples and places. In this respect geography on the one hand resembles the science of anthropology, with its descriptions of particular cultures, and on the other hand resembles the synoptic discipline of history, with its recounting of particular human events.

Like history, geography has wide integrative sweep, utilizing and coordinating knowledge from many other disciplines, including the physical sciences, the life sciences, the social sciences, and (in historical geography) history. The major organizing principle of geography is *place* rather than *time,* as in history. Geography is less synoptic than history in that the meanings integrated come largely from the empirical realm (except for historical geography) and not from the esthetic, synnoetic, and ethical realms. On balance, then, it is probably best to regard geography as essentially an empirical discipline with a strongly concrete and integrative emphasis.

The conflict in psychology, between those who study what nature has made of man and those who study what man has made of himself, is not marked in social science. Natural science is concerned with the objective processes of nature, the science of man with the creation and creations of persons. Social science deals with the world of culture and society, a world of which human beings are themselves the architects. For this reason the kinds of abstractions which apply to the world of all material things or even of animate beings generally cannot suffice for the description of the human world.

Still, the social sciences are not without inner tensions and growing pains. Sociology has struggled to become free of its earlier associations with social reform, just as psychology has fought free of its earlier philosophical and religious ties. Anthropology in coming of age has had to go beyond its previous largely exclusive preoccupation with primitives. Perhaps the most serious problem of the social scientists has been to avoid value judgments, as objective scientists are supposed to do, and yet not nullify the relevance of their knowledge to real human concerns. [1] Because of the present fluid state of these fields it is particularly important to be aware of the tentative and historically conditioned character of the following attempt to epitomize two representative social science disciplines.

Each of the special social sciences is concerned with somewhat

[1] On the problem of vitality and relevance in social science research see C. Wright Mills, *The Sociological Imagination,* Oxford University Press, Fair Lawn, N.J., 1959.

different aspects of human life. Of the five disciplines listed above, anthropology is the most comprehensive, including studies of all aspects of the man-made world, from languages and tools to law, manners, and religion. One of its branches, physical anthropology, properly belongs to biological science, and another, archaeology, is most closely allied to the synoptic discipline, history. Sociology is also comprehensive, but more restricted in range of concepts and methods and thus better suited than anthropology to illustrate social science as a distinctive domain of inquiry. Social psychology may be regarded for our purposes as belonging to sociology. Political science is still in a highly fluid state, making it difficult to characterize briefly. Economics is relatively precise and affords an excellent illustration of a more specialized description of human behavior than is found in anthropology and sociology. On these grounds it appears reasonable to limit the present illustrative treatment of the field of social science to the two disciplines of sociology and economics, brief characterizations of which will serve to indicate some of the modes of thought found in social science generally.

Sociology is a relatively young science concerned with extremely complex matters. It is not surprising, therefore, that many differences occur in ideas and techniques of investigation in the discipline and that precise and stable formulations are rare. The following sketch should be taken only as one illustration of the patterns of thought in this field.

Max Weber defined sociology as "that science which aims at the interpretive understanding of social behavior in order to gain an explanation of its causes, its course, and its effects." [2] In this definition two features particularly deserve comment. First, the subject matter of sociology is *social behavior*. For Weber, the term "behavior" is used to refer to subjectively meaningful action. Reflexive, instinctive, and automatic kinds of behavior are excluded. Behavior is distinctively human only when a person acts consciously and deliberately, with purposes and ends in view, and is motivated by certain attitudes and feelings. Furthermore, the behavior in question is "social" in the sense that it is oriented toward the conduct of other persons. Thus, conduct exclusively

[2] *Basic Concepts in Sociology*, tr. by H. P. Secher, The Citadel Press, New York, 1962, p. 29. Reprinted by permission of the publisher.

in relation to inanimate objects or animals does not belong to sociology, which is concerned with interaction among persons, each of whom takes account of others as individuals with attitudes and expectations toward himself. Even though the subject matter is social interaction, the distinctive sociological mode of analysis is to refer to the meaningful experience of individuals, which alone can yield understanding of behavior.

The second noteworthy point in Weber's definition centers in the phrase "interpretive understanding." The subjective intentions which determine social behavior can be understood only if the scientist by an act of imaginative projection puts himself intellectually and emotionally in the position of those whose behavior he seeks to explain. While such interpretive criteria need not be inconsistent with scientific objectivity, they are far from the elemental objectifications which make physical science data universally confirmable, and they underscore the autonomy of sociology as a discipline with its own unique concepts, methods, and varieties of empirical meaning.

An essential part of any scientific inquiry is the creation of conceptual categories suitable to the subject matter investigated. In sociology most of what is studied is familiar to everyone in everyday experience, e.g., social relationships, customs, values, and institutions. In this regard sociology differs from most other sciences, which are largely concerned with unusual and unfamiliar phenomena. The sociologist must therefore make a special effort to devise new and more precise ways of speaking about relatively familiar matters.

By way of illustrating the method of precise sociological definition of otherwise commonsense ideas, three of Weber's definitions may be cited.

A social relationship . . . will be known as "open" to those on the outside, if, and insofar as, participation in the mutually oriented social conduct, relevant to its subjective meaning, is, according to its system of authority, not denied to anyone who is inclined to participate and is actually in a position to do so. [3]

A "corporate organization" is an aggregative social relationship char-

[3] *Ibid.*, p. 97. Reprinted by permission of the publisher.

acterized by an administrative staff whose activity is oriented exclusively and continuously to achieving the goals of the organization. [4]

By "power" is meant that opportunity existing within a social relationship which permits one to carry out one's own will even against resistance and regardless of the basis on which this opportunity rests. [5]

In commenting on the definition process (as he would not feel obliged to do in physics or biology, for example) Weber remarks: "The apparently 'laborious' definition of these concepts is an example that what is 'self-evident' is rarely thought out clearly, for the very reason that it appears obvious." [6]

Some of the major concepts in sociological analysis are indicated in the italicized words of the following summary statement:

A *social group* is a system of social interaction, whose members cooperate toward common goals and recognize certain *social norms* specifying rules of behavior, rights, and obligations, violation of which brings *sanctions* in the form of loss of cooperation, diminished prestige, and specific penalties. *Social structure,* which refers to the relatively stable modes of human interrelation, is determined by *differentiated social positions,* to which attach certain *roles* (obligations within the social system) and *status* (rights and privileges relating to authority, remuneration, immunities, and prestige). A *reference group* is a group the conception of which is part of the individual's basis for appraising his own social situation and expectations. Reference groups are an important factor in determining subjective meanings, intentions, and hence social behavior.

Social norms are *institutionalized* when they are accepted by a large proportion of the members of the social system, are internalized, and sanctioned. A *social institution* (e.g., marriage or the system of exchange) is a complex of institutionalized norms. These norms are the basis for ensuring *conformity* and *social control,* and they also measure social *deviation.*

A *society* is a social group which occupies a definite territory, is perpetuated largely by sexual reproduction within the group,

[4] *Ibid.,* p. 115. Reprinted by permission of the publisher.
[5] *Ibid.,* p. 117. Reprinted by permission of the publisher.
[6] *Ibid.,* p. 98. Reprinted by permission of the publisher.

possesses a comprehensive *culture* (including characteristic thought forms, beliefs, values, norms, customs, institutions, and symbolic systems), and does not form a subgroup of any other group (i.e., is independent). Every society has various subsystems which exist to meet basic *functional needs,* e.g., the family for social self-perpetuation, the economy for adaptation to the material environment, the polity for the attainment of social ends, and such systems as the press, courts, and religious organizations for the integration of the society.

Any social structure or partial structure (mechanism) may be analyzed as to *function* or *dysfunction,* by which is meant the degree to which it does or does not fulfill social needs. Functions are *manifest* or *latent* depending on whether they are intended and recognized or not. Sociological inquiry in large part consists in the analysis of the functions and dysfunctions of various social structures and mechanisms. Particularly important is the study of such major social subsystems as kinship groups, economic organizations, political structures, and religious associations.

The process of learning a culture, called "socialization," takes place by social interaction, through which *internalized objects* are built up. Included among these internalizations are the many roles which define the system of duties toward others, and these enter into the structure of the developing *social self.*

The members of any social system are generally assigned implicitly or explicitly to certain *rank orders* on the basis of qualities, relations, and performance. A group of families among whom intermarriage is generally regarded as appropriate, whose prestige ranking is about the same, and who interact socially on the basis of equality, comprise a *social class.* Occupational, ethnic, and religious groups may also be ranked as to prestige levels. A variety of instruments have been developed for measuring and predicting prestige levels in any given society. The various forms of social stratification may be analyzed as to their functions and dysfunctions. Of importance also is the study of social *conflict* and *integration* in intergroup relations and of *social mobility,* by which a person's social rank may change, either as a result of personal performance or by the establishment of new social relationships.

Finally, *social change* can be analyzed in terms of the concepts of structure, function, and social needs. While no exact
laws of social behavior have yet been formulated, some insights
may be gained into the basis for individual conformity and deviation and for the transformations that take place in cultures, institutions, norms, roles, and rankings as a result of internal stresses,
environmental factors, or external pressures.

Thus, the chief aim of sociology is to provide an array of
relatively precise descriptive and explanatory categories for understanding the exceedingly diverse and complicated phenomena of
social behavior. The subject matter studied comprises every kind
of social interaction, and the basic method of inquiry is the construction of conceptual schemes revealing the structures of social
groups and the functions that these structures subserve.

From sociology we turn to economics as a second illustration
of the social science domain. Economics differs from sociology in
that it is a more specialized discipline. Sociology deals with social
behavior in general, while economics deals with only one department of such activity. The special concepts and methods applying
to economics are a consequence of this limitation of subject
matter.

Paul A. Samuelson defines economics as "the study of how
man and society choose, with or without the use of money, to
employ scarce productive resources to produce various commodities over time and distribute them for consumption, now and in
the future, among various people and groups in society." [7] The
central fact around which all economic thought and action turns
is that human beings have unlimited wants but only limited resources. From this disparity arises the problem of *scarcity* of *goods*
and *services,* i.e., of things that people want. Economics is not concerned with scarcity in any absolute sense, but only in relation to
people's desires, which appear to be without bounds. Economic
behavior therefore pertains even to the most wealthy societies,
because the degree of affluence is never such that people do not in
some respect want more than they have.

---

[7] *Economics: An Introductory Analysis,* 5th ed., McGraw-Hill Book
Company, Inc., New York, 1961, p. 6. Reprinted by permission of the publisher.

The fact of scarcity necessitates acts of *choice* as to what and how much shall be produced, by whom, with what resources, and by what methods, and to whom the products shall be distributed. These are the fundamental economic problems in any society, and different economic systems are devised to deal with them. Many different economic arrangements are possible, and the decision as to what system of production and distribution is used depends upon many considerations, including historical precedents, cultural patterns, geography and natural resources, population, intellectual, scientific, and technical development, religious beliefs, and political factors. For the most part the facts and generalizations of economics apply to particular kinds of economic systems and not to economic behavior in general. A comprehensive understanding of the subject requires the use of *comparative* methods, in which similarities and differences between economic systems (e.g., primitive, feudal, capitalist, and communist) are analyzed.

Because economic activity is a consequence of decision concerning matters of public import, economics is called a "policy science." That is to say, it deals with problems belonging in the realm of social policy. This does not mean, however, that the economist as such makes recommendations or decisions regarding public policy, for the meanings characteristic of his discipline are descriptive and not normative, i.e., they disclose what *is*, what *can be,* and *how* any goal may be reached, not what *ought* to be done (the latter pertains to the field of ethics).

To some extent all the social sciences are policy sciences since all are concerned in some way with the deliberate artifacts of culture (e.g., social institutions) rather than with the given facts of nature. In this respect meanings in the social sciences are similar to those in the realm of symbolics, and the empirical and symbolic domains overlap. As we have seen, languages are cultural artifacts designed for effective communication. That is, they are instruments for social coordination, just as are the various social inventions (including those of economic life) studied in the social sciences. It has already been mentioned that linguistics is a branch of anthropology and that the only difference between the study of language and of linguistics is that the former is directed at the effective practical mastery of particular symbolic systems, while the latter is concerned primarily with generalizations, comparisons, and theoretical explanations about language. Of all the sciences, economics is perhaps the most like language in that considerable emphasis is placed on studying the structure of particular conventional systems of production and exchange rather than on the general theory of such systems.

That the nature of the meanings in a field can be of great practical import and not only of speculative interest is well illustrated in the history of economic thought. Classical economics was conceived after the fashion of a natural science, in the belief that the laws of exchange were laws of nature and that the economic destinies of man were guided by forces beyond his making or control. This physiocratic position underlay a laissez-faire approach to economic life, which eventually proved unrealistic and socially disastrous. It is now widely recognized that economic systems are human constructs, that economic life is subject to social determination, and that economic problems can be solved by deliberate policy decisions. This shift in economic theory from the status of a natural science to that of a policy science has had profound and far-reaching effects on the organization of production and distribution in the modern world.

The starting point for all consideration of economics is *natural resources* (land) and *population*. All material wealth is drawn from the bounty of the earth and is appropriated by the people who inhabit the earth. The raw materials of the land are extracted and transformed for human use by means of *labor*. The productivity of labor is greatly increased by *specialization* of function and the *division of labor* among the various specialists. The products of labor are the *goods* and *services* that people need and want. Goods are of two broad kinds: *consumer* goods (like food and clothing), which are directly used for the satisfaction of wants, and *capital* goods (like machinery and houses), which are used to sustain or increase productivity. An increase in capital goods requires a temporary sacrifice of consumer goods, but in the long run the larger capital outlay should make possible a considerably higher output of consumer goods.

Since every person needs many kinds of goods and services,

and not only those that he himself produces, the division of labor characteristic of all developed societies requires some system of *exchange* by which the production of each worker may be distributed to many others in return for a share in their products. The most influential social invention yet devised for effecting this exchange is the *market* system, in which the distribution of goods and services is determined by factors of *supply* and *demand*. Goods and services in the market are assigned *prices,* which under conditions of *perfect competition* are determined by the intersection of the two curves relating supply to price and demand to price, respectively. Different forms of analysis apply to situations of imperfect competition, of which the extreme case is complete *monopoly*. In the market system prices are assigned not only to commodities, but also to labor as *wages,* to the use of land and capital goods as *rent,* and to invested funds as *interest,* the rates of each being determined by supply and demand factors just as in the case of commodities.

The conduct of the market may be greatly facilitated by the use of *money,* which provides a convenient medium of exchange (all goods and services being thus reducible to a common standard of value), a unit of accounting, a "store of value," and a standard for deferred payment. Money may be in the form of commodities (e.g., gold or other metals), or more conveniently in various kinds of paper notes.

From the standpoint of understanding and control, the use of money is of far-reaching importance, for it permits economic activity to be measured mathematically. Because of the money system, qualitative preferences can be quantitatively assessed, and the powerful resources of mathematical computation can be brought to bear on the study and management of economic processes. The methods of economic analysis are at many points comparable to those of physics, where measurement and quantification are also of the essence. A considerable part of economic reasoning consists in the construction of ideal models, on the basis of certain simplifying assumptions (e.g., perfect competition), and the deduction of expected consequences, which can then be compared with observed economic behavior. If the observations do not agree with predictions, the theoretical model may be abandoned, or it may be refined and new testable predictions determined, or its range of applicability may simply be circumscribed. Because of the quantification effected by the use of money, economics is more amenable than any other social science to the use of precise theoretical models and the mathematical formulation of its principles and laws.

Economic activity is not, however, controlled simply by an automatic market mechanism constituting an interactive system similar to the matter-energy configurations of physics. The economy is part of a larger social system, and economic man is an abstraction from the more complex reality of social man. Hence, economics includes the study of (1) *business organizations,* including proprietorships, partnerships, and corporations, with their various systems of capitalization, ownership, and control, (2) *labor unions* and the processes of determining wages, hours, and conditions of work through collective bargaining, strikes, and other procedures, and (3) *government,* with its power to control economic life through (*a*) direct government expenditures, (*b*) taxation, (*c*) money and credit control using the banking system (Federal Reserve open market operations, discount rate policies, reserve requirements), (*d*) wage and price controls, (*e*) subsidies, (*f*) regulation of manufacturing, investment, transportation, and trade, (*g*) social security provisions, and (*h*) international economic policy (tariffs, foreign aid, trade agreements, and cooperation with world or regional organizations).

The most distinctive feature of contemporary economics, in comparison with earlier economic thought (prior to about 1930), is this recognition of the whole social context in which economic behavior occurs. The classical study of market mechanisms (microeconomics) is now being complemented by the analysis of total economic patterns (macroeconomics), using such concepts as *national income, national product* (gross or net), *price level, wage level, rates of saving* and *investment,* and rates of *economic growth.* These concerns, which originally came to the fore in attempting to control the *business cycle,* have now been incorporated in a comprehensive system of economic thinking that recognizes the possibility of deliberate social control of production and distribution in accordance with appropriate public policies regarding security, stability, freedom, and justice.

Methodologically, it should be added that economics as a modern policy science depends heavily upon descriptive statistics for providing a picture of population trends, prices and inventories of various commodities, volume of trade, wages for various types of work and distribution of workers by occupation, levels of interest, rent, income, saving and investment, money in circulation, and all the other data required to make wise decisions, whether individually, in private associations, or in government.

This sketch of the field of economics provides a fitting conclusion to our discussion of science as a realm of meaning. The study of economic processes combines the mathematical and mechanistic considerations of the physical sciences, the organismic ideas of the life sciences, and the distinctive human factors of the human sciences. Moreover, as conventional schemes, economic systems are related to the basic symbolic forms, while as social inventions, they are related to the created forms of the esthetic realm, to which we turn next.

THE THIRD REALM: *Esthetics*

12

MUSIC

Just as the empirical meanings in the sciences are essentially different in kind from the conventional meanings in the symbolic realm, so the esthetic meanings in the arts differ in kind both from symbolic and from empirical meanings. The chief feature distinguishing esthetic meanings from symbolic and empirical meanings is the *particularity* of the former. Symbolic meanings are *general* in the sense that the conventional forms are devised to serve as bearers of meaning in an indefinite number of instances. Symbol-systems are formal types in which the structural pattern alone matters and not the particular concrete instance of utilization. Similarly, science is general in the sense that the particular data of observation are not the goal of inquiry, but only the raw material for generalization and theory formation. Knowledge in language is primarily of general patterns of expression, which may be used in a great variety of particular contexts. Knowledge in science is ideally of general laws and theories, connected with observable particulars by way of prediction and verification.

In the esthetic realm, on the other hand, the object of knowledge is the singular particular form. The primary concern is not with types of things—not with kinds and classes of things—but with unique individual objects. Essentially, every esthetic object is incomparable. To classify it is to engage in an activity which is empirical, or perhaps philosophical, rather than properly esthetic.

One may raise the question whether esthetic meanings really deserve the name of knowledge at all. This is a matter on which opinions differ. Some prefer to limit the term "knowledge" to the strictly discursive and cognitive fields (i.e., mathematics and empirical science). Others prefer a wider reference, comprising meanings in the other realms, including the esthetic. The question is not of much importance. What is important is that by whatever name they are called, the distinctive meanings in each of the realms be acknowledged and understood. If the narrower interpretation of the term "knowledge" is preferred, a broader concept such as "understanding" may be used for the arts and other non-empirical fields.

Aristotle made a useful distinction between the *theoretical* or *speculative intellect* belonging to mathematics, science, and philosophy and the *practical intellect* [1] belonging to art and morals. The spheres of practical intellect may further be divided into the activity of *making,* which belongs to the arts, and the activity of *doing,* which belongs to morality. The understanding of art, therefore, is of making particular things and of particular things made. In other words, meanings in the arts refer to particular *works,* i.e., individual things which have been brought into being as a consequence of work.

Esthetic meanings are gained by *acquaintance* and not by *description,* as in the case of empirical meanings. Each work of art contains its own meaning and speaks for itself. Its significance cannot be embodied in separable symbolic patterns, as in the sciences. Knowledge in science is *about* kinds of things in certain of their aspects. Understanding in the arts is *of* particular things in their wholeness. Scientific knowledge is *mediated* by general symbolic forms. Esthetic understanding is *immediate,* referring directly to the objects perceived. Empirical knowledge is mediated

---

[1] Here "practical" is used in a broad sense, to refer to any active transformation of things, not merely to "utility" in the ordinary sense. Thus, "practical" as here used includes the activity of the "fine" artist as well as the craftsman.

by general *concepts*. Esthetic understanding is attained in direct *perception*. The content of scientific knowledge is expressed in *propositions,* statements that may be called true, false, or probable, or as holding within certain limiting conditions. Esthetic understanding is not contained in propositions, but in particular presented objects. While esthetic objects may contain propositions, as in the case of poetry and drama, these propositions merely contribute to the content of the work of art, and their truth or falsity is not the measure of the esthetic meaning of the work.

Moreover, descriptive propositions may be used to give information about a work of art, such as its origins and effects, the processes used in making it, and the designer's intention. Such information does not in itself yield esthetic understanding. It may, however, call attention to perceptual features in the work which would not otherwise be noticed and in this fashion become relevant to the esthetic meaning.

Another difference between science and art has already been treated in the discussion of symbolism in Chapter 7. The language of science is discursive, aiming at precise literal descriptions organized according to the principles of ordinary logic and reaching perfection in the formulas of mathematics. The language of art, on the other hand, is nondiscursive, symbolical, and metaphorical, and is organized according to the different logic of presented forms. Furthermore, the language of science is more readily separable from the expressions in which it is employed than is the language of art, where expressive materials and expressive content are virtually inseparable. Thus, it is possible to have well-developed autonomous disciplines of mathematics and ordinary grammar, but not of the languages of music and painting.

For a philosophy of meaning, the really crucial distinction is between empirical and esthetic meanings and not between knowledge of natural things and of things made. For, on the one hand, the sciences regularly deal with things made, and, on the other hand, one may have esthetic understanding of natural objects. Man-made products (i.e., works of art, in the broad sense) are properly studied in physics, chemistry, and the social sciences (especially anthropology). Also, the natural world of stars, plants, and people is an endless resource for esthetic delight. The essential distinction in type of meanings is between the descriptive, generalizing approach to things in the empirical realm and the immediate attentive perception of individual objects in the esthetic realm—in either case regardless of whether the things described or perceived are man-made or natural objects.

The fields of science and art are therefore by no means mutually exclusive. One may find deep esthetic meaning in things which are studied scientifically, for example, in interesting crystal formations or in the ritual patterns of a primitive tribe. The theoretical structures of science may be themselves esthetically admirable. Likewise, things which have been made to yield esthetic delight, such as buildings or the sounds of a symphony, can be analyzed empirically, and the activities of the creative artist can be subjected to scientific scrutiny. The empirical and esthetic realms are thus not divided by the nature of the objects treated or by ostensible subject matter, but by the kinds of understanding gained—the difference being between the general-descriptive and the individual-perceptive modes.

Esthetic meanings are herein treated in connection with a study of the arts because it is through the arts that esthetic understanding is most directly and deliberately cultivated. Of particular significance in this regard are the *fine arts,* traditionally comprising these seven: music, poetry, painting, sculpture, architecture, dance, and drama, which have been commonly regarded as the main source of the esthetic heritage of mankind. Actually, of course, nature provides far more extensive resources for esthetic experience, and the many artifacts constructed for other than esthetic purposes (in the "practical" arts and crafts) exercise a much more pervasive influence on the esthetic consciousness of mankind than do the fine arts. Nevertheless, the fine arts are particularly suitable for the study of meanings and for the special attention of educators because they provide the basis for the analysis of distinctive varieties of esthetic signification in the most pure and unambiguous forms and because they are an excellent foundation for the explicit pursuit of esthetic meanings through education. The fine arts are to the esthetic cultivation of mankind what the pure sciences are to the general development of empirical competences.

Following this preliminary general orientation to the esthetic domain, we shall now proceed to consider several major varieties of esthetic meaning within the fine arts, beginning with the field of music.

The subject matter of music consists of individual *musical compositions*. A "musical composition" is a patterned sequence of sounds which has a beginning and an ending and is deliberately created for an esthetic purpose—that is, to be listened to for its own intrinsic interest and not for any ulterior utilitarian ends. The meaning of each musical composition belongs to that composition alone and is not derived from its membership in any collection of such compositions.

Music is similar to language, in that both consist of patterned sound-sequences. The essential difference is that the sounds of music are not formed into conceptual symbols which communicate discursive meanings. Musical sounds directly impart their own qualitative meanings; they do not stand for ideas, as do the elements of intelligible speech.

Because music is made up of sounds, any given musical work is ephemeral; it is gone as soon as the last note has been sounded. In order to make re-creation of the work possible, a composition may be recorded by means of some sound-reproducing device, and it may be put into written form using certain conventional notations. The written score can then be read by performers, who render the composition with more or less fidelity to the composer's original intention for the benefit of other listeners. While composing, performing, and listening are substantially different activities, calling into play quite different skills, all three embody the same kinds of musical meanings. Using the medium of sound, the composer fashions the forms of musical meaning by the power of his creative imagination. The performer reconstructs those meanings, employing sound-producing instruments appropriate to the composition. The listener responds to these meanings in the corresponding patterns of his own feeling-states. The perceptual content is similar to all three; only the initiatives and the modes of active participation are different.

A musical work is a pattern of sounds and silences. The sounds may include irregular and complex vibrations called "noise" (such as produced by percussion instruments), "vocables," that is, the sounds of speech (in songs), and "tones," which consist of regular and relatively simple vibrations. Each tone is characterized by "pitch" (measured by its fundamental frequency of vibration), "tone color" (depending on the distribution of subsidiary frequencies, or harmonic vibrations), "loudness" (measured by the amplitude of vibration), and "duration."

The pitches used in music may vary over the entire range of audible frequencies, just as in speech an indefinite variety of phonetic elements is possible. Ordinarily, however, just as only certain phonemes are used as the sound basis for a given language, so in music certain distinguishable tones are selected as the basis for composition within a given musical tradition. For example, most European and American music of the last few hundred years has been based upon some selection of tones from the *chromatic scale* (the successive notes on a piano).

Although musical scales are arbitrary conventions, they are not ordinarily adopted without a rational basis. The *diatonic scale,* for example, consists of a succession of *octaves,* each of which contains seven distinct tones and follows the same pattern of whole and half steps (depending upon the mode, e.g., major and minor), the frequency of vibration doubling in the ascent from one octave to the next. The chromatic scale results from inserting half steps between the whole steps of the diatonic scale, yielding twelve tones to the octave. A *whole tone scale,* with six distinct tones, results from using only whole steps in passing through the octave.

Most music in the Western world has been so constructed that in any given section of the composition one particular tone (the *key* tone or *tonic* of the scale) serves as a kind of basis of orientation or reference for all the other tones. Different compositions may be written in different keys, and modulations from one key to another may be made within a composition. It is also possible to construct *atonal* music without any such reference tones. In music of this type some principle other than tonality is adopted to lend coherence to the work. Non-Western music is generally constructed on a different basis from that of the West and therefore sounds odd to those accustomed to ordinary Western tonality.

Actual musical tones seldom consist of a single frequency of vibration. The *fundamental* vibration is nearly always accompanied by *harmonic* vibrations whose frequencies stand in simple numerical ratios to the fundamental. The relative amplitudes of these constituents of the tone are responsible for its *color* or *timbre,* and these amplitude patterns are consequences of the structure of the instrument used for producing the sound. Musical understanding includes familiarity with the many kinds and shades of tone color and with the varieties of musical instruments employed (including the human voice). These instruments range from simple pipes, membranes, and strings, through more complex systems of the same, controlled by keys and valves, to the newer electronic instruments based on the oscillations of electrical circuits.

Music comes into being when tones are organized into significant patterns, and the understanding of music results chiefly from sympathetic attention to these patterns. The most fundamental musical patterns have to do with *rhythm,* that is the time relationships of tones. *Meter* is the pattern of regularly recurring accents, indicated by the *time signature* (e.g., 4/4, 5/4, 6/8, signifying four or five quarter-note beats or six eighth-note beats per measure). *Tempo* is the number of beats per minute, indicating the speed of the music. Rhythm goes beyond meter and tempo, and properly refers to the entire temporal organization of tones into phrases and the larger musical forms produced by the patterned combination of phrases.

The meaning of music is most intimately connected with the rhythmic sense, which in turn is directly related to the fundamental human experience of *time.* Time is measured by movement, rooted in the human organism in the regular pulses of the heart and in the periodicities of breathing, with its recurrent cycles of cumulation, tension, and release. The meaning of music is not simply a matter of intellectual comprehension. It is also an act of organic response in which the vital rhythms upon which life depends are brought into relation to the sound patterns of the music. Roger Sessions sums up this idea as follows: "Music is significant for us as human beings principally because it embodies movement of a specifically human type that goes to the roots of our being and takes shape in the inner gestures which embody our deepest and most intimate responses." [2]

An organized succession of tones constitutes a *melody,* which is also referred to as a *voice part,* whether or not it is actually sung. A composer working out a melody, an instrumentalist attempting to play it, or a listener seeking to understand it, may profit greatly by voicing the melodic line because in so doing his whole being is caught up in that rhythmic flow of sound which is the soul of the music.

The basic unit of melody is the melodic *motif,* an elemental tonal pattern that is capable of expansion and development into larger sequential structures. Motifs are stated, contrasted, and restated in hierarchies of rhythmic patterns comprising *phrases* (some complete, others incomplete, leading on to further resolutions), *periods,* and a great variety of more complex *melodic forms,* such as stanzaic, binary, ternary, song, rondo, dance, etc. These melodic constructions are analogous to the patterns of discourse built up in prose and poetry using words, phrases, clauses, sentences, and paragraphs as parts of literary compositions.

Combined tones formed by sounding two or more tones simultaneously constitute *chords.* Different combinations of tones produce quite different effects, with varying degrees of *consonance* and *dissonance,* depending on the simplicity or complexity of the ratio in which the respective tonal frequencies stand. Chord patterns are an important part of musical structure. They are closely connected with tonality because the tones from which chords are constructed are selected from the scales in which the music is composed. Chords are also connected with rhythm, some being "chords of movement," because of their dissonance and the sense of incompleteness produced by them, others being "chords of repose," because of their consonance and the resulting sense of finality.

The weaving together of different sound patterns yields musical *texture.* Melodies accompanied by chords constitute *harmonic texture,* while melodies combined with other melodies comprise *contrapuntal* or *polyphonic texture.* Music which is only

[2] *The Musical Experience,* Princeton University Press, Princeton, N.J., 1950, p. 19. Reprinted by permission of the publisher.

a single melody is called "monophonic," and music which has one melody with chords is called "homophonic."

In general, the sounding together of tones is called "harmony," whether as combined melodies or as chords. Harmony lends depth and richness to musical expression that is not possible using only single notes in temporal sequence. Melody and harmony together permit the construction of a two-dimensional manifold of sound in which the horizontal melodic lines are associated with vertical harmonic distributions, and the whole is visually represented by the form of the two-dimensional musical score.

Just as complex melodies are built up from melodic motifs by expansion, repetition, and contrast, so melodies and chords may be combined into successively larger musical patterns. The larger forms have been classified into such traditional categories as minuet, scherzo, rondo, theme and variations, passacaglia, fugue, and sonata, each with its characteristic structure. For example, the form of the first movement of the classical sonata consists of three main parts: exposition (usually repeated), development, and recapitulation, the exposition using two or more closely related keys with two or more contrasting themes, which are further elaborated in the development and finally restated in a single key in the recapitulation. An introduction may precede the exposition and a coda may be added as a final summing up. A complete musical composition may consist of a combination of several of these larger forms. Thus, a classical sonata, string quartet, concerto, or symphony usually consists of three or four movements, of which the first is in the sonata (or "first movement") form.

While the analysis and classification of musical forms is important to the musicologist, such theoretical knowledge does not in itself constitute musical understanding, which also requires direct sympathetic awareness. Preoccupation with theory sometimes interferes with the comprehension proper to music by diverting attention from the hearing of the work itself to ideas about the work. Nevertheless, musical meaning is communicated by the sound patterns which the theorist discerns and names, and anyone who seeks musical understanding or hopes to teach it needs a knowledge of the structure of sound that is the source of musical delight to the practiced listener. The value in the conceptual study of musical forms is in the direction of attention to esthetic possibilities hitherto unnoticed or otherwise only imperfectly sensed.

The ultimate object of esthetic attention in music is not the several forms and qualities disclosed by analysis, but the musical composition as a whole. Hence, if a piece of music is to qualify as a composition worthy of esthetic interest, it must have a certain organic unity among its parts. It may not be simply an aggregate of separate elements, no matter how interesting each element may be in itself. The principle of unity in variety is central in all esthetic endeavors. The source of significance in all of the arts—and indeed also of esthetic delight in natural objects—is in the weaving of contrasting parts into a single complex whole.

The meanings of a musical composition rest principally on its *musical ideas,* a term referring to those tonal or rhythmic patterns that provide the points of departure for the composition or for an episode or aspect of the composition. A "musical idea" may be a motif, which becomes the basis for larger melodic development, or a chord from which further harmonic elaborations grow. It may also be a rhythmic figure worked out in a variety of interesting modifications and contrasts. Musical ideas are the source of organic quality in the composition in that they lend it its distinctive character as a unique whole and embody its characteristic internal directions of growth. They are the formal factors binding the elements of the composition into a whole so as to impart a sense of life and motion.

Enrichment of experience through music depends upon openness to the boundless variety of possible musical ideas. A person's musical understanding is unnecessarily impoverished if he limits himself to certain traditional, conventional, and habitual musical patterns as being the only ones he considers authentic or admirable. Anyone who wishes to enlarge and deepen his esthetic insight must practice receptivity to unfamiliar musical forms (including the initially strange forms of non-Western music), listening to them hospitably and without preconceptions, until such inherent power to delight as they possess makes itself felt. Each work should be invited to speak its own message and to stand on its own merits alone, for it is in the perception of the singular work of art, and not in the conceptual classes to which the abstractive intellect may assign it, that its esthetic meaning consists.

Musical understanding in the final analysis is consummated in love. As earlier pointed out, although a knowledge of music theory, including an ability to analyze patterns of rhythm, melody, harmony, and tone color—the basic elements of all music—may be helpful, such rational competence does not in itself disclose esthetic meanings. Such meanings derive from the cultivation of self-forgetful delight in the direct contemplation of the patterns of musical statement, contrast, accent, progression, repetition, and variation that critical analysis describes.

13

THE VISUAL ARTS

The term "visual arts" will be used here to designate the fields of painting, drawing, graphic arts, sculpture, and architecture, in which the artist shapes tangible materials into objects of esthetic import. These works differ from music in having a degree of individual permanence. They are not composed of ephemeral sounds that persist only in memory and need to be re-created again and again by skilled performers. A painting, a drawing, a lithograph, a sculpture, or a building is made of relatively enduring materials, and, though it may be copied by repeating the original design or represented in a variety of reproductions, the original of each work of art (except in the graphic arts) is regarded as the one authentic instance of that work, all other copies or representations of it being considered secondary and derivative.

Just as the sciences all belong within a single category of meaning because they have in common the goal of empirical description culminating in generalizations, laws, and theories, so all the arts have in common the aim of creating singular objects that articulate significant patterns of subjective feeling. Again, as the sciences differ on the basis of subject matter described, so the arts differ in respect to the use of materials from which the works of art are constructed. Musical meanings are characteristically those produced when the materials used are sounds. Meanings in painting, drawing, and graphics differ from those in music because of the considerable differences between the properties of sounds and pigments (or pencil, ink, crayon, etc.). The import of sculpture is a consequence of using materials distributed in three dimensions rather than on a plane, as in painting, drawing, and graphics, and architectural meaning results from working with materials so organized as to yield perceptual delight by looking at the object, by moving in, around, and through it, and by dwelling in it. The other arts, to be treated in the following two chapters, are characterized by still other uses of materials.

Painting, drawing, the graphic arts, sculpture, and architecture, though differing in significant respects, are alike in being arts in which enduring materials are organized in significant spatial patterns. Because of this common basis, most of the same fundamental concepts can be used for characterizing the methods and structure of all these fields. In these arts the primary mode of perception is *visual* rather than *aural,* as in the case of music.

It is sometimes said that the visual arts are "arts of space," while music belongs to the "arts of time." It is certainly true that the temporal organization of tones is the clue to musical import and that the spatial organization of materials is the basis of the visual arts. Yet the assignment of arts to space and time cannot be made absolutely. For space is not irrelevant to music, nor time to the visual arts. The qualities of music are influenced by the spatial arrangement of players (as in an orchestra or choir), and the difference in quality between binaural and monaural sound perception is a function of the spatial separation of the two ears, yielding a feeling of "depth" rather than "surface" in the sound. Likewise, full visual understanding is not achieved instantaneously. The significance of a painting, drawing, lithograph, sculpture, or building is revealed step by step in time, as one visually explores the work, just as a musical composition unfolds moment by moment in the succession of tones. Nevertheless, a major difference still exists between the two domains in respect to time. This difference lies in the fact that the visual work in itself determines neither the content nor the rate of sequential impressions, as music does.

Similarly, the spatial arrangement is obviously essential to the meaning of a visual work, but only a subordinate contributory factor in a musical performance.

As in the case of music, the proper subject matter of knowledge in the visual arts is the *individual work*. Comparisons of one work with another, classification of works according to type, school, or style, and information about the circumstances of construction or the effects of exhibition are not in themselves of esthetic concern. Such factual data may be relevant to esthetic understanding, but only if they are used as a means for more insightful direct perception of specific works. The art historian, E. H. Gombrich, begins and ends his book on *The Story of Art* [1] with the remark that "there is really no such thing as art. There are only artists," by which he intends to emphasize the individuality of art as opposed to the generalization of science. One might better say that from a strict esthetic viewpoint there are not even artists, but only particular works of art. These works in turn give rise to a variety of individual esthetic intuitions as different persons perceive the works at different times and under different circumstances.

Recalling Aristotle's distinction between the speculative and practical intellect, it is evident that in the arts the connection between means and ends is much closer and inseparable than in science. Knowledge in science is gained through observation and experimentation using appropriate techniques and instruments. But once the knowledge is secured, the means used to gain it recede from view. In the arts this separation is never so clear, for the work of art bears the sensible impress of the means used to create it. Science results in independent ideas; artistic activity culminates in sensible objects in which the esthetic ideas are inseparably embodied. Hence, in the study of art, materials and techniques play an essential role.

The successful artist in any given field is a person who thinks well with the *characteristic materials* of that field. Thus, the musical composer is skillful in thinking with sounds. The painter articulates his inner life through the medium of paints. The sculptor reveals his intuitions in metal, clay, or marble. The

[1] Phaidon Publishers, Inc., New York, 1958, pp. 5, 446.

architect speaks volumes with wood, brick, stone, steel, or any number of other building materials. Similarly, in the dance and drama the artist works through the medium of bodily movement and action, and in literature the esthetic idea is embodied in words.

What holds for the creative artist also applies, though with somewhat less force, to any person who seeks to understand a given art form. No one can intimately comprehend works in a given field unless he cultivates an immediate feeling for the basic qualities, possibilities, problems, and limitations of the materials from which objects in that field are made. Such feeling is best, or perhaps only, gained by actual practice in manipulating the kind of stuff with which the artist works. No such demand attaches to the student of science, who may possess an excellent descriptive knowledge of things without any direct acquaintance with the construction of the instruments used in experimental inquiry. In science such acquaintance is, of course, valuable supplemental knowledge, but it is not of the essence as it is in the arts.

Mastery in the arts grows out of prolonged imaginative experimentation with material media in order to exploit most fully the expressive possibilities of the substances used. Oil paint is a medium which can be applied in many different ways, transparently or opaquely, with smooth or rough surfaces. Different effects are obtainable with tempera or water colors. In drawing, the artist may use pen and ink, crayon or charcoal, a sharp, hard pencil or a blunt, soft one, smooth or rough paper, and a variety of techniques in applying the coloring substance. In the graphic arts the medium is of even more decisive importance than in drawing and painting. Prints may be produced from woodcuts, engravings, lithographs, stencils, or etchings (the plates being made either by acid or by the dry point process). Sculptors make use of a great many kinds of materials which they form by a number of different techniques, the most common of which are carving, modeling, casting, and construction. In architecture the kinds of materials used are manifold, and they are put together in many ways, including such traditional construction patterns as posts and lintels, arches, vaults and domes, and (particularly in modern steel structures) cantilevers and trusses. Each technique in planning the building is used to satisfy the requirements of space spanning, area enclosure, volume creation, and secure support.

This brief statement indicates only some of the principal materials and techniques used in the visual arts. Many others could be added, such as collage, mosaic, stained glass, ceramics, tapestry, and photography. Art forms are as various as are the kinds of material substances and the imaginations of ingenious designers. The fact to be emphasized is the significance of the material used in the construction of the work of art and, consequently, the importance for the education of esthetic sensibility of direct familiarity with matter and technique.

The materials of the work of art do not, of course, in themselves embody its meaning. Its significance depends, rather, on the manner in which the materials are organized, that is, upon the *formal* properties of the work. The esthetic feeling evoked by a painting, print, sculpture, or building is a result of the qualities of its constituent materials as they are put together in a patterned whole.

This interrelation of material elements to form an esthetic whole may be illustrated by considering some of the typical concepts used in the analysis of a painting. The forms and relationships of *line* in a painting express both structures and movements. Some line patterns suggest harmony and ease, others suggest conflict and harshness. Some give a feeling of rigidity, others of flexibility. The sense of movement in the picture is conveyed by the way in which the eye is led in rhythmic fashion from one part to another by the continuity of the lines.

Color is another important expressive factor, both in its basic qualities of hue, saturation (relative vividness), and value (relative lightness or darkness), and in its distribution in the painting. The color qualities in themselves arouse characteristic emotional responses, and by their arrangement in degrees of contrast or continuity affect the sense of movement in the picture, expressing agitation or repose, excitement or serenity. The color values produce balanced and contrasting patterns of *light* and *shade,* which are both inherently expressive and contribute to the sense of *volume* in the picture. The feeling of volume is further induced by line contours which effect closure rather than ending abruptly. The color and line treatment can likewise create the appearance of *mass,* some patterns yielding an impression of lightness and delicacy, others a feeling of weight and solidity.

The illusion of *depth* in a painting is necessary if the two-dimensional canvas is to produce the three-dimensional effects inherent in volume and mass perception. If the artist wishes to express the feeling of a single unified space, he uses a system of *perspective,* based on the apparent diminution in size (or color and distinctness) of an object as it recedes into the distance. Depending on the perspective relations employed, the space created may be a peaceful or a dynamic one. Instead of a single space, the painter may choose to represent more than one space on the same canvas, inviting the eye to move unceasingly from one area to another without reference to any one fixed point of view. The depth element in a painting is frequently analyzed by means of a series of apparent *planes,* parallel or intersecting, into which imagination discerns the components of the picture to be organized.

Finally, the way in which lines, colors, light and shade, volumes, masses, and planes are interrelated defines the *composition* of the painting. Relevant to composition are the relative proportions of light and dark, horizontal and vertical, curved and straight, the relation of the size and shape of the painting as a whole, in its *frame,* to the size, shape, and locations of the parts of the design, and the various aspects of balance, symmetry, and contrast among its constituents.

Similar analytical concepts apply to the other visual arts. Contours and surfaces yield feelings of mass and volume in sculpture, and the shapes and distribution of stationary materials may produce a sense of tension or repose, equilibrium or movement, harmony or struggle. Light and dark, smooth and rough surface texture, and the color of materials used also contribute to the expressive effect of the work of sculpture. Even though a sculpture is not framed, like a painting, the work gives a sense of encompassing volume within which the solids and voids are organized to form a composite whole.

In architecture the design of a building is to a large extent analyzable in terms of series of parallel and perpendicular planes, although domes, arches, and other curved lines and surfaces may also enter into the pattern. The proportion of horizontal and vertical components is particularly important in giving the effect of lateral movement or of ascent. Some buildings are organized so as to induce feelings of quiet respose, others of tense striving. In some cases the composition is simple and regular, with an obvious central volume surrounded by symmetrically distributed volumes. In other cases the composition is more complex and irregular, yet with some organizing pattern that relates the volumes in a unified whole. Colors, light and shade (including the arrangement of doors and windows), and texture of materials (walls, roof, doors, etc.) also contribute to the feeling created by the building.

In architecture a factor of particular significance is the relation of the structure to its environment, both natural and manmade. Since the esthetic effect of the building depends on the context in which it is placed, the architect needs to plan his design with due consideration for the landscape setting and for other structures in the vicinity. Finally, the form of the building also needs to be planned both with due regard to the uses for which it is intended (including provision for possible changes of use) and with concern for the esthetic integrity of the structure as a source of continuing perceptual delight, not merely of practical utility in the narrow sense. A building can be esthetically significant and still be *functional* if "function" is understood to include a wide range of human responses rather than merely those of productive efficiency.

Up to this point we have considered the meaning of a work of art by reference to its material qualities and the design by which the material components are organized into a patterned whole. The question now is whether or not these material and formal meanings exhaust the significance of the work. Does the work express something more than the immediate perceptual effects of the organized sense materials? Clearly what a person sees in an art object depends considerably on his previous experience. His perceptions of the object arouse associations affecting the appearance of the object to him. One of the most perplexing problems of esthetics is how to distinguish associations that are appropriate to a work of art (and therefore esthetically relevant) from those that are not. *Impressionistic* critics hold that any and all associations are appropriate and that a work of art means whatever the viewer feels in perceiving it. *Formalistic* critics, on the other extreme, hold that the meaning of the work consists in its intrinsic material and formal properties and not in any associations of the observer. The positive values in both extremes can be preserved in a position that allows for associations disclosing relationships within the work itself that are confirmable in the perception of all who view it with openness and sympathy.

The question of meaning in works of visual art is especially critical in respect to the matter of *representation* or *imitation*. There is a long tradition in esthetic theory according to which a work of art is considered an imitation of other things either concretely existing or subsisting in an ideal realm. Plato regarded the artist's creation as twice removed from reality, as a copy of an existing thing, which is in turn a copy of an ideal form (the only true reality). A widespread commonsense view is that the proper aim of the painter or sculptor is to imitate real objects, the worth of his work being measured by how faithfully he represents them.

The trouble with the imitation theory is that it unduly restricts the range of admissible meanings. If an artist wishes to represent some actual thing, there need be no objection to his doing so. Many of the greatest paintings and sculptures have achieved a high degree of verisimilitude. On the other hand, there is no reason why all paintings and sculptures *must* look like something else. In fact, a first principle of esthetic meaning is that the significance of what is perceived refers to the unique object and not to any relationships beyond itself. One does not ordinarily expect a musical composition to imitate anything else. Nor is the architect's handiwork usually supposed to represent any other object. Why, then, should a painting or a sculpture have to conform to the design of something outside itself? It would appear essential to the freedom of the artist that no such requirement be imposed.

One of the great achievements of modern art has been the liberation of painting and sculpture from the limitations of representationism. It is important for the student of the arts to be taught from the beginning that the meaning of a drawing, a painting, or a sculpture is not necessarily or principally contained in the answer to the question "What does it look like?" Its meaning consists in the perceived design—in a unique pattern of colors, lines, surfaces, volumes, light and shade, which express certain intrinsic and singular qualities of the object.

When representation is rejected as the criterion of esthetic worth, it becomes much more difficult to make reliable and defensible critical judgments about works of art. The artist is freed to fashion anything to which his fancy inclines him, without being held to account by the world of existing things. Still, critical choice is not excluded, for the sovereign esthetic criterion remains, namely, the power of the work to create delight in the attentive and sympathetic beholder. This ultimate esthetic criterion is the basis on which in the long run the meaningful may be distinguished from the meaningless among works of art. The works of enduring worth demonstrate their power to arouse interest and love in generation after generation of viewers, while the flood of oddities and mediocrities make their fleeting impressions and pass into oblivion.

In music the musical idea (e.g., any melodic motif, rhythmic pattern, or harmonic design that provides a basis for the organic development of the composition) was presented as a useful concept for analyzing musical meanings. Somewhat analogously, in the visual arts it is helpful to consider the *artistic problem* which a particular work is designed to solve. The artist's problem is to use his materials to express an *esthetic idea,* that is, to achieve certain perceptual effects. There is no limit to the range and kinds of admissible problems. The problem may be that of accurately representing some existing natural object, but it need not be. Indeed, more usually the problem is to create something entirely new, organizing materials into forms that gain heightened interest from the fact that they transcend the demands of nature and ordinary utility. The purpose of the artist is to achieve perfection in the solution of his particular problem, that is, to organize his materials in just the right way for the embodiment of his perceptual idea. The success of the work is then to be judged with respect to the artist's problem and not with respect to some other problem that may be implicit in the viewer's preconceptions. If this principle is kept in mind, it may be possible to discern valuable meanings in works of art that would be obscure to perception guided by extraneous expectations.

One of the best ways of gaining an understanding of the variety of possible problems and solutions in the visual arts is to study the history of art. Since the painters, sculptors, and architects of a given period and place have often shared similar problems, it is possible to use certain common interpretive categories to discern the intention of many different individual works of art. Such historical generalizations can be helpful in guiding the viewer to a better direct perception of the individual works. The following illustrations suggest the nature of these historical generalizations.

Primitive art was often connected with magic. Its function was not primarily to give pleasure, but to open channels to supernatural powers. Hence, an understanding of particular primitive art forms may be enhanced by studying the magical rituals of the tribes concerned.

Ancient Egyptian art was developed within the context of a highly organized social system. It was correspondingly stylized according to certain formal conventions. The purpose of the artist was to preserve everything in clarity and completeness. Thus, his pictures were meant to function more as maps than as direct visual representations of things. The resulting pictorial art was accordingly conceptual rather than perceptual in its effect.

Classical Greek art, on the other hand, was characterized by deep human feeling. The great Greek sculptors had a profound interest in the natural forms of things, particularly the human body. Greek painters and architects discovered foreshortening, and thus developed a perceptual art instead of the essentially conceptual Egyptian type. Another preoccupation of the Hellenic artists was the problem of presenting a vivid sense of movement in a painting or a statue. This problem was successfully solved in the classical period by the appropriate dynamic organization of surfaces, contours, and volumes.

The practical-minded Romans were less concerned than were the Greeks with harmony and beauty and more with the accurate rendering of details. Their civic aims are evident in their lifelike representations of political leaders and culture heroes, and in their great public buildings, which served as symbols of imperial pomp and power.

Medieval Christian artists were chiefly interested in using their talents to communicate the Christian message. Hence, they abandoned the humanism and naturalism of the classical Greeks in favor of something like the Egyptian objective of clarity and completeness, but now aimed at persuasively teaching the Christian faith. The medieval Christian artist also learned to portray what he *felt,* rather than what he *knew* (as in ancient Egyptian art) or what he *saw* (as in Hellenic art), and this objective opened up wholly new channels of expression.

Norman and Romanesque church architecture of the twelfth century, using imposing masses of stone, expressed the idea of the *Church militant,* while the Gothic style of the thirteenth century, using stone and glass in a framework calculated for maximum strength with minimum bulk, yielding a sense of weightlessness and uplift, expressed the idea of the *Church triumphant.*

In the late thirteenth century Giotto rediscovered the art of creating an illusion of depth and opened a new era by painting in such a way as to make the stories told by his pictures seem real and present. The International Style of the fourteenth century represented interest in delicate and beautiful things and was based upon the practice of careful observation of natural objects.

In the fifteenth century the problem of depth was solved by the architect Brunelleschi's discovery of perspective, which was quickly taken up by painters. In the same period Jan Van Eyck invented the art of painting with oils instead of tempera, thus providing a medium for the more faithful representation of things with full scientific accuracy.

The Renaissance flowering of interest in the real world culminated in the great Italian artists of the sixteenth century, such as Leonardo, Michelangelo, Raphael, and Titian. Leonardo solved the problem of making a painting seem alive by his invention of *sfumato*—blurred outline and mellowed colors inviting the observer's imagination to supply the living quality of the figure. Michelangelo, as sculptor, solved the problem of making his figures appear as though a living form had been released from a block of stone. In painting, Raphael achieved masterful effects of simplicity and serene beauty through skill in composition, and Titian consummated the art of attaining a sense of unity.

El Greco in the late sixteenth century foreshadowed future reactions against correctness of representation, presenting visions that led the imagination far beyond the confines of ordinary reality. Men like Caravaggio, Velásquez, and Rembrandt in the seventeenth century presented an honest naturalism in contrast to the formal idealism of such painters as Carracci and Reni.

Following the artificiality and decorativeness of the eighteenth-century Baroque and Rococo and the rationalism and moralism of the Enlightenment, the visual arts participated in the revolutionary upheavals of the late eighteenth century, and artists began to revolt against standard styles and traditional subject matter. In the nineteenth century for the first time art became separated from the common life. Artists sought to express their own individuality, freely choosing their own problems. Delacroix, Millet, and Courbet chose to represent reality with all its pathos and without sentimentality. Manet chose to show how things *look,* apart from knowledge of how they *ought* to look. Monet and the other Impressionists set down interesting designs of light and color suggested by things, in complete disregard of the standard criteria of suitable subject matter, balanced composition, and accurate drawing.

With Cézanne an autonomous modern art came to fulfillment. In accord with his example, artists devoted themselves zealously to the exploration of what Clive Bell called "significant form," in its most various manifestations, from the Expressionism of Van Gogh, and the Primitivism of Gauguin and Rousseau, the Cubism of Picasso and Duchamp, and the abstract Constructionism of Mondrian, to the Surrealism of Dali. The goal of the modern movement is to liberate the artist from the necessity of working at only one problem, such as copying nature faithfully, so that he may enrich the life of all by opening up new worlds of esthetic meaning through the power of his creative vision.

These few examples from the history of art suggest something of the richness of possibilities for endeavor in the visual arts. For our purposes the lesson to which they point is not primarily that art is conditioned by its historical setting (though that is doubtless true) but that artists and their works need to be understood in the light of their specific aims and not in terms of any universal and permanent standards of validity. For the last word about a work of art, like the first, is that its meaning consists in what its organized materials uniquely express.

14

THE ARTS OF MOVEMENT

Music and the visual arts have been considered first in the present section because they are the most highly developed, most widely understood, and, in a sense, the "purest" forms of esthetic expression. However, these arts are not primary, either historically or in relation to human nature. The earliest and most elemental of all the arts is the dance. The dance is the primordial art because the instrument employed in it is the human body itself, and because bodily movement is fundamental to all human existence.

The *sense of movement* is inherent in every human activity. To be alive is to be able to respond—to be moved and to move. All perceptions of the surrounding world are accompanied by motor reactions. Every experience, whether primarily of feeling, thought, or volition, engages the whole person, including the interconnected system of muscles, nerves, bones, tissues, organs, and internal secretions. No other instrument is as elaborate, sensitive, and intimately responsive as the human body. This is why the arts of movement are so important for the expression and perception of human meaning.

The term "arts of movement" is intended to include all intentional activities, undertaken for esthetic purposes, in which the desired expressive effects are communicated by the movement of the human body. Obviously movement also occurs for other than esthetic reasons, as in daily work, eating, locomotion, and social activities, and much of what a person must learn relates to the motor skills required for the successful conduct of daily life. The special value of the arts of movement, and particularly of the dance, is that they afford opportunities for the deliberate and concentrated cultivation of bodily potentialities without limitation by the exigencies of practical life.

The arts of movement are the foundation for the learnings which take place under the broad heading of "physical education." The program of instruction in this field is ordinarily centered around individual and team sports and gymnastic activities, with the dance being at most one among many options. Closely related are the fields of health education and of recreation. All these fields are concerned with promoting the vigor of the human organism, neuromuscular skills, good interpersonal behavior, emotional balance and control, and sound judgment. While these objectives extend beyond the esthetic concern which is proper to the arts, it is still true that the arts of movement, and particularly the dance, provide the main key to methods and meanings in health, recreation, and physical education.

The fundamental concept of the arts of movement is the *organic unity* of the person. Health means wholeness, and the goal of education may be regarded as personal wholeness. From this standpoint the classic duality of mind and body is rejected. A person cannot think without a body, nor are his motor responses independent of thought. If learning is to be organic, provision needs to be made for activities in which the intellectual and motor components of experience are deliberately correlated. This union of thought, feeling, sense, and act is the particular aim of the arts of movement and of the fields of health, recreation, and physical education. Nowhere else is the coordination of all components of the living person so directly fostered, nor the resulting activity so deeply rooted in the unitary existence of the person.

It was pointed out earlier that meanings in the arts are immediate perceptions rather than the mediated conceptions of the discursive fields. Of all the arts, the arts of movement best exemplify this immediacy, since the person's own body is the instrument of expression and response. Here perceptions arise from the felt tensions and rhythms of the organism itself, without objectification in any nonhuman thing. Thus, the meanings communicated are, so to speak, flesh of our flesh and bone of our bone. They interpret the life of persons at the very wellsprings of organic being.

The materials of dance are *movements,* perhaps with assistance from music, costumes, stage settings, architecture, and lighting. These supplementary materials are all subordinate to movement and are only justified insofar as they enhance the presentation of the inner life of dynamic conflict and resolution, lift and decline, as it is objectified by bodily movements. The movements of the dance are designed to express definite inward purposes, moods, and attitudes. They are not random and haphazard, but controlled so as to convey ideas of the ebb and flow of feelings and emotions. They are intelligible forms with their own characteristic presentational logic. They make visible the subjective life of persons by means of a series of symbolic gestures.

Unlike music, which has a highly efficient system of notation, the dance has traditionally had no written form. Consequently, dance designs have largely had to be transmitted directly from person to person instead of impersonally through graphic transcriptions. As a result, the accurate recovery of long discontinued forms is impossible, protracted declines in the condition of the art have been difficult to avoid, and the preservation and diffusion of dance achievements have been hindered. Only in the twentieth century have satisfactory systems of dance notation begun to be developed (as in the work of Rudolph Laban, the author of a comprehensive system of notation for indicating movement).

As an art form, dance is closely related to music. Though originally music was used only as an accompaniment to dance, it long ago became established as an independent art in the Western world. The forms devised to solve musical problems are ordinarily not suitable for dance, and musical ideas are not always translatable into corresponding forms of movement. Nevertheless, complete dance does involve voice as well as movement, and appropriate subordinate musical accompaniments are often composed for the dance.

The connection between dance and drama is even closer than between dance and music. Music is a disembodied expression of emotions that dance expresses bodily. Drama, on the other hand, embodies emotions in the persons of characters, while the dance aims at *typifying* human emotions. Dance is a composition of movements that express kinds of feelings, while drama is composed of *actions* that portray events of human significance.

The dance shares with all the arts the quality of *abstraction*. That is to say, the meanings expressed are not merely accidental, subjective, and personal. They are intended as objectifications of inner experiences having universal import. They are not of the same nature as the abstractions of the sciences, which are contained in conceptual generalizations. Rather, the meanings conveyed in the dance and in the other arts are communicated in particular sensuous presentations. Their perceptual vital connotations are contained in specific organic forms capable of being understood by other sensitive and receptive persons because the feelings conveyed are deeply rooted in the basic structure of human nature.

These meanings are also *idealizations*. They are not meant to reproduce nature nor to imitate commonplace actions, which are in no need of artistic expression. The forms of art offer a re-shaping or transformation of nature that exalts, clarifies, and concentrates perception through significant abstraction. The artist creates a new world in which human potentialities not fulfilled in the natural world can be realized.

In the dance, as in every other art, the expressive forms tend to crystallize into traditional formulas. Historical, geographic, and ethnic factors enter into the development of standardized *styles* in art. Thus, even though the impulses of artistic creation are universal, the particular forms of expression are influenced by circumstances of time and place. This fact of stylization imposes two obligations on those who seek to communicate esthetic meanings. First, attention should be directed beyond the forms to the inner life they are designed to express. Second, interpretations have to be offered so that the artistic style of a group of people can become meaningful to persons living in a different time or culture. Such translation across group lines requires an imaginative and sympathetic attempt to participate in the life of the other people so that their unfamiliar artistic idioms may become intelligible. The goal of understanding alien styles of dance is not, however, merely conceptual in quality, yielding knowledge *about* other people and their ways. It depends on the ability to make the appropriate *motor* responses to the forms presented. The characteristic meaning of the dance consists in the direct experience, whether as a dancer or as a spectator, of the sense of movement that the forms of the art objectify.

Contemporary dance as an art form is of two main types: ballet and modern expressive dance. In ballet the objective formal qualities are emphasized; in the expressive dance the chief concern is the communication of emotion. In the ballet more or less standard codes of movement are used, and particular motor skills are exploited to the full; in the expressive dance the crystallization of forms is minimized, and the direct relation of movement to life experience is emphasized.

The ballet is a particular kind of theater dance developed during the Renaissance. It suffered stylistic ossification and became a mere decorative adjunct to the opera, until it was rescued and given its independent place as a theater art by Jean George Noverre in the mid-eighteenth century. After another period of decay in the nineteenth century, it was again revitalized in the present century by Michel Fokine, whose cardinal rules may be summarized as follows: (1) Let there be no ready-made routines. (2) Each ballet shall be a unified dramatic sequence without extraneous passages. (3) Expression is to be effected by means of the whole body, not by stylized hand gestures. (4) The *corps de ballet* is to participate integrally in the dance and not serve merely as a decorative background. (5) Music, scenery, and costumes are to serve with the dance in fulfilling a single esthetic purpose. The essence of these rules is the principle of organic vitality: the insistence that the dance express living experience through an integrated sensuous pattern.

According to John Martin, the soul of ballet is *idealistic abstraction,* and its body is *dynamic equilibrium,* in which "the dancer becomes a sensuous sentient object maintaining balance against all hazards, inviting and even extending these hazards far beyond the margin of safety and meeting them effortlessly in evidence of a dominion over the inertias and circumscriptions of realism." [1]

The classical ballet has its own *vocabulary of movement*. There are five fundamental positions of the feet, five corresponding positions of the arms, others for the hands and head, eight directions of the body, seven types of movement (bending, stretching, rising, jumping, gliding, darting, turning), and various climactic poses used to finish sequences of movement. Additional effects can be achieved by the dancer rising on the toes. From these various elements an inexhaustible variety of movement designs can be created.

The dynamic equilibrium of the ballet is achieved within a gravitational field. The postural standard from which all departures are made is that of the vertical body supported by the legs as a single solid column, with the feet as a stable base. As parts of the body are moved from this neutral position, compensatory movements are made by other parts to maintain gravitational equilibrium. The support of the legs is dramatized in a great variety of ways, the arms participate in the development of designs, and the orientation of the head and the facial expression are made to harmonize with the larger body movements. In all cases the movements and postures are felt as emanating from the whole body as a dynamic unity and not simply from separate body parts.

The modern expressive dance emerged as an art in the present century through the revolutionary work of such artists as Isadora Duncan, who saw the dance as a projection of the inner life of a dancer, and Mary Wigman, who first developed expressive dance as an objective art with clear dramatic form. These modernists in the field of dance, like their counterparts in music (e.g., Arnold Schönberg and Igor Stravinsky) and in the visual arts (e.g., Paul Cézanne and Frank Lloyd Wright), aim to liberate the artist from subservience to standard forms, particularly from the obliga-

[1] *Introduction to the Dance*, W. W. Norton & Company, Inc., New York, 1939, p. 217. Reprinted by permission of the publisher.

tions of verisimilitude, so that he may create new and unfamiliar ideal abstractions for the enrichment of the world of human meanings.

The method of the expressional dance differs from that of the ballet in that, rather than starting with a given vocabulary of movement and using it to display the dancer's powers, as in the ballet, the point of departure is the emotional life of the dancer, whose goal is the presentation of a *significant emotional concept* through formal movement materials created *extempore* for that specific purpose. The primary equipment of the modern dancer is a body trained for strength, control, plasticity, and responsiveness. The training required is physical education in the organic sense: the development of skill in bodily responses in perfect correlation with relevant intellectual and affective factors within the whole person.

As stated earlier, the emotion expressed by the dancer is not merely an individual subjective impulse. The dancer is not supposed to move under the compulsion of immediate private emotional pressures. He has to learn to remember, re-create, and objectify significant human emotions so as to evoke similar responses in other people. This mastery of *emotional objectification* is the heart of dance technique.

The native realm of the dancer in all types of dance is *space,* both the particular space around the body and the general space in which he moves. Movement through space introduces the factor of *time,* and since the movement must take account of gravity, *weight* also enters as an essential element. However, space, time, and weight in the dance are perceptual categories—the stuff of immediate inward experience—and not general metrical standards as they are in the conceptual formulations of the physical sciences, where the same three factors also occupy a central position.

In the arts of movement the organization of space, time, and weight has symbolic import. For example, the basic body attitudes in dance are sometimes described metaphorically as those of "arrow," "wall," and "ball," connoting respectively such feelings as piercing, dividing, and turning inwards. Movements upward may signify aspiration, downward submission, across the body seclusion, outwards awareness and welcome, backward retreat,

forward initiative and purposefulness. When directional movements such as these are accompanied by compensatory shifts in
weight, quite different expressive effects—with more tension and
complexity of emotion—are achieved. For example, movements
along diagonal directions (from the standpoint of the body imagined as in a horizontal cube) produce more tension than do
movements in the vertical and horizontal directions, because of
the required weight redistributions. Each body orientation has
its natural expressive possibilities, which the dancer seeks to ex-
plore and to realize through his movements.

The *expressive qualities* of movements can be analyzed in
terms of the qualities and combinations of the various motion
factors. The weight factor may vary on a scale from heavy to light,
the space factor from direct to flexible, and the time factor from
sudden to sustained. Different combinations of these factors produce different qualities of movement. For example, a heavy, direct,
sudden movement (a punch) differs in quality from a heavy,
direct, sustained movement (a press) or a light, flexible, sustained
movement (a float).

Being able to analyze movements is, of course, no indication
that they are understood inwardly and that one has learned to
respond to them with his own whole being. Nevertheless, conceptual analysis of perceptual forms may be helpful in directing
attention to the essentials of what is to be learned through the arts
of movement. Such intellectual formulation is also necessary in
arriving at an understanding of the distinctive kinds of meaning
in these arts and their place within the whole enterprise of
teaching and learning.

In the arts of movement, as in the other arts, the goal of creation
is the making of significant individual works of art, and the perceiver's aim is to understand the import of those works in their
uniqueness. Thus, in the dance the object to be created and understood is the *individual dance composition*. For the making of such
works no fixed rules of method apply. They are the offspring of
creative imagination, in response to the urgencies of vital expression, using the natural powers of the human organism itself
as materials.

Concerning the method of invention in the arts of movement,

one begins with some kind of stimulus, such as a *movement idea,* a verbal concept, a visual image, or a sound, which starts an expressive movement flow. This flow comprises *movement motives* and *movement phrases,* analogous to the melodic motives and phrases in musical composition. Using these elements, *themes* are developed, with repetitions and variations to supply the continuity and contrast essential in every significant esthetic object. The boundaries and divisions of the composition are marked by *climaxes,* produced by final thrusts, intensifications, or sharp contrasts.

Above all, what makes the composition a work of art is its organic quality. It is a whole, with beginning, middle, and end and with parts so interfused and interdependent that none could be omitted without damage to the others. It is not a collection of isolated elements. It is a creation expressing the organic rhythms of the living person. The logic of its development reflects the inner dialectic of personal life, in which each new element is assimilated within a system with basic organic integrity and continuity. Thus, the forms of the dance exhibit intrinsic relationships growing out of the immediacy of the inner life rather than the extrinsic relationships that characterize arbitrary constructions and conventional abstractions.

A final factor of great importance in the arts of movement and in the larger related fields of health, physical education, and recreation is the element of *play.* Whether or not particular play activities fall within the province of the arts as such, the typical meanings inherent in play belong to the esthetic realm. A consideration of play therefore helps to reinforce and illuminate the meanings characteristic of the several fields of artistic creation.

The classic treatment of the philosophy of play is Johan Huizinga's *Homo Ludens: A Study of the Play Element in Culture.* [2] Huizinga demonstrates that play is not a minor and incidental form of human activity appropriate only to children and to adults in their times of relaxation, but that it is a primordial civilizing force influencing every field of cultural endeavor. He shows that the play element is clearly evident in language, in law, in war, in the pursuit of knowledge, in philosophy, in religion,

[2] Beacon Press, Boston, 1955.

in poetry, in music, and most particularly in the dance, the perfect exemplification of play.

Huizinga's analysis of the essentials of play discloses eight features of meaning in this field. First, play is *free,* not obligatory. The player chooses to participate in the game, just as the artist deliberately elects to create his works of art and the perceiver of the works voluntarily enjoys them.

Second, play is concerned with a *make-believe* world, and not with ordinary, everyday life. Play, like the arts, effects a transformation of existence. By the power of imagination a new order of things is created in which the complexities and frustrations of concrete actuality are overcome in the ideal abstraction of a game or a work of art. Play is not designed to enable one to adjust to the real world or to help him meet ordinary wants and needs. It is, rather, a kind of ecstasy lifting up the participant to a realm of freshness and extraordinary delight.

Third, play occurs within a *limited space and time.* A game, like a work of art, is a definite finite object with a beginning and an end. It is a complete, individual whole. Like a picture, it has a frame, and like a symphony, it has its proper duration.

Fourth, play has *order.* It is not random activity. A game is an organized pattern of events, a structure with its own inherent logic. The order of play is not primarily that of ordinary discourse or of science; it belongs, rather, to the perceptual idealizations of the esthetic realm—of forms presented for the immediate enjoyment of the experiencer.

Fifth, play lives on *contest* and *tension.* Players struggle with one another to win the game, not for personal gain but for the love of the activity itself. The player strives for excellence. His aim is prowess in the chosen form of contest. His satisfaction consists in playing the game well, as the artist also seeks perfection in the making of his works, devoting himself without reservation to the service of his art.

Sixth, play proceeds according to *rules* which are absolutely binding on the players in the game. The worst sinner in play is the spoilsport, who rejects the rules, and not the cheat, who implicitly acknowledges the rules in attempting to conceal his breaking of them. The rules comprise the constitution of the play society, the binding element making possible a disciplined form of conjoint activity. The arts reflect this aspect of play to the extent that certain artistic conventions are adopted as the agreed basis for artistic construction and interpretation. In both play and art, of course, the principle of freedom requires that the rules be voluntarily adopted and that new sets of rules may be invented without limit.

Seventh, play activities tend to form *enduring communities.* The temporary associations of the play group lead to long-term voluntary associations. Similarly, though works of art are individual esthetic objects, artistic activity leads to persisting schools and movements, which are influential in determining the cultural atmosphere of civilization.

Finally, play associations tend to be *esoteric* and *secret.* They give their members a sense of being privileged "insiders," and the life shared is regarded as something special, different from the ordinary life of the public world. Belonging to such groups seems to fulfill a deep hunger in human beings. The esoteric voluntary associations of play are perhaps the best answer to the pernicious in-group/out-group distinctions of race, class, and religion. Similar benefits may also flow from the esoteric associations of devotees in the arts, who by voluntarily combining in groups of persons with similar esthetic concerns both preserve freedom and secure the benefit of social reinforcement.

Summing up, the arts of movement are the source of esthetic meanings in which the inner life of persons is objectified through significant dynamic forms using the human body as the instrument. These meanings, which are expressed in purest form in the dance arts, are also the basis for physical education conceived as the development of mature psychophysical coordination. The goal of such education is personal wholeness, or organic well-being of mind and body, which is the essence of health. An important element in the achievement of health is the spirit of play, which has proved to be a powerful force in the creation of culture in all its aspects. Thus, the arts of movement, physical education, and health and recreation activities are all closely interrelated resources for the enrichment of esthetic meaning, both in individual persons and in the life of society.

15

LITERATURE

Of all the arts probably the most widely influential in the communication of meaning are the arts of literature. Since language is a highly developed means of expression for purposes of general communication, the literary artist has the advantage of employing a commonly accepted and widely understood medium. In contrast, music, the visual arts, and even the arts of movement, make use of symbolic forms not so generally understood.

On the other hand, the use of language as the medium in the arts of literature also creates special difficulties for literary understanding. Though the same vocabulary and grammar apply to literature as to other kinds of meaning, as in science, personal relations, and ethics, the uses of language in the several realms are not of the same logical types. Hence, literary meanings may more readily be confused with meanings in other fields than can meanings in such fields as music, painting, and the dance, in which the medium is not language. It is easy, for example, to read a poem incorrectly as though it were a statement of fact, while one could hardly do the same for a sonata. However, the possible confusion in the uses of language in the language arts does parallel the confusion in the visual arts between esthetic presentation and literal visual representation.

A major problem in the study of literature is to distinguish the various functions of language. Language used for esthetic purposes conveys different meanings from language used for non-esthetic purposes. Unless these distinctions are carefully made, literature cannot be rightly interpreted and its intended meanings will be missed or distorted.

As stated in Chapter 7, the literary use of language is *non-discursive*. Even though the same vocabulary and syntax are used in literature as in ordinary discourse, the connotation of the verbal symbols is different. In literature, language is deliberately exploited for its *expressive* effect rather than to indicate, denote, or describe things for practical purposes. In everyday discourse language is a tool of social adjustment—an effective means of organizing human energies for dealing with the natural and human environment. Literary language, by contrast, is used to stimulate *contemplation*. The literary work is to be enjoyed for its own sake and not for any extrinsic ends. Its language is intended as itself a source of esthetic delight and not as a means to any other end, whether practical (as in everyday affairs and in the technical fields) or theoretical (as in the pure sciences).

A central concept in the art of literature (as, indeed, in every art) is *imagination*. Literary language is used imaginatively rather than literally. A work of literature is not meant as a series of literal propositions, but as a construction designed to stimulate the imagination of the reader. The term "imagination" does not necessarily imply the use of language to evoke mental images, though this effect may occur. The term is intended to refer more broadly to the use of language to create new forms of experience—"worlds of the imagination"—which are not meant to represent ordinary actuality, but to effect a transformation of everyday experience. Literary language, regardless of the particular forms of composition in which it is used, is essentially *fictional*. It is not designed to convey literal truth, but to present significant invented objects for imaginative contemplation.

As in the other arts, works of literature are *ideal abstractions*.

No matter how "realistic" a work may appear, it is an idealization in the sense that certain aspects of experience are abstracted from concrete actuality for special emphasis. Each work is deliberately designed for certain esthetic effects and never merely to recapitulate the haphazard, contingent quality of concrete actuality.

The subject matter of literary study is primarily the *individual work*—whether poem, novel, play, or essay. Each such work is a unique whole, with its own proper beginning, middle, and end. Literary understanding, from the esthetic point of view, consists in the perception of the work in its singularity, as a particular complex organization of verbal symbols communicating ideational, emotional, and sensuous meanings pertaining to that one work alone. The esthetic function of literature is to provide individual objects for serious nonacquisitive contemplation.

The effects of literature, of course, usually extend beyond the esthetic realm. For example, a great deal of empirical knowledge may be acquired in reading novels or seeing plays. In fact, literature is one of the best sources of insight into personality and culture. Fiction is sometimes a more valuable source of information about the natural world than even the literal factual descriptions of science. Literature may also be used for a variety of practical purposes, such as emotional therapy, moral instruction, and ideological persuasion. Though all these functions may be performed by literature, they are incidental to the unique literary function of providing objects of esthetic interest. All the other purposes can be served by other means: factual information by empirical descriptions, catharsis of emotion by psychotherapy, character training by moral education, and shaping of commitments by political, philosophical, and religious instruction. Only literature itself can provide the distinctive esthetic values communicated by the particular patterns of language comprising individual literary works.

A preliminary phase of literary scholarship consists in establishing as clearly as possible the content and circumstances of composition of the works to be read. The determination of content is the task of *textual criticism*. In the writing down and subsequent reproduction and transmission of a piece of literature many opportunities for error and uncertainty may arise. In the work of textual editing of manuscripts and printed materials the scholar uses all available evidence to produce a text that is as close as possible to the intention of the author. In the case of old, obscure, or widely dispersed writings the text may be difficult to establish and the results only moderately probable. In other cases the text may be virtually certain.

The study of the circumstances of composition (sometimes referred to as *higher criticism*) may provide further information of value in understanding a literary work. Included here are such matters as date, authorship, authenticity, place, occasion, and historical context. The evidence used to ascertain these factors may be both *external* (drawn from outside the work itself) and *internal* (gained from an analysis of the language, style, allusions, and explicit statements in the work).

Textual and higher criticism are highly developed forms of literary scholarship, depending upon a variety of special disciplines, including archaeology, paleography, bibliography, and linguistics, as well as upon knowledge of such more general fields as history, science, and philosophy. Nevertheless, it is clear that the meanings resulting from such critical scholarship are empirical and not esthetic. Hence, the student of literature who knows only how to edit a text and how to determine such facts about it as chronology, authorship, and purpose is only on the threshold of literary understanding. In themselves these investigations do not yield distinctive literary knowledge, but only information that may be useful later in gaining such knowledge.

Once the text and the circumstances of composition are established as well as possible, the next step is to investigate the meaning of the work. René Wellek and Austin Warren, in their incisive *Theory of Literature* [1] distinguish two kinds of approach to the study of literature: the *extrinsic* and the *intrinsic*. According to the extrinsic approach, a piece of literature is to be interpreted in relation to the biographical, psychological, social, economic, political, and ideological factors presumed to have influenced it. Contrariwise, under the intrinsic approach the start-

[1] Harcourt, Brace & World, Inc., New York, 1942. The analysis in the present chapter draws heavily upon Wellek and Warren's book.

ing point for literary scholarship is the structure of the literature itself rather than the external factors.

From the standpoint of a critical philosophy of meaning, the intrinsic approach is clearly the more essential because it presupposes the distinctness and relative autonomy of literary understanding in the esthetic mode. However, this judgment does not exclude the study of extrinsic factors, provided they are shown to be relevant to the intrinsic significance of the work itself, as the following discussion of some of the main types of extrinsic factors will indicate.

A literary work cannot rightly be interpreted simply as a fragment in the *biography* of the author. Art is not simply a means of self-expression. It is not merely symptomatic of the artist's personal feelings. It is, rather, the objectification of a communicable inner life. When a novel, poem, or play does make use of materials from the author's life, these materials are transformed for literary purposes. The value of the literature is entirely independent of how nearly its content corresponds to the biographical facts. Thus, while biographical knowledge may help to explain allusions in an author's works, the chronology of his writings, and the relationship of the work to the works of other writers or to the events of the time, these factors are not in themselves esthetically significant. They are esthetically relevant only as they disclose perceptual qualities in the work itself that might otherwise go unnoticed.

Similarly, the *psychology* of literary composition tells nothing about the esthetic meaning of literature. The fact that an author composed his work for neurotic reasons or that his work reflected certain personality characteristics may provide interesting psychological data, but no basis at all for esthetic judgment. Nor is the psychological truth of a novelist's or dramatist's characterizations of any inherent artistic value. Psychological information can contribute to esthetic understanding only if it permits the discrimination of qualities and relationships that might otherwise be perceived less clearly. For example, certain aspects of the structure of *Hamlet* may well be illuminated by Ernest Jones's psychoanalytic interpretation of the play, and Kafka's novels may likewise remain esthetically obscure without the insight into them provided by depth psychology.

Sometimes literature is unintelligible apart from the *social, economic,* and *political* situations which it reflects. To the extent that this is the case, the proper literary meaning of a work depends upon understanding these extrinsic factors. Yet it is an error to evaluate any work as literature on the basis of its contribution to any social goals (as, for example, the Marxists do). Being "true to life" may or may not advance artistic worth. All that social factors do is to provide materials for the creation of literary values; they do not themselves determine those values.

In like manner, while a study of the history of *ideas* may yield valuable information for the interpretation of literature, works of literary art are not intended as philosophic treatises and are misjudged if so regarded. Like all the other extrinsic factors, intellectual movements and philosophic reflections can be utilized by authors in the construction of literature for esthetic purposes. I is only in relation to these purposes that such factors may be considered relevant.

Finally, it is not even justifiable to explain literature by reference to the *other arts.* For example, literature is sometimes linked with music or painting as exemplifying a certain spirit (e.g. Romantic or Baroque). Each art evolves in its own way, in accordance with its own tempo and internal structures. Despite the common characteristics of the esthetic mode, each field within the arts is relatively independent of the others in its historical career and none can be interpreted in terms of the others. Thus, nonliterary esthetic factors are also extrinsic to the art of literature and belong to literary interpretation only where they contribute to the esthetic significance of particular literary compositions.

The central fact is that the objects of knowledge, in the art of literature, are particular verbal patterns designed to serve specific literary purposes. The significance of each work inheres in its own structure. The import of the work itself does not refer to the subjective experience or intention of the author nor to the sum of the readers' reactions. The meaning of the work is a system of intersubjective values, that is, of perceptual abstractions that the work has the power to evoke in all who read it attentively and sympathetically.

In certain respects the intrinsic structure of literature is similar to that of music. In both cases *sound* is an integral part of the esthetic effect. While the sound of music is nearly always physically audible, the sound of literature may be either audible (as in recitations and in drama) or, more commonly, heard only with the "mind's ear." In both music and literature sound contributes to esthetic effect both by the inherent qualities of the sound elements and by the relations between these elements. The study of inherent sound qualities as they contribute to esthetic effect in literature comprises the topic of *euphony*. Much of the delight of literature consists in the immediate sensuous appeal of the words used.

The relation between the sounds expresses the sense of time, which is fundamental in literature as well as in music and the arts of movement, and indeed in all the arts. The key concept for the relational element of sound is *rhythm*. Rhythm is so important because it is deeply rooted in nature, with its alternations of day and night, of seasons, and of growth and decline. Human life is experienced as a cyclic alternation of work and rest, conflict and reconciliation, contrast and resolution. Language itself exhibits rhythm in the patterning of words, phrases, clauses, sentences, and larger complexes. Literature differs from ordinary language in exploiting much more fully the rhythmic possibilities of language, by greater regularity in the stress distributions and by a variety of other phonetic and syntactical devices, including *rhyme* and *alliteration*. Rhythm is sometimes thought to apply only or mainly to poetry. Actually it is an essential feature of all types of literary art, whether prose or poetry.

Rhythm is a general term referring to the varied patterns that give a work of art organic quality. Much more limited and specific is *meter*, which refers to the patterns of rhythm in poetry. The study of poetic meter is *prosody*. The classical graphic model of metrical analysis uses as units *feet* with two or three syllables each, either short (unaccented) or long (accented), such as iamb (u–), trochee (–u), anapaest (uu–), dactyl (–uu), and spondee (––). Other systems use musical notation, acoustical methods, or formalistic treatment of the patterns (Gestalt) of whole sentences. Whatever the method used, the goal of metrical analysis is to illuminate the sound and time relationships in the poetry in order that the maximum esthetic effect of the work as a whole may be enjoyed.

Beyond the rhythmic and metrical factors, in which literature has much in common with music, literature also makes use of the rich semantic resources of language. In fact, it is on this resource of meaning that the special quality of literature as an art depends. As already pointed out, the literary use of language differs from its practical and scientific uses in not being tied to literal reference. The art of literature depends upon the possibility of using language *figuratively,* i.e., nonliterally and nondiscursively.

Figurative usage is of several kinds. Literary *images* are particular perceptions (presentations) which also stand for something inner and ideal (representations). Images may be connected with visual, auditory, olfactory, kinesthetic, thermal, or any other type of sensation. *Symbols* likewise are objects that refer to something other than themselves and that are also for contemplation in their own right. They differ from images chiefly in that they are less occasional and more recurrent. Thus, images to which certain meanings are regularly attached may become symbols. A third basic literary concept, which overlaps both image and symbol, is that of *metaphor.* Here a sensuous image that means one thing is used to refer to something else that bears an inner likeness and to which attention is drawn by the nonliteral reference. Inherent in metaphor (as indeed in all figurative use of language) is a principle of *analogy*—an intuition of qualitative likeness between different things—and of *double vision* in which two distinct but related things are held in creative tension in the imagination.

The imaginative quality of literary expression is further exemplified in the use of *myth.* In literary theory this term does not refer, as it does in common parlance, to a false or fantastic story, but rather it refers to the narrative presentation of archetypal, eternal, ideal, or eschatological meanings, in terms of events in the sensible space-time world. Myths are an expression of important social meanings through concrete images. They convey a picture of the shared convictions of a community of the faithful, whether or not the community is regarded as religious in the traditional sense. Thus, one can speak of the "myth of progress" or the "myth of the master race," as well as the Jewish myth of creation or the Christian myth of the Second Coming of Christ.

In the complete literary work the various patterns of sound and of imagery, symbol, metaphor, and myth are organized into a single expressive whole. The resulting works are of various kinds. Modern literary theory usually divides them into *fiction* (including novel, short story, and epic), *drama* (prose or verse), and *poetry*. Such genre distinctions may be made on the basis of outer form (metrical and structural patterns) and of inner form (purpose, attitude, and tone). They are somewhat arbitrary, and are today considered fluid and descriptive rather than (as formerly) rigid and prescriptive. Since the meaning of the individual work, in the organization of its elements into an expressive whole, is the objective of literary understanding, classifications by genre, analyses of style, ordering by periods, and other such activities of technical literary scholarship are useful (like extrinsic criticism) only as they help the reader to discover the values inherent in individual works and not if they take the place of esthetic perception of the works themselves.

In all the arts, including literature, the esthetic excellence of the work is a consequence of skillful *composition,* in which contrasting elements are brought together into a whole which conveys a powerful "illusion of reality." While the goal of literature is not an accurate representation of life, such as literal descriptions can provide, the artist does aim to present a convincing portrayal of human existence. In narrative fiction, for example, the meaning is expressed by a *plot* (a series of episodes organized with appropriate scale and pace to tell a compelling tale), by *characterization* (in which, using a variety of methods, the persons whose destinies are interwoven in the plot are vividly presented), and by *setting* (the environment in which the plot occurs and through which the characters express themselves). Other forms of literature use a great variety of other methods of composition to achieve the desired literary effects.

In summary, literature is the art in which language is the medium of esthetic expression. The subject matter of literary study is the individual literary work, which is a figurative particular presentation of significant intersubjective abstractions. To understand literature it must be studied intrinsically to discover the unique patterns of sound, rhythm, meter, and semantic figuration as they are used in the creation of singular unitary compositions. Extrinsic factors may also add valuable insights, but only as they are employed to illuminate the inherent structure of each work itself.

Introduction to Realms Four and Five

The three realms of knowledge described thus far in Part Two all comprise disciplines and groups of disciplines that are familiar in organized academic and scholarly life. Schools and colleges offer courses in language, mathematics, the sciences, and the arts, and recognized professional societies exist for the promotion of knowledge in these fields. The same is true of the sixth realm (synoptics) comprising the disciplines of history, religion, and philosophy.

The fourth and fifth realms, now to be considered, do not fit neatly into this pattern. So unfamiliar is the domain of personal knowledge within the prevailing system that a new term, "synnoetics," seemed required to represent it. Furthermore, the synnoetic realm is not constituted by a set of standard academic disciplines, corresponding to the constituents of the symbolic, empirical, esthetic, and synoptic realms. Instead, the exposition of synnoetics requires the use of an assorted selection of movements growing up within disciplines belonging to other realms, chiefly psychology, literature, religion, and philosophy. It is not customary to offer courses in relational insight, personal knowledge, or existential awareness, nor are there standard scholarly associations devoted to the pursuit of such knowledge.

A similar situation pertains with respect to the ethical realm. To be sure, moral meanings are studied in moral philosophy, and ethics—the critical analysis of moral judgments—is one of the standard branches of the discipline of philosophy. Nevertheless, the advancement of knowledge in the ethical sphere does not occupy a place in academic and scholarly affairs parallel to the study of language, mathematics, science, art, history, and philosophy. (Religion, like morals, has ambiguous standing among the fields of knowledge.)

Among all the realms, the two dealing with personal and moral knowledge are at one and the same time the most essential and the most problematical. They are the most essential because they deal with elemental human meanings that sustain all other knowledge. They go most directly to the core of personhood and color every type of understanding. Because they are so elemental they are also problematical. The personal and moral types of knowledge are not abstract and objective to the same extent as the other types are, and therefore they are more affected by the contradictions and perplexities of concrete human existence. For the same reason, expert knowledge in these fields is not concentrated in distinct professional academic associations to the same extent as knowledge in the other realms. Moreover, the conflicts and uncertainties of personal and moral knowledge exceed those in any other kind of knowledge.

The awkwardness of this situation has been a matter of serious concern in the working out of the present philosophy of the realms of meaning, and no claim is made that the difficulties in the analysis here presented have all been eliminated. This introductory note is to acknowledge that questions still remain and that they are evident to the author, as they will undoubtedly be to the reader.

How shall we deal with the special problems posed by these two realms? It could be argued that the two do not fit neatly into the general scheme because they do not belong in any scheme of knowledge. It may be urged that personal understanding and moral judgments are not in any definable sense knowledge, that no canons of criticism and validation can be devised for them, and that no communities of disciplined inquiry can arise to deal with such matters.

Against this argument it can be urged that it is difficult to escape the perennial persistent claims of personal insight and of moral consciousness. Moreover, as will be shown in Chapters 16 and 17, logical inquiry reveals that these two realms have distinctive logical features that do not permit them to be subsumed under any other realms. If they do not seem to qualify as knowledge, it may be that the criteria of what counts as knowledge need to be broadened and more precise distinctions among the varieties of knowledge need to be made. The possibility of expert understanding in these realms can also be defended, both by reference to the great seers and prophets of mankind and to certain movements within professional scholarship itself.

Perhaps the seeming strangeness of the personal and moral fields among the academic realms reflects some limitation in the scholarly world itself. Academic man feels relatively secure with the problems of language, science, literature, history, and the other traditional fields of learning. He can objectify, abstract, and master or manage ideas in these domains. He cannot so easily claim mastery in the realms of personal understanding and moral judgment, for these are precisely the domains in which managing and manipulating must give way to acknowledging, accepting, obeying, and making sacrifices. The more searching demands of synnoetics and ethics tend to drive men of knowledge into the more manageable realms of symbolics, empirics, esthetics, and (for the most daring) synoptics.

Accordingly, the reason these two kinds of knowledge do not appear to fit neatly into the structure may not be due to any deficiency in them, but to the one-sidedness of the academic world, which results from timidity and resistance to dealing seriously and persistently with concerns that touch the core of personal being. If such is the case, the solution to the problem posed by these realms lies in giving special attention to the development of disciplined insight in them.

Actually the problem of these fields may not be caused by the weakness in the world of scholars alone. The difficulties may arise out of the human situation itself, in which everyone, scholar and nonscholar alike, is involved. The one-sidedness of the academic world, to the extent that it exists, mirrors the one-sidedness of society generally, in its reluctance and inability to deal effectively with the elemental personal and moral demands of life.

If this view of the situation is correct, the awkwardness introduced into the scheme of knowledge by including the personal and moral realms should serve as a stimulus to greater responsibility for disciplined inquiry in these fields and to deeper concern for their place in the program of general education.

THE FOURTH REALM: *Synnoetics*

16

PERSONAL KNOWLEDGE

All meanings consist of certain discriminations, organizations, and interpretations of experience. Each realm of meaning includes aspects of experience of a particular logical type which result from special kinds of selection and focusing within the complex totality of experience. Language meanings have to do with conventional patterns of symbolization. Scientific meanings concern empirical abstractions, generalizations, and theoretical formulations. Esthetic meanings deal with ideal abstractions contained in particular non-discursive presentations.

We now turn to a fourth realm, in which the selection and organization of experience is of a distinctively different logical kind from the three thus far considered. These meanings will be designated by the term "synnoetics." Briefly, this term refers to meanings in which a person has direct insight into other beings (or oneself) as concrete wholes existing in relation.

The general nature of synnoetics as a distinct realm of meaning may be made clear by indicating the main respects in which it differs from the other three realms thus far discussed. Knowledge in symbolics, empirics, and esthetics requires *detachment*, while synnoetic meaning requires *engagement*. In the first three realms the knower stands apart from what he knows. In the latter he effects a direct meeting.

Knowledge in symbolics, empirics, and esthetics is *objective,* or better, it depends on a *subject-object relationship.* Synnoetic meanings relate *subjects* to *subjects.* Objectivity is eliminated and is replaced by *subjectivity,* or better, *intersubjectivity.* Intersubjectivity also has a place in language, science, and art, but it differs from the intersubjectivity of personal insight in being based on common reference objects. That is to say, in the former realms the intersubjectivity is indirect and triadic; in the latter it is direct and diadic. In synnoetic understanding the separation between subject and object is overcome and a personal meeting takes place.

Synnoesis does not occur, of course, wholly without mediation. Subject relates to subject by a variety of means of communication, including ordinary language and perhaps even more often by the many sorts of nondiscursive symbolic forms. No realm of shared meaning can dispense with language of some kind. What is distinctive about synnoesis is that in this realm the function of the symbols used is to effect a relationship between the communicating beings themselves (or within themselves in the case of intrapersonal reflection) and not to establish a common orientation to some third objective entity. This is what was meant above by calling synnoesis diadic instead of triadic.

Meanings in this personal realm are *concrete* rather than *abstract,* as in language, science, and art. Language meanings are abstract in the sense that they are concerned with classes of sounds, semantic elements, and grammatical structures. Science meanings depend on concrete experience, through sense observation, but consist of the abstractions of classifications, generalizations, laws, and theories. Meanings in the arts are ideal abstractions presented in particular created works. In contrast with these, personal meanings are concrete in the sense that relational understanding is not a fragment, a perspective, or a transformation of some other more complete experience. Rather, it is itself the prototype of experience in its wholeness or concreteness.

Michael Polanyi [1] points to this basic quality of concreteness in his discussion of the personal element in all knowledge. He distinguishes between "explicit knowledge" such as occurs in the abstract formulations of science and even of everyday descriptive discourse, and "tacit knowledge," which is unformulated and is the basis for making sense of experience, i.e., for "understanding." "The structure of tacit knowing," says Polanyi, ". . . is a process of *comprehending*: a grasping of disjointed parts into a comprehensive whole." [2] This knowing by wholes has long been recognized by the Gestalt psychologists. What Polanyi does is to transform Gestalt insights into a comprehensive theory of knowledge in which the active participation of persons is primary: "According to the theory of Personal Knowledge, all meaning lies in the comprehension of a set of particulars in terms of a coherent entity —a comprehension which is a personal act that can never be replaced by a formal operation." [3] Again, ". . . the knowledge of a comprehensive entity is an understanding, an indwelling and an association. . . ." [4]

In contrast to the realm of personal knowledge, symbolic, empirical, and esthetic meanings are impersonal. Language is for everybody's use, science is public knowledge, and art is presented for all to behold. Personal knowledge, on the other hand, is always on a one-to-one basis. It is not predicated upon the idea of "anyone" or "whosoever," but on confrontation with the singular being. Impersonal meanings presuppose the interchangeability of persons. Personal relations presuppose the uniqueness of the persons who enter into relation.

Language, science, and art are concerned with *essences,* while personal knowledge is *existential.* That is to say, the former fields deal with various kinds and qualities of being, while the latter has to do with *being itself,* that is, with concrete existence. To be is to be in relation. There is no such thing as absolutely solitary existence. The very concept of isolation has significance only

[1] See his *Personal Knowledge,* The University of Chicago Press, Chicago, 1958, and *The Study of Man,* The University of Chicago Press, Chicago, 1959.

[2] *The Study of Man,* p. 28. Reprinted by permission of the publisher.

[3] *Ibid.,* p. 49. Reprinted by permission of the publisher.

[4] *Ibid.,* pp. 65–66. Reprinted by permission of the publisher.

against a background of others from whom one is separated. Separateness is relative nonbeing; all dividing of things depends upon their prior being in relation.

Having thus broadly characterized the synnoetic realm of personal knowledge, we proceed to a consideration of how these meanings are acquired and of some distinctive methods and concepts in this realm which may assist in teaching and learning such meanings.

For the most part, personal knowledge is not developed through formal instruction. It is a consequence of the basic fact of human association, beginning with the family and extending out in ever-widening circles to relationships in community, occupational life, and even with people in other nations and cultures. The quality of personal meanings therefore depends upon the nature of the common life, particularly upon the earliest and most intimate associations in the family, between parents and children.

Although personal knowledge is largely a product of ordinary social experience, it is not without benefit of theoretical study and concentrated consideration by specialized inquirers. However, those who are recognized as leaders in the practice and interpretation of meanings in this realm do not form as coherent and identifiable a company as do the linguists, scientists, and artists, respectively, in the first three realms of meaning. The subjectivity inherent in personal knowledge inhibits the formation of groups of persons who adhere to common objective criteria of meaning in this realm. Even more relevant is the fact that in personal understanding concern for critical theoretical judgments may militate against intersubjective awareness, somewhat as in the case of the arts, where overemphasis on critical evaluation may interfere with appreciative perception. Moreover, in personal insight the simplest and most untutored people can be as competent as, or even more competent than, people who have devoted much time and thought to the perfecting of this aspect of life. The same cannot be said of linguists, scientists, or artists, all of whom become demonstrably expert through the deliberate cultivation of their specialized pursuits.

In spite of this somewhat embarrassing situation concerning

practical expertise in the realm of personal knowledge, the insights of those who have considered the subject deeply may still be effective in making provision for the optimum development of these meanings. This assumption is necessary if the educator is not to abandon all hope and responsibility for improving the quality of human meanings at the deepest personal level.

Those who have been most concerned professionally with personal relations come mainly from four fields of endeavor, namely, religion, philosophy, psychology, and literature. As general disciplines the first two belong within the synoptic realm (see Chapters 19 and 20 below), the third within the empirical realm (see Chapter 10 above), and the last within the esthetic realm (see Chapter 15 above). Though workers from these fields provide most of the ideas for the understanding of personal awareness, the essential logic of meanings in this realm is neither that of the synoptic, the scientific, nor the esthetic disciplines, except insofar as the synoptic disciplines by their very nature integrate meanings from the other realms, including the synnoetic.

A classic discussion of the meaning of personal knowledge is found in the writings of Martin Buber. [5] According to Buber, fullness of being consists in *relation*. Relations are of two kinds: "I-Thou" and "I-It." I-Thou is a "primary word," not in the sense of a spoken utterance, but as a creative event. I-Thou arises out of the "reality of combination." I-It, on the contrary, arises out of separation. I-Thou, being primary, is not produced by the conjunction of a prior "I" with a prior "Thou." Rather, I-Thou is the primordial reality from which "I" and "Thou" are derived by abstraction. Thus, the infant's earliest life consists in relation, and only gradually are the self and the other discriminated as separable beings. On the other hand, I-It *is* derived from setting together "I" and "It." First comes the "I" (derived from I-Thou) as existing over against things (It), and from these two put in the relation of subject to object comes the I-It.

Buber adds that the "I" of I-Thou is not the same as the "I" of I-It. In being separated and then impersonally reconnected a fundamental alteration in the quality of being takes place. The "I" of I-Thou is a connected person with subjectivity; the "I" of

[5] See especially his *I and Thou*, Charles Scribner's Sons, New York, 1958.

I-It is a differentiated individual who is a subject over against a world of objects.

In the I-Thou relation the attitude of manipulation is absent. One does not try to *use* the other with whom he stands in relation, but rather affirms and respects the other's being. Others in relation are not objects to be comprehended, categorized, or abstracted. Relation is a state of being, not an emotional condition or an experience (both of which presuppose the isolation of the subject as over against objects). In the I-Thou relation others are set free to be themselves, not to be what I will them to be. At the same time, persons in relation are responsibly concerned for others, seeking their well-being, living to serve, to heal, to teach, and to strengthen them in every possible way that does not contradict their freedom.

Freedom is a central concept in the analysis of personal knowledge. Here freedom does not mean anarchy—the autonomy of isolation—nor does it mean release from responsibility by being submerged in social activities. It means the power to be and to become through relationships in which the integrity and worth of each person are responsibly affirmed by the others with whom he is associated.

Another fundamental concept in personal relations is *love*. Love is also an ambiguous term. In the present connection it does not refer to a subjective experience, state of feeling, or passion. It means simply the reality of the active, caring, responsible relation of an "I" to a "Thou." The antithesis of love is not hate, which still manifests a kind of relation, but indifference, the cold exclusion of others by behaving as if they did not exist.

Although personal relations are usually thought of as occurring between human beings, in Buber's view they may also take place in our life with nature and in our spiritual life. One can regard the objects of nature as objects to be used and consumed (the I-It relation), or as beings in themselves, to be respected and loved (the I-Thou relation). This personalization of relationships with nature is the basis of animism and of the more sophisticated view (panpsychism) that everything existing has an inner consciousness. It also underlies the principle of noninjury of any living thing in Eastern religion—a principle that also governs Albert

Schweitzer's basic ideal of "reverence for life." As for life in the spiritual sphere, Buber holds that every I-Thou relation is grounded in a relation to the eternal Thou and hence that all authentic personal relations are rooted in the life of the spirit.

The primacy of relation is emphasized in a way somewhat different from Buber's in the naturalistically oriented social psychology of George Herbert Mead. [6] Mead holds that the *self* is created by social interaction, in which the developing person internalizes the roles he sees others around him taking and the reactions of others toward him.

... there are two general stages in the full development of the self. At the first of these stages, the individual self is constituted simply by an organization of the particular attitudes of other individuals toward himself and toward one another in the specific social acts in which he participates with them. But at the second stage in the full development of the individual's self that self is constituted not only by an organization of these particular individual attitudes, but also by an organization of the social attitudes of the generalized other or the social group as a whole to which he belongs. [7]

In this process of self-making through taking the role of the other, Mead holds that language plays an essential part. "Language in its significant sense is that vocal gesture which tends to arouse in the individual the attitude which it arouses in others, and it is this perfecting of the self by the gesture which mediates the social activities that gives rise to the process of taking the role of the other." [8] This observation supports the position assumed in the present work that language meanings are used to express the meanings in each of the other realms, including the synnoetic.

The concept of relation is at the core also of the thought and practice of the psychiatrist Harry Stack Sullivan. According to Sullivan, "The field of psychiatry is the field of interpersonal relations, under any and all circumstances in which these relations exist . . . *a personality* can never be isolated from the complex of interpersonal relations in which the person lives and has his

---

[6] See *Mind, Self, and Society,* ed. by Charles W. Morris, The University of Chicago Press, Chicago, 1934.

[7] *Ibid.,* p. 158. Reprinted by permission of the publisher.

[8] *Ibid.,* pp. 160–161. Reprinted by permission of the publisher.

being." [9] Insofar as he is a scientist, the psychiatrist's goal is description and generalization. But the personal relations about which he theorizes are themselves concrete intersubjectivities. Sullivan holds that since a self is made up of the reflected appraisals of other people (as Mead also maintains), the quality of a person's life is deeply affected by the quality of the relationships with the significant persons (e.g., parents, siblings, teachers, peers) with whom one lives. If a person has been rejected by the significant persons, he will tend to develop a self-rejecting personality. If he has been welcomed, he will tend to develop a confident, self-accepting personality. In this connection Sullivan stresses the significance of love in the growth of healthy personality. His definition of love recalls the one earlier given in the discussion of Buber's position: "When the satisfaction or security of another person becomes as significant to one as is one's own satisfaction or security, then the state of love exists. So far as I know, under no other circumstances is a state of love present, regardless of the popular usage of the word." [10] Reminiscent of a somewhat similar point made by Polanyi, Sullivan goes on to urge the fundamental importance of personal relations for the proper development of all other meanings: "It is only when the world expands as a tissue of persons and interpersonal relations which are meaningful that knowledge becomes truly significant, and learning becomes a serious attempt to implement oneself for one's future life." [11]

The field of investigation in which the most extensive conceptual schemes for the interpretation of the meanings inherent in personal relations have been devised is psychoanalysis. Actually, the principal aim of psychoanalysis is not theoretical understanding, but therapy. The therapist is chiefly a practitioner in the art of helping emotionally disturbed people to improve the quality of their personal relations, the goal being to foster the kind of mature love described in the foregoing paragraphs. The emotionally ill person is essentially one whose relational meanings are

[9] *Conceptions of Modern Psychiatry,* W. W. Norton & Company, Inc., New York, Copyright 1940, 1945, 1947, and 1953 by The William Alanson White Psychiatric Foundation. Reprinted by permission of the publisher.

[10] *Ibid.,* p. 20. Reprinted by permission of the publisher.

[11] *Ibid.,* p. 21. Reprinted by permission of the publisher.

distorted, and the restoration of health depends on the rectification of those meanings. Psychoanalysis thus represents a developed theoretical and technical discipline in which expert deliberate instruction in personal understanding is undertaken. Some of its leading methods and concepts are therefore of special relevance to the present study.

The basic method of psychoanalysis is the reeducation of the client through reliving past relationships in association with the analyst. Under the expert guidance of the analyst, who claims to understand the ways of the psyche and the manifold causes of deviation from the path of mature love, the patient is given insight into his behavior problems and help in developing better habits of personal response.

According to orthodox Freudian theory, every person is endowed with certain instincts, such as hunger and sex, which demand satisfaction within a physical and social environment that to some extent necessarily conflicts with and frustrates those instincts. The source of instinctual energy (particularly the sexual energy or *libido*) is the *id*. The id is regarded as part of the *unconscious*, an aspect of the personality below the level of conscious mind required to explain the many irrational features of human behavior as the person seeks to adjust his instinctual life to the restrictive environment.

The Freudians view the personality as possessing, besides the id, an *ego* and a *superego*. The ego serves as a mediator between the id and the outside world, adjusting the subjective demands of the former in accord with the objective demands of the latter. The superego represents the standards, ideals, and moral demands of society that have been incorporated into the psyche. The ego balances the demands of the superego with those of the id in terms of the *reality principle*. In the mature person the ego maintains a proper balance within the psyche and between the psyche and the outside world, preventing both the anarchy of unrestrained impulses and the tyranny of a rigid and fearful conscience.

In the Freudian view the development of personal relations revolves around the *Oedipus complex,* which concerns the problems arising from the child's sexual desire for the parent of the opposite sex, together with the fear and hatred of the parent of the same sex. The healthy solution of the Oedipal situation is for the child's unrealistic and normally frustrated desire for the parent of the opposite sex to be replaced by an identification with the parent of the same sex and for the superego to develop as the internal monitor of right relationships with both parents.

Psychoanalysts have described a number of typical *mechanisms* or *dynamisms,* meaning habitual processes by which the person either unrealistically or realistically attempts to come to terms with his various conflicts and frustrations in interpersonal relations. Among these are the following: *introjection* or *incorporation* (the ego perceiving itself as having the character of some external entity), *projection* (ascribing some quality of the ego to external objects), *denial* (refusing to recognize an unpleasant reality), *fixation* (the persistence at one level of development of patterns characteristic of an earlier level), *regression* (return to behavior patterns belonging to an earlier stage), *sublimation* (changing the aim of an impulse without blocking its gratification, by the discovery of alternative outlets), *repression* (exclusion of painful materials from consciousness), *reaction formation* (the development of socially acceptable attitudes and habits directly opposed to certain repressed impulses), *undoing* (the doing of an action opposite to a former action, the doing of which caused psychic distress), *isolation* (disconnecting unpleasant memories from their emotional associations), *displacement* (shifting emotional energy from one object to another), *asceticism* (denial of impulses), and *intellectualization* (linking impulses with rationality so as to render them more controllable).

The goal of therapy is to enable a person to effect more satisfactory relationships by understanding the mechanisms he habitually uses in the conduct of his own life and by substituting more mature and realistic ways of feeling and acting for the immature and unrealistic remainders of infantile behavior. The ideal adult, who is described by Freudians as having a *genital* character, is able to love fully and freely and to utilize his emotional energies creatively and widely through sublimation rather than having them used up in unproductive defense mechanisms. Those who fall short of such maturity remain fixed at earlier stages, namely, the *phallic* (typically showing aggressiveness as a defense against castration anxiety), the *urethral* (typically with competitiveness as a defense against shame connected with urination), the *anal* (typically manifesting parsimoniousness and compulsive cleanliness due to unresolved toilet training problems), and the *oral* (typically associated with strong dependency behavior continuing the effects of early oral deprivation).

The foregoing sketch of certain important psychoanalytic concepts is included to indicate the type of ideas that can be used for the understanding and improvement of meanings in the realm of personal knowledge. No attempt need be made to indicate the nature of the many other psychoanalytic concepts used by such interpreters of Freud as Alfred Adler, Carl Gustav Jung, and Otto Rank and by such neo-Freudians as Karen Horney, Erich Fromm, Harry Stack Sullivan, Abram Kardiner, and Clara Thompson. [12] Suffice it to say that the field of psychoanalysis is rapidly changing and that new theoretical constructs are continually being developed to meet changing cultural conditions and in response to new insights into the nature of human relationships. Many of the newer analysts have broken away from the strongly instinctual (and particularly the sexual) orientation of the Freudians and from their heavy emphasis on influences in the infancy period as the principal determinants of personality.

The term "personal knowledge" includes not only relations with other persons (and even things, as Buber points out), but also relations with oneself. The intimate connection between the two has already been indicated in showing how the self is formed in interaction with other persons. On the other hand, some students of human nature are primarily concerned with the relation of the self to itself, i.e., with self-knowledge, regarding such understanding as fundamental and intersubjective relations as derivative. This latter view is generally characteristic of the Existentialists, who have developed extensive conceptual schemes for interpreting the meaning of personal existence. Among these thinkers are the philosophers Søren Kierkegaard, Martin Heidegger, Karl Jaspers, and Jean Paul Sartre.

[12] For a valuable survey of the various theories, see Gerald S. Blum. *Psychoanalytic Theories of Personality,* McGraw-Hill Book Company, Inc., New York, 1953.

The basic principle of the Existentialists is that reality is in *concrete existence,* not in essences, as rationalists maintain. In personal existence "to know" and "to be" are one and the same. Such knowledge is not gained by detached contemplation, but in active living. A person *is* what he *does;* his existence is determined in the acts which he performs.

Above all, for the Existentialist, a self is related to itself in *freedom.* The being of a person consists in being free. Sartre says that a person is a "project," that is, an existence created by deliberately propelling oneself forward into the future. A person is what he wills to be. He makes a "leap" toward existence. He is defined by the choice of his ends. The choices by which a person makes himself is an absolute "either/or." However, it necessarily occurs within specified circumstances. A person cannot make the world anything he wants it to be, but he cannot escape the necessity of making *his world* whatever he wills it to be. A person is completely free to confer whatever meaning or value he will on his presented environment and on the past as it comes to him in memory and tradition. No one is determined by outside forces; they only constitute the materials out of which, in absolute freedom, one must fashion his existence.

Thus, according to the Existentialists, one knows himself through his *decisions.* One is what he decides to be. Unfortunately, they hold, it is impossible to discover any objective basis for decision, for the choice of what I shall be depends upon me, the chooser, and not upon any external factors. Furthermore, says Sartre, I am *responsible* for what I decide, both for myself and for all other persons. I am responsible for others because my choice affirms the value of what I choose, and this value applies both to myself and to all mankind. The fact that I must choose and bear responsibility for myself and others and that I can have no objective assurance that my choice is right throws me into *anguish.* Existentialists hold that anguish is an inescapable consequence of freedom. It differs from fear, which refers to threats in the external world. Anguish comes from having to create myself for myself and others without any external direction.

We constantly seek to flee from anguish by regarding ourselves as things rather than persons and as determined rather than free. But this very attempt to escape is evidence of the underlying anguish. We try to hide the uncomfortable truth from ourselves, but the trying itself bears witness to our predicament of undetermined decision. In our choices we are alone, without excuse, condemned to be free, responsible at every moment for creating anew both ourselves and the world as it is for us.

Existentialists differ on the question of whether or not there is any ultimate solution to the human predicament, in some realm of transcendent being. Kierkegaard and other religiously oriented thinkers affirm ultimate salvation in the decision of faith. Atheistic Existentialists like Sartre, on the other hand, emphasize the fundamental *absurdity* of existence, in the sense that the choices by which being is determined have no justification beyond themselves and that death in the end negates all meaning, since meaning resides in subjectivity and death terminates the subject. Whatever their view of the ultimate, all Existentialists agree on the primacy of freedom and on the person as destined to choose, without benefit of determination beyond the self.

The Existentialists tend to be critical of psychologists and psychoanalysts for trying to understand personal knowledge of the self and of others in terms drawn from empirical science. In effect, the Existentialists assert that meanings in the realm of personal relations are of a different logical order from the empirical meanings of the scientific realm. In Chapter 10 the differences between psychologists who analyze human behavior by the methods of natural science and those who use distinctively personal categories like "self," "purpose," and "consciousness" were pointed out. The latter type of psychologist is actually close in his concerns to the realm of meaning discussed in the present chapter. The essential difference is that the scientific psychologist, whatever his methods and categories, is interested in generalization and theoretical explanation rather than in the concrete subjectivities of personal encounter. The latter concern may, of course, govern the work of the practicing psychologist or psychoanalyst, whose aim is healing and education rather than general explanation. In fulfilling their goals, though scientific generalizations and theoretical models may well prove of great use, the personal meanings take precedence over the theoretical ones.

The Existentialists believe that the categories and methods of psychology and psychoanalysis tend to blur the distinction between the empirical and the personal realms and that concepts unique to the latter realm are required. To this end, Sartre seeks to develop what he terms "existential psychoanalysis." Like empirical psychoanalysis, his discipline is based on the principle that a person is a totality, not a collection of parts, and that in all behavior a person expresses his whole self. He further agrees with the traditional psychoanalytic approach in being concerned with particular situations, with activities of all kinds, no matter how apparently trivial, and with the prelogical grounds of behavior. He differs in rejecting the idea of the unconscious and in making the idea of original choice basic. He believes that general, abstract explanations of human conduct do not touch the reality of deliberate human decision. He also believes that the ordinary psychoanalysts' concern for past factors in behavior obscures the fact of instant, abrupt changes in orientation that do occur and that a person inwardly knows are always possible. It is in this knowledge of radical freedom that the intrinsic meaning of being a person consists, and it is this insight that the Existentialists believe the ordinary psychoanalysts lose in their attempt to apply the fundamentally different logic of general descriptions to personal meanings.

Out of the meeting of psychology (particularly psychotherapy) and Existentialism has come a movement called "existential psychology," whose adherents aim to combine the valuable results of empirical and clinical psychology with the ontological insights of philosophical Existentialism. In this union there may be the foundations of a discipline in which a full understanding of personal knowledge can be achieved.

Existential psychology, like Existentialism itself, draws upon the *phenomenological* principle that understanding of persons is possible only if the other is accepted at face value—as he appears —and without bringing to the experience one's own predispositions and judgments. To know another is to be related to him in openness and acceptance and not with preformed categories and evaluations. While one cannot escape his own thought structures, he can learn to attend to the other and to perceive the other in the other's own terms.

Rollo May [13] suggests several contributions that he believes the existential approach can make to psychology. Of first importance is the emphasis on will and decision, which is central to such thinkers as Kierkegaard, Schopenhauer, Nietzsche, Bergson (in his concept of the *élan vital*), and William James (in his concept of the *will to believe*). The affirmation of decision need not negate determining factors in human behavior. The essential point is that in every circumstance the person must make some choice of what he will do with what is presented to him.

A second contribution is in the development of the idea of the ego, the self, or the person. Behind the many manifestations of the psyche, some unity or identity of being is presupposed. According to May, "logically as well as psychologically, we must go behind the ego-id-superego system and endeavor to understand the 'being' of whom these are different expressions." [14] An example of such a unitary concept of the self is available in Gordon Allport's idea of the *proprium* discussed in Chapter 10.

A third contribution of existential thought concerns the constructive functions of *anxiety* and *guilt*. Every person is anxious because, in Paul Tillich's phrase, he must struggle for "the courage to be" against the constant threat of "nonbeing." The freedom of the existing person consists precisely in his responsibility to fulfill potentialities that are not yet in existence and that are not foreordained. Because he is free and responsible, he incurs guilt when his choices lead to impoverishment of being rather than to its fulfillment, that is, to isolation and estrangement rather than to meeting and love.

Finally, existential thought affords valuable insights into the understanding of *time*. The personal measuring of time is quite different from that of abstract physical measurement. Real time is a correlate of freedom, in which creation is possible. A person is a being who both remembers and anticipates. That is, he is

[13] Rollo May (ed.), *Existential Psychology*, Random House, Inc., New York, 1961.

[14] *Ibid.*, p. 47.

related not only to himself as present, but also as past and as future. In this way the nonbeing of the past and the future are incorporated by the free decision of the person into the being and becoming of the present.

Existential psychology is particularly helpful in making clear the intimate interconnection of relations between persons and a person's relation to himself. The meaning of personal knowledge comprises both self-relations and relations to others, and neither is possible without the other. Psychotherapy emphasizes the interpersonal aspect, Existentialism the intrapersonal aspect. Existential psychologists, together with such religiously oriented thinkers as Paul Tillich and Martin Buber, show that the understanding of the self and the understanding of relationships with other selves are indissoluble.

In addition to the movements of thought from philosophy, religion, and psychology already cited, *literature* is a resource of great value in the development of personal knowledge. In fact, all the arts may contribute to this kind of understanding. One of the principal values of the arts is that by objectifying human subjectivity they may enhance self-insight and the knowledge of intersubjective relations.

It should be noted that while the arts can aid in the deepening of personal knowledge, the distinction between personal and esthetic meanings still holds. It is one thing to perceive a poem or a play esthetically, as an objectified abstraction of a type of subjectivity, and another thing to use that esthetic insight synnoetically, as a resource for deepening one's understanding of real existential relations between unique beings. In Denis de Rougemont's fine definition of art as a "calculated trap for meditation," this connection between esthetic presentation and personal insight is clearly expressed.

The same connection is also evident in the frequently noticed but seldom defined ideal of "sincerity" in the arts. I. A. Richards interprets sincerity to mean "obedience to that tendency which 'seeks' a more perfect order within the mind," leading one "to act, feel, and think in accordance with 'one's true nature.' " [15] When

[15] *Practical Criticism*, Harcourt, Brace & World, Inc., New York, 1929, pp. 270–271.

a work of art becomes a means of coming to understand one's own true nature, esthetic meaning culminates in personal knowledge, in this case of the self by the self.

For most people, literature is more influential than any other cultural resource for growth in personal knowledge. Drama, poetry, the novel, and biography exert profound effects on the consciousness of human relatedness. This consciousness is doubtless affected far more by imaginative literature than by the combined forces of all the personalistic, existentialistic, and phenomenological psychologists, theologians, and philosophers. Moreover, the literary tradition in personal knowledge extends back to antiquity. The great works of literature always have provided models for meditation on the deepest relations between the person and things, other persons, and self.

Great literature is a revelation of life, a moving portrayal of the human condition in its heights and depths. It is concerned with human beings in both their strengths and weaknesses, with the ideal possibilities they glimpse and exemplify from time to time, and with the actions through which they seek to realize their destinies.

Each of the major literary forms can contribute to personal knowledge. One thinks of the revelation of life afforded by Walt Whitman's poem "Song of Myself" or T. S. Eliot's poem "The Hollow Men," by Fedor Dostoevski's novel *The Brothers Karamazov* or J. D. Salinger's novel *Catcher in the Rye,* by the autobiographical *Education of Henry Adams,* by Ralph Waldo Emerson's *Essays,* or by Dante Alighieri's epic of epics, the *Divine Comedy.* There are many works, in many languages and times, that have helped form the personal understanding of mankind.

Among the several types of literature, drama especially stands out as a means for growth in personal insight. Aeschylus' "Prometheus Bound," for example, is a story set in a mythological framework, about a hero who suffered because he dared to defy the arbitrary commands of the gods in order that he might bring the benefits of civilization to mankind. It is a story of universal relevance to persons in their struggle to reconcile creativity and convention, freedom and necessity, love and duty. Again, in Shakespeare's *King Lear,* one can see by means of the various characters the revelation of personality running the gamut from nobility to foolishness, modesty to arrogance, generosity to greed, loyalty to treachery, compassion to cruelty, love to hate, honesty to deceitfulness. Through such drama one more clearly understands that human beings are extremely complex mixtures of qualities and that virtue and vice are not simply separable, but paradoxically interwoven.

Great drama is a portayal of life in its reality, bringing into high relief what happens in different circumstances everywhere every day. Not only in plays, but in all human life, if one has eyes to see, great strengths are spoiled by fatal flaws, pride leads to a fall, innocent love suffers, and personal loyalty in the end helps to save the state.

In tragic drama one sees that man's greatest problem is himself, because of his misuse of the highest and most characteristic human gift, namely, freedom. In tragedy it is revealed that man is self-willed, ambitious, and in search of self-justification, faced as he is by the threat of eventual nullification through death. But it is also made clear that the retributive judgment that comes upon the tragic hero because of his misdeeds need not simply destroy him. He becomes a hero precisely because through his trials he *learns*. The theme of tragedy is education, at the deepest personal level. Suffering can teach. It can effect a purgation that in some degree removes the stain of guilt. It is a source of self-knowledge in which the protagonist comes to a more complete understanding of his own being. In these many ways the insights of tragic drama parallel those of the Existentialists, who are also concerned with the paradoxes of freedom and the demand placed on every person to create a meaningful life in a world full of contradictions and absurdities.

Comic drama, too, can contribute much to personal knowledge. Some critics suggest that comedy may, in fact, be a more authentic source of personal knowledge than tragedy. Nathan Scott argues that the tragic hero is an extremist who forgets that he is a man and not an angel. Therefore, Scott thinks, tragic man cannot serve as well as comic man to reveal the whole truth about the human situation.

. . . the point that comedy is always making (is) that we are not pure, disembodied essences, that indeed we are not pure anything-at-all, but that we are men and that our health and happiness are contingent upon our facing into the fact that we are finite and conditioned and therefore subject to all sorts of absurdities and interruptions and inconveniences and embarrassments—and weaknesses. This is, we might say, the courage that the comic imagination requires of us. [16]

Thus, works in literature and in the other arts may be of great value in stimulating synnoesis, i.e., understanding of the human situation. Such works have always served this personal knowledge function, and they continue to do so. Today they powerfully supplement the more direct and professionalized work of psychoanalysts, personal and existential psychologists, and theologians, already discussed.

In brief, meanings in the synnoetic realm are subjective (and intersubjective), concrete, and existential. They arise in the I-Thou encounter, in which the other is accepted in freedom and love. Persons grow to healthy maturity through their encounters with others. But choices may be made in which the relations of freedom and love are denied. In that event personal meanings are impaired, relationships become manipulative and impersonal, estrangements and fragmentations occur, and the self loses its integrity and creativity. To restore personal and interpersonal wholeness, therapeutic methods have been devised, together with theoretical models of the human psyche that are intended to guide the practice of healing. These conceptual patterns, enriched by insights from phenomenology, Existentialism, theology, and, above all, from literature, provide a basis for disciplined understanding in the synnoetic realm, making possible reliable education in a domain that is of fundamental importance for the life of man and society.

[16] Nathan A. Scott, Jr., "The Bias of Comedy and the Narrow Escape into Faith," *The Christian Scholar*, vol. XLIV, no. 1, Spring 1961, pp. 9–39.

THE FIFTH REALM: *Ethics*

17

MORAL KNOWLEDGE

The essence of symbolic meanings is formal convention, of empirical meanings factual description and explanation, of esthetic meanings individual significant perceptual forms, and of synnoetic meanings concrete existential intersubjectivity. The essence of ethical meanings, or of moral knowledge, is *right deliberate action,* that is, what a person *ought voluntarily to do.*

The distinctive logic of ethical meanings may be made clear by comparing and contrasting it with the logic of meanings in each of the four realms hitherto discussed.

Language is a social invention that has been developed for purposes of communication. That many different symbolic conventions are possible is shown by the many different languages actually in existence. It does not make sense to say that one *ought* to use one language rather than another, except in a hypothetical way. Thus, it is proper to assert that *if* one is to communicate effectively in a society of English-speaking people, he ought to speak English rather than any other language. But this hypothetical sense of "ought" is not what is meant by the moral "ought." Language meanings are ethically neutral. Symbolic conventions are arbitrary constructions to which the question of moral right and wrong does not properly apply. When we speak of using the "right" word or grammatical construction, we simply mean that the usage in question conforms to customary practice or is accepted by those who for some reason or other are acknowledged as language authorities in the society.

In the empirical realm meanings are factual. Since facts simply *are,* it does not make sense to ask whether they are *right.* A scientific proposition is true or false or probable. It is not right or wrong in an ethical sense. To be sure, an empirical statement may be said to be right in the sense that it is a correct statement of the facts, but this has nothing to do with moral obligation. One may properly ask whether a given state of affairs is morally right, as, for example, whether certain existing social practices are morally right. The factual statements may be right, in the sense that they truthfully represent the actual situation, but the conditions they report may at the same time be morally wrong (or right).

This distinction between empirical meanings and ethical meanings is of great importance. If it were more clearly understood, much confusion about ethical questions would be avoided. Two centuries ago David Hume made the distinction clear when he pointed out that one can never correctly make an inference from what *is* to what *ought to be,* nor vice versa. Fact and moral obligation are of essentially different logical orders. From the fact that people actually *do* behave in a certain way, it does not follow at all that they *should* behave that way. Similarly, from the assertion that a given kind of action is right, it does not follow at all that the action is in fact done by anybody.

In the present century Hume's insight was further reinforced by the influential work of G. E. Moore, who argued that all attempts to reduce values to facts are instances of the "naturalistic fallacy." [1] This fallacy is committed whenever one *defines* value concepts in factual terms, as for example, when the statement "This is good" is said to *mean* "This gives me pleasure." The first statement asserts that something is valuable, or praiseworthy, or desirable, all of which meanings are logically different in kind from the factual import of the second statement. The statement of value is logically independent of and incommensurable with

[1] *Principia Ethica,* Cambridge University Press, New York, 1959.

(though not necessarily inconsistent with) the statement of fact.

The relative independence of ethical and empirical meanings follows from the fact that it makes sense to ask of any existing state of affairs, whether or not it is a state of affairs that is good or that ought to exist. Thus, "This is good" cannot *mean* "This gives me pleasure," because it is entirely in order to ask "Well, is it good that this gives you pleasure?"—a question that would be pointless if the good were properly definable as the pleasant, since a negative answer would then be self-contradictory.

The naturalistic fallacy applies not only to definitions of value in terms of natural facts such as pleasure, happiness, and success, but even to definitions using transcendent facts, as in some traditional theological systems. For example, Moore holds that one commits the naturalistic fallacy if he asserts that "right" *means* "what God wills," for it is not self-contradictory to assert that some command of God is not right, i.e., that God ought not to will that action.

The rejection of the naturalistic fallacy preserves the logical integrity of ethical meanings by not allowing them to be absorbed into the empirical realm. One can make ethical evaluations of any matter of fact because moral judgments do not occupy the same realm of meaning as empirical statements.

There are, however, competent theorists who hold that ethical statements, though not reducible to factual statements, actually do not have any cognitive meaning at all. A. J. Ayer in *Language, Truth, and Logic* [2] limits knowledge to empirical, mathematical, and logical meanings and holds that ethical statements are neither true nor false but merely expressions of personal preferences. Thus, they are merely disguised imperatives or ejaculations. Similarly, Charles Stevenson argues that "as a working model, you might regard 'this is good' as meaning 'I approve of this; do so too'—for in saying that something is good one means, partly, that one approves of it and, partly, that one wants one's hearers to approve of it as well." [3]

[2] 2d rev. ed., Dover Publications, Inc., New York, 1952.
[3] Charles L. Stevenson, *Ethics and Language,* Yale University Press, New Haven, Conn., 1944, p. 21. Reprinted by permission of the publisher.

Stephen Toulmin [4] takes the position that the difference between empirical and ethical meanings is to be understood in terms of the uses or functions of language. Empirical language is used to modify expectations, i.e., to state predicted consequences. Ethical language, on the other hand, is used to alter feelings and behavior so as to produce the most harmonious satisfaction of desires and interests. Furthermore, Toulmin holds, ethical concepts are not used, as empirical concepts are, to designate *properties* of things. Instead, they are *gerundives,* by which is meant that they are based on the idea of *worthy of.* The value-concept "truth" is a gerundive, because it means "worthy of credence." Similarly, "excellent" and "beautiful" mean "worthy of admiration," and "right," means "worthy of doing." Thus, gerundive concepts enter into science and art as well as into ethics, since one ought to believe what is factually true and one ought to admire what is esthetically admirable, just as one ought to do what is right. However, moral judgments are directly and exclusively of the gerundive type. They are only indirectly pertinent to science and art, in which the central substantive meanings are concerned with descriptions and presentations, respectively, rather than with statements of obligation to believe or admire.

Turning next to the esthetic realm, ethical meanings differ from esthetic ones in that the latter arise out of disinterested perception, while the former are concerned with active personal commitment. In the arts things are *made* for purposes of contemplation. In ethics acts are *done* for purposes of participation. Furthermore, esthetic objects are unique individual works with their own intrinsic excellence, while moral acts are generally thought to exemplify universal principles of obligation. In this respect ethical meanings are like the principles and generalizations of science.

The most important difference between esthetic meanings and ethical meanings, as between empirics and ethics, is that in the former the basic ethical idea of right or obligation is absent. Like a fact, an esthetic object simply *is.* There is no question of "ought" about it. It is presented for contemplation, and its perceptible

---

[4] See *The Place of Reason in Ethics,* Cambridge University Press, New York, 1960.

qualities make themselves felt in the perceiver. One may or may not contemplate the object and one may or may not respond favorably. One need have no sense of responsibility for artistic production or appreciation and no guilt is incurred in connection with one's esthetic experiences. In the case of moral conduct this esthetic neutrality does not apply. Everyone is obliged to do right, and if one fails to do so, he incurs guilt. Moral conduct is a universal responsibility, and the requirement to accept moral principles is generally considered far more seriously and urgently than is the requirement to approve of particular works of art.

The relative independence of art and morals rests upon keeping clear the logical distinction between meanings in the two realms. Trouble results when the distinction becomes blurred. Art suffers when moral judgments take the place of esthetic criteria. In that event censorship flourishes, the expressive freedom of the artist is violated, and works of art become standardized tools of social control. Moral principles are esthetically irrelevant, and when they are introduced as factors in artistic production and criticism, the works of art are inevitably impoverished and esthetically corrupted. On the other hand, when morals are assimilated to esthetics, right and obligation disappear altogether, and morals become a matter of taste and style. Then an act is regarded as right if it is fitting, pleasing, or satisfying. The test of the good is then taken to be balance or harmony, and it is held that there are no universal principles of obligation, but only individual acts whose worth is judged by the intrinsic delight they afford. Some traditional hedonistic and utilitarian systems of ethics, in which (committing the naturalistic fallacy) the good is defined in terms of pleasure, harmonizing of interests, and maximizing happiness, illustrate this assimilation of ethics to esthetics.

To maintain the relative independence of the esthetic and ethical realms is not to deny the propriety of judgments from one realm to the other. Works of art may quite properly be judged by moral principles to ascertain their effect upon conduct. Conceivably it may even prove desirable to prohibit the making and exhibition of certain works of art on moral grounds. But such moral judgments have no bearing on the esthetic significance of the works themselves. Similarly, it is quite in order to evaluate moral principles from an esthetic standpoint, showing what styles of life ensue and to what degree harmony, balance, and satisfaction are realized, provided it is understood that these legitimate judgments of taste are not the basis for judging the rightness of the actions prescribed.

Finally, we may compare meanings in the ethical realm with meanings in the synnoetic realm. Both are realms of decision, commitment, and active engagement. While particular moral decisions are made in concrete existential situations, the moral principles implicit in making such decisions are abstract and general. Thus, moral choice has both personal and impersonal elements. It is personal in that the whole being of the person is expressed in the decision to act. It is impersonal in that the morality of the act is not a function of the person in his singularity, but of the situation. Ethical meanings also differ from personal knowledge in not having to do with unique person-to-person encounters, but with decisions to which universal claims are attached.

Above all, ethics differ from personal understanding in respect to the element of obligation. Personal relations, like facts and perceptual forms, simply *are*. The relation of one person to another is the awareness of a presence, the I-Thou meeting. Such relationships are not founded on duty, but on love and communion. Obligation involves judgment of what is, on the basis of an ideal. Personal relations are consummated in what presently is. Love presupposes unconditional acceptance rather than critical evaluation and action aimed at improvement.

The autonomy of the ethical realm vis-à-vis the synnoetic realm of personal awareness and encounter does not render either domain impervious to the other. While one can properly make moral judgments about personal relations, the significance of the latter is not determined by the former. Likewise, while moral conduct can be criticized from the standpoint of personal relations, the ethical meanings are not determined by synnoetic factors.

The realm of ethics, then, is *right action*. The central concept in this domain is *obligation* or what *ought to be done*. The "ought" here is not individual but a *universal* principle of right.

Moral action presupposes *freedom*. Ethical meaning does not attach to coerced, purely habitual or mechanical, accidental, unconscious, or compulsive action. It is conduct that is deliberately executed as an expression of what one is committed to personally. Such action is self-determined rather than determined by outside factors. In this respect, personal knowledge (of the self) is essential to ethical meanings since personal maturity is the ground of freedom. Being a free person is prerequisite to moral action, but not all free action is moral. Thus, personal maturity is a necessary but not a sufficient condition for right conduct.

The concept of ethics sketched here clearly goes far beyond the restricted idea of the subject matter of morality as concerned only with certain special classes of actions, e.g., sexual relations, property rights, and truth-telling. *All* voluntary actions whatever are properly subject to moral judgment, regardless of how trivial or important, public or private, they may be and regardless of any conventions by which morality may be limited in ordinary understanding. The ethical domain is not defined by what conduct is about, but by the fact of its being deliberate and subject to the judgment of right and wrong.

Like personal insights, ethics is everybody's business. Ethical considerations enter into every department of ordinary life. As in the case of personal knowledge, it is difficult to identify the moral expert. There is no discernible class of persons who are specialists in good conduct, as there are specialists in language, science, and art. Nor is there any clear road to moral mastery, as there is in these other fields. The ancient Socratic question "Can virtue be taught?" continues to be asked.

On the other hand, there are acknowledged moral leaders, to whom many look for moral direction and inspiration. The great religions of mankind have brought forth their prophets, saints, and seers—Moses, Isaiah, Akhnaton, Gautama Buddha, Confucius, Jesus, Muhammad, Francis of Assisi. National life produces heroes who become exemplars of moral courage—Joan of Arc, Robert Bruce, Abraham Lincoln, Robert E. Lee, Mohandas Gandhi. Humanitarians like Elizabeth Fry, William Wilberforce, Robert Owen, Jane Addams, and Jacob Riis arise to awaken consciousness of social injustices. Moral philosophers, too—Socrates, Marcus Aurelius, St. Augustine, Blaise Pascal, John Locke, Immanuel

Kant, John Stuart Mill, John Dewey—have made contributions
to moral leadership by the articulation and critical analysis of
moral standards.

Important as these leaders are, they are not the principal
source of moral guidance for the average person. By far the most
significant sources of such influence are the laws and customs of
society. The conscience of a society is embodied in the traditions
of civility by which the common life is governed. Certain standards
of conduct are taken for granted as the basis of the social system,
and a variety of sanctions are used to encourage adherence to these
standards. Obedience to laws and customs is not, of course, always
right. Nevertheless, accepted social standards are intended to provide guidance for conduct, and they do embody much well-tested
moral wisdom.

The content of the moral tradition covers every aspect of the
common life. Beliefs about what is right and wrong are the very
foundation of culture and civilization. Five main areas of moral
concern deserve special notice. First, there are certain basic *human
rights,* which describe conditions of life that it is believed ought
to prevail. For example, the Constitution of the United States
acknowledges such basic rights as the following: trial by jury, in
which the accused is given information on charges and the right
to confront witnesses and have counsel; right of habeas corpus;
freedom from ex post facto laws; freedom of religion, speech,
press, assembly, and petition; right to bear arms; protection against
arbitrary search and seizure; protection against double jeopardy
and self incrimination; due process of law; and freedom from cruel
and unusual punishments. An example of a more comprehensive
statement of rights is found in the "Universal Declaration of
Human Rights" proposed by the General Assembly of the United
Nations in 1948. The fundamental human rights, no matter how
stated, are those that are intended to secure the freedom, integrity,
and dignity of the person as a person against unjust coercion of
any kind.

A second area of primary ethical interest is that of *sex and
family relations.* Since the family is the elemental social institution in which persons are born and nurtured, it is essential that

the relations between the sexes and among the members of the family be carefully considered and wisely ordered. It is to this end that moral codes dealing with these matters are elaborated.

Other social relationships are the subject of a third set of moral traditions. Included among these are such matters as relationships among and within *class, ethnic, racial, religious,* and *vocational* groups. Every culture has its distinctive expectations and regulations about what is right and wrong in these relationships.

The last two major areas are those of *economic* and *political* life. The former has to do with property rights and with the equitable distribution of goods and services, that is, with matters of *distributive justice,* while the latter is a matter of the just deployment of *power.*

Each of the last four areas ultimately refers back to the matter of basic human rights, since the appropriate organization of society from an ethical standpoint is the one which is *just,* that is, which gives each person what is due him, or what he ought to have. The unjust social order, whether exemplified in family, vocation, exchange, or civic relations, is one in which the person is deprived of his basic rights arbitrarily and without justification.

Since progress beyond the accepted standards of society depends upon criticism and the discovery of new moral possibilities, adherence to law and custom is not a sufficient basis for moral conduct. Still, it is essential to recognize the place of tested tradition in ethics, for only thus can the special relevance of the common life (and of the "ordinary person") to moral insight and the normal means of ethical education be understood. Ordinary people, rather than a corps of specialists, are the guardians and practitioners of morality, because moral conduct has to do with right action in everyday affairs and with the basic terms for the common life. Moral conduct is the source of the common good, for which everyone, and not a particular group of professional moralists, is responsible. Moreover, right conduct *can* be taught, and is continually taught, not by experts who profess the subject of ethics, but by participation in the everyday life of society according to the recognized standards of that society. Such learning constitutes ethical education insofar as the standards engendered by law and custom are deliberately appropriated as the chosen principles of a person's own conduct.

Since morality is everyone's business, it is natural that the language of morals should be ordinary language. In this realm no special technical concepts are required to express the intended meanings. Contemporary analytic philosophers are making a valuable contribution to ethical clarity in their appeal to ordinary language usage as the clue to ethical meanings. They point out, for example, that when a person says "This action is right" he clearly does not mean the same as "I enjoy doing this" or "You should do this." If he meant the latter two assertions, he would have made them instead of saying what he said, which means something different. In the field of ethics, then, common language usage is the basis for the expression of meanings.

Despite this emphasis on common understandings in the ethical realm, there is still a place for ethical theory, that is, for reflection on what ethical understanding is and how it may be improved. Since moral judgments are practical rather than theoretical, the person who knows ethical theory is not on that account more moral than he would be without such knowledge. This contrasts with the case of the scientist who in knowing the theory of his subject *ipso facto* becomes a better scientist. The ethical case parallels that of the artist and of the person in his ability to relate to himself and others in that theory is not of the essence of understanding the subject. The same holds for the person who is fluent in a language without knowing its theory.

The special value of ethical theory, like theory in all the other realms of meaning, is in guiding teaching and learning. If one knows precisely what an ethical meaning is and how moral judgments may be criticized and justified, reflection may be directed with maximum effect to developing moral competence.

How, then, should moral deliberation take place? What are the methods of ethical inquiry, either in solitude (where, finally, the moral decision is formed) or in association with others who may have conflicting convictions about what ought to be done?

To begin with, since moral conduct has to do with decisions

to act in particular situations, wise choice presupposes clear understanding of what the situation is. The one who is required to act
needs to know the context of his action—the circumstances and
conditions in which his decision is to be made. The moral problem
is of the form: What ought I to do in this situation? To solve it one
has to be clear as to what is given in the setting where choice
occurs. In short, before a person can know where to go, he needs
to understand where he is starting from.

Having defined the situation, the next step in the inquiry is
to construct in imagination a series of possible decisions to be
made and courses of action to be taken. Conduct is not moral if
one acts without due deliberation, does what first comes to mind,
follows precedents automatically, or chooses on the basis of accidental factors. The improvement of conduct depends upon the
habit, in making each decision, of bringing into consciousness a
range of different possibilities from among which a selection can
be made. The imagined courses of action can be original constructions, like those of a playwright or novelist who invents the plot
of his drama, or they may be suggestions drawn from the actions
performed by other persons (or by oneself) in analogous circumstances.

Up to this point no distinctively moral element has entered
in. The situation and the possibilities of action are matters of
fact, not of obligation. Now comes the moral question per se:
Which of the possible courses of action is the right one for me to
take? There are three main types of ethical theory upon which
the decision may proceed, namely, the *subjectivist,* the *formalist,*
and the *teleological.*

According to the first type, the idea of right is defined in
terms of some subjective feeling-state. That is, the right choice is
defined as that which gives one the most pleasure or satisfaction.
In effect this position simply dismisses the moral question as
meaningless because the idea of right is absorbed into an idea of
fact, namely, what pleases or satisfies wants. The chooser is asked
to give up the moral search (which, it is assumed, will inevitably
be fruitless) and unashamedly pursue the natural way of self-
interest.

This first method of treating the moral problem is open to the criticism that it contradicts the entire moral experience of mankind and the persistent intuitions of the moral consciousness. As pointed out earlier, about any interest or desire pursued it always seems appropriate to ask, "But *ought* I pursue it?"—a question that would be pointless if the subjectivist approach were to be accepted.

The other two kinds of approach to the evaluation of the imagined possibilities of action presuppose the autonomy and distinctiveness of the ethical realm and point to specifically moral resources for guiding choice.

The second type of theory is *formalistic,* because the criteria of rightness are certain formal principles of action. According to this theory, there are universal standards of conduct by which decisions should be made. The study of these principles and the methods of applying them to particular cases is the subject of *casuistry.* Examples of moral principles are the Golden Rule, Kant's Categorical Imperative, and the Ten Commandments. The first two are completely formal in that they do not refer to the kind of action but only to the demand for reciprocity and universalizability, while the Decalogue deals with certain specific classes of actions that are held to be intrinsically right or wrong.

In making decisions on a formalistic basis the various possibilities of action are evaluated by means of relevant formal principles. The question of relevance is determined by the kind of action contemplated. The principle used as a standard must refer to the same kind of action as the one being evaluated. In making the application the difficulty arises that moral principles are general, while moral decisions are particular. It is necessary to decide whether principles are to be maintained absolutely and without limitation or whether the particular circumstances alter the demands of the general rule. Sometimes, too, more than one principle applies to a particular situation, and a decision must be made as to which rule to apply and, if both, how they may be reconciled. Such questions as these fall within the province of casuistry.

Under the formalist approach the moral inquirer needs an array of standards to which he can turn. These are found chiefly in the accepted traditions of the society in which one lives. They are available in the teachings of the great religious leaders, in sacred literature, and in the writings of moral thinkers. They are to some extent embodied in historic charters and constitutions, and their particular applications are continually being worked out in the law and the courts. [5]

Another important source of principles is admired persons who in their own lives exemplify the meaning of good conduct. Probably no other influence to good behavior is as powerful as the example of a man who embodies the principles to which he is committed. Thus, when Aristotle set about stating the principles of right conduct in his *Ethics,* he simply described how an Athenian gentleman acts. The good life, he said in effect, is attained in acting the way good men act. In the same way, the Christian community has, for the most part, found its ideal of conduct in "the imitation of Christ"—the principle of action is to act the way Jesus did. The followers of the Buddha and of Muhammad the Prophet have adopted analogous procedures.

Useful as the formalist approach to moral decision is, it has its difficulties and limitations. One problem has already been suggested, namely, that of application to the particular situation. Formal principles tend to be empty. The morality of the deed may be more a function of what is done, particularly and substantively, than of the form of doing it. One may assent to the principle of loving his neighbor, but still not know what loving concretely means nor who his neighbor is in a given instance.

Formalism also tends to degenerate into legalism, i.e., mechanical and literal keeping of rules as ends in themselves. The law loses its spirit and becomes letter. Obligation becomes the burden of duty rather than willing response to the sense of rightness. Duty for duty's sake or for the sake of the principle is in fact contrary to the fundamental meaning of morality as action freely chosen for the sake of the right.

Another problem with formalism is that it may provide no

[5] It is not implied here that the laws of a society are identical with moral principles. To a large extent laws are rules of practice designed to further the ends of society. They are moral only insofar as the ends to be served are morally conceived. The present point is simply that the laws of society are in fact often used as moral rules in making decisions.

criteria for judging between possible courses of action to which different moral principles are relevant. Each mode of behavior may be judged as right by its own relevant principle, but still no basis may exist for deciding which mode to elect. This difficulty may be avoided only if moral principles are organized in a hierarchy of increasing generality, so that when two proximately independent kinds of action are at issue, a more general principle comprising both kinds of action can be invoked. Such comprehensive principles as the Golden Rule provide standards of this broad type allowing discriminations between actions ostensibly different in kind, to which different particular rules apply.

The most perplexing difficulty of all with the formalist approach to moral judgments is the problem of the choice and justification of the principles themselves. Perhaps the major problem in moral decision is not in testing imagined possibilities against a set of principles, but in the selection of principles to be used as standards. Many offer themselves as leaders, authorities, and exemplars. Which among them are the true authorities? Laws and traditions differ from culture to culture. Which are worthy of acceptance as moral guides?

One solution to the problem of authority is offered in the theory of *conscience*. It is said that every person is endowed with a native *intuition* of the right which, if he attends to it and obeys it, will enable him to know right from wrong. Moral principles are simply generalizations of what men have heard with the ear of conscience, and they may be checked for authenticity by any person who sincerely and persistently seeks to know and do what is right.

Other theorists hold to a *natural law* view of moral principles. According to this view, generalizations about right conduct can be made on rational grounds; there are certain self-evident truths about conduct that can be justified with certainty by rational reflection alone. Thus, certain rationalists of the Enlightenment held "these truths to be self-evident, that all men are created equal, that they are endowed by their creator with certain unalienable Rights, that among these are Life, Liberty, and the pursuit of Happiness." The natural law of morality is believed to be as real and certain as the natural law of fact discovered in empirical inquiry, although the former is a law of obligation which may be disobeyed, while empirical laws describe what necessarily occurs, without any possibility of disobedience. The natural moral law is a normative, prescriptive law in the domain of freedom. The natural law of science is a factual, descriptive law in the domain of necessity.

Another answer to the problem of authority is the doctrine of *revelation*, according to which certain principles are authenticated on the basis of the supernatural circumstances attending their disclosure. If miracles, signs, and wonders are believed to have accompanied the giving of the law, and if these indications are guaranteed by a powerful and respected institution with a long and impressive history, the authority of the revelation is difficult for many people to call into question.

Unfortunately, conscience, reason, and revelation have not proved to be clear, unambiguous, and universally acknowledged guides. The moral intuitions of the most earnest, reasonable, and well-intentioned people differ, and what are supernatural proofs to one group of believers are considered superstitions by another group. The fact of persistent disagreement on moral questions is the rock on which all claims to infallible authority, whether in intuition, reason, or revelation, come to grief.

On the other hand, the problem of disagreement should not be exaggerated to the point where one throws in the sponge with the subjectivists and denies that moral claims have any meaning apart from personal feeling-states. There *are* certain principles, such as the duty to keep promises and to tell the truth, which are universally acknowledged. Furthermore, apparent differences in principle may actually be differences in application under different circumstances. Moral judgments are necessarily relative to situations, and in that sense *ethical relativism* is justified. It can also be argued that because of human limitations no one can know what is really right and that different principles are varying approximations to the right, each with some measure of authenticity but each also limited by the particular biases of the persons and groups who accept it.

Perhaps the best solution to the problems presented by formalism is to adopt the third of the basic ethical theories, namely, the *teleological* one. According to this position, the rightness of an act is judged according to the consequences of doing it. If the consequences are good, the act is right; if they are evil, the act is wrong. Thus, the primary category in teleological ethical theory is *good* instead of *right,* which is primary in formalism.

Using the teleological method, one makes his choice by considering what the different possible lines of action are likely to lead to and by weighing the relative worth of the several consequences. The right action is then the one that produces the best results. This method is also useful in deciding between moral principles. Those laws or rules are best that, on the whole, yield the best consequences when applied.

The teleological method, of course, does not so much solve the moral problem as shift its basis from judgments about right to judgments about good. To use the method effectively, one has to be able to evaluate the worth of consequences. Much of the appeal of the teleological approach lies in the fact that many people think they can know and agree better on what is good than on what they ought to do, and hence that they can resolve the question of right by determining what course of action is the most likely to lead to the agreed good consequences. This analysis of means to ends is the basis for the pragmatist theory of valuation. [6]

If it is assumed that the good is defined as what gives pleasure, success, or any other state of affairs, then the teleologist commits the naturalistic fallacy of identifying a fact with a value. To avoid this, the meaning of desirable consequences must be interpreted as an *ideal*. This concept of ideals is fundamental to teleological ethical theory. It means a state of affairs that is worth bringing into being, "a consummation devoutly to be hoped for." An ideal is not an actuality, not a fact, but a possibility that *ought* to be realized, a potentiality it is *desirable* to actualize.

From the teleological standpoint, then, moral decision requires a set of ideals to serve as standards of reference in the evaluation of consequences—a realm or kingdom of ends that define what is worthy of effort, sacrifice, and devotion. The sources of these

[6] For a classic statement of this position see John Dewey, *Theory of Valuation,* The University of Chicago Press, Chicago, 1939.

ideals are essentially the same as the sources of moral principles earlier suggested. The moral traditions of mankind contain visions of the good life that have compelling power on the actions of men. For use in moral decision, these goods need to be arranged in hierarchical order so that conflicts among lesser goods may be resolved by reference to goods on a higher level.

Unfortunately, there appears to be no sure means of demonstrating what the ideal life really is, so that everyone will agree. There continue to be differences in conceptions of the good, just as there are differences in conceptions of the right. Conflicts may be due to the fact that no common basis for values exists, and that the good is simply another name for what people happen to want. If that is so, the moral problem is dismissed as a pseudoproblem. [7] Again, conflicts may be due to the complexity of the problems of evaluation and the need for much fuller thought and discussion. That is, the good may be accessible to mutual understanding but difficult to establish.

Or, the persistence of disagreements may be a result of an ingrained egocentricity in human beings that biases their judgments in favor of their own interests and makes universal agreement difficult or impossible (in contrast to the field of empirical science, where self-interest is not involved to the same extent, making consensus possible). This is the position taken by theologians who affirm a doctrine of original sin, or of inveterate self-centeredness. [8]

The goal of universal consensus is itself an ideal deeply rooted in the moral consciousness. It is this ideal which persistently stands in the way of surrendering to an easy subjectivism— a toleration of all values as personal preferences, not subject to moral judgment. One way of establishing an ideal of the good that can be universally acknowledged and used to counteract the egocentric bias is to appeal to *essential human nature* as the ultimate criterion of the good. This approach is in effect a species of *natural law* ethical theory, applied to ends rather than to kinds

[7] This is the subjectivist position once more.

[8] See, for example, Reinhold Niebuhr, *The Nature and Destiny of Man,* Charles Scribner's Sons, New York, vol. 1, 1941.

of action. The highest good for man is taken as the maximum fulfillment of human potentialities, or as realizing what is deepest and most essential in human existence. [9]

It might seem, and it is frequently so argued, that referring the good to the nature of man opens the possibility of an empirical ethical theory, since human nature is a matter of fact. This conclusion is erroneous because the standard here is not actual empirical human nature, but "ideal" or "essential" human nature. These terms, and ones like "maximum fulfillment" and "deepest," do not refer to facts, but to values. They are gerundives rather than descriptions. "Essential human nature" is not a natural *fact* but an *ideal* that is appropriate to human beings.

The present study suggests a basis for articulating an ideal of human nature. It has been indicated throughout that the distinctive goal of human existence is the realization of *meaning*. If this is accepted, then the good life consists in the realization of meanings, in all realms: in the ability to communicate intelligibly and forcefully, to organize the experience of sense into significant generalizations and theories with predictive power, to express the inner life in moving esthetic constructions, to relate with others and with oneself in acceptance and love, to act with deliberate responsibility, and to coordinate these meanings into an integrated vision and commitment.

Such an ideal of what human life can be and ought to be is consistent with the facts of human experience and with the persistent visions of universality, truth, beauty, love, duty, and integrity that have come down in the moral traditions of mankind. It states a goal, based on the study of human potentialities, by which the consequences of actions may be assessed, and hence provides a solid ground for moral decisions. On this foundation, it would seem, a defensible and productive theory of morals can be established—a theory according to which the entire educative endeavor is seen as a moral enterprise aimed at the consummation of human life through the increase in meaning in all its realms.

[9] This is the approach used by certain ethically oriented psychologists like Erich Fromm and Abraham H. Maslow.

THE SIXTH REALM: *Synoptics*

18
HISTORY

In this final section of Part Two we consider a sixth realm of meanings, *synoptics*. This term comprises meanings having an *integrative* function, uniting meanings from all the realms into a unified perspective, that is, providing a "single vision" or "synopsis" of meanings. The chief synoptic disciplines are history, religion, and philosophy. Each achieves the integration of meanings in a different way: history by imaginatively re-creating the past, religion by the disclosure of ultimate meanings, and philosophy by the critical interpretation of expressed meanings. Since these ways are more diverse than are the ways of the different fields in any other realm of meaning, it might seem better to treat each as a separate realm. While there would be no serious objection to doing so, the three may be treated as belonging to one realm in that, for all their differences, they share the one fundamental purpose of integrative or synoptic understanding. They differ only in the manner of effecting the intended integration.

The central category in the field of history is *time*. To understand history is to understand the meaning of temporality, and vice versa. The subject matter of history is *what happened in the past,* or, more precisely, *human events of the past.* Thus, history is not concerned with time in general, but with past time. The appropriate mode of discourse for history is the past tense.

Time enters into other realms of meaning also, but not in the same way as in history. Time in the empirical descriptions of science is simply an impersonal measure of rates of change. The clock is a mechanical instrument for organizing the data of observation according to certain intelligible patterns. Similarly, in language and in the arts, time has to do with formal dynamic relationships within discourse or in esthetic objects. In personal relations time enters as the existential reality of being and becoming, but not as located in an objective sequence. In ethics, while time is a factor in the situation where decisions are made, the standard of judgment is timeless. History alone gives to time its integral meaning. It unites the abstract objectivity of parametric impersonal time in science, and rhythmic time in language and the arts, with the concrete subjectivity of time in personal relations and particular moral decisions, yielding a realization of *whole time,* in which particular unique happenings actually occurred.

The unit of historical inquiry, in which the full significance of time is revealed, is *the event, happening,* or *episode.* An "event" is something that happened once upon a time. The task of the historian is to describe, order, and interpret events.

Events are *concrete.* They are not abstractions, i.e., aspects of complete things. They are themselves existential wholes. Many elements are united in the actuality of any given happening. Each event begins, proceeds toward its end, and is completed. In a sense it is a finished work, a whole occurrence. The integrative nature of history follows from the concreteness of events as the basic units of historical inquiry. If the historian is to present what actually happened, he must bring together the various aspects of human experience into significant wholes, relating past occurrences in the light of all the ingredients that go into the formation of a complex real-life happening.

History differs from science in this concern for the concrete, singular event. Science aims at generality, history at describing unique events. Both are rooted in *actual fact,* but in science the facts are the basis for generalizations and theories, while in history the particular facts are the final objects of knowledge.

History is like art—especially literature—in that its goal is particular unique presentations in the form of convincing stories. The events of the past are recounted in an imaginative way so as to move the reader by their drama and by their universal human appeal. History is unlike art in that, although its works are imaginatively constructed, they are intended as disclosures of the actual world and not of a fictional world. Imagination enters into the manner of telling the story, not as the fabrication of events that never actually occurred.

Creative imagination also enters into scientific constructions, which, like historical accounts, relate to the actual world. But the creations of science (and of art) are imaginative *abstractions,* the former having reference to actual things, the latter to fictions. The creations of the historian, on the other hand, are ideally not abstractions but concretions, and they refer to actuality rather than to fiction. Since no one history can relate the fullness of any event, every account is necessarily a partial abstraction emphasizing certain aspects that the historian considers most significant. Nevertheless, the ultimate goal of history is to tell the *whole* story about what happened. Hence, the historian cannot follow the artist's practice of deliberately presenting abstractions for the sake of creating certain responses in his readers.

Actually, the goal of a complete history, even of one event, is never attainable. The whole truth about anything is infinitely complex and can never be told. Hence the historian, who is a finite being writing for an audience of finite beings, has to tell a partial truth. The critical question for the historian concerns the grounds for selecting what he will include in his account. The artist's grounds for selection are esthetic effect, the historian's are fidelity to the facts. The historian's task is to decide which limited materials will most faithfully represent the infinite concrete truth about what happened.

One other difference between art and history is noteworthy. Works of art are complete compositions, each with a beginning, middle, and end, and as esthetic objects they are independent from all other things. Events, too, are particular happenings, and a history consists of accounts with an ostensible beginning, middle, and end. On the other hand, this discreteness and apparent completeness in the case of history are due to practical limitations rather than to the nature of the subject. Every event is part of a whole world of interconnections, and every historical account is a fragment of the infinitely rich story of the past. It is quite appropriate to frame a picture as an expression of its finite perfection and incomparable uniqueness. The happenings of history cannot be framed. They are necessarily immersed in the infinite stream of time and bound up in mutual ingredience with an infinity of other happenings.

It was stated above that the subject matter of history is *human* events of the past. "Natural history" belongs to science rather than to history, because it is not concerned with time in the full historical sense, but with the temporal succession of occurrences according to the laws of nature. Historical time applies to events that have occurred as a result of human decision. Nicolas Berdyaev makes a distinction between the "true time" of concrete historical action and the "false time" of mechanistic abstraction. [1] Benedetto Croce also emphasizes the essentially human content of history in calling it "the story of liberty," [2] and R. G. Collingwood, in *The Idea of History* [3] writes, "What kinds of things does history find out? I answer, *res gestae:* actions of human beings that have been done in the past."

This essential human reference of history is what links it with the realms of personal and moral knowledge. The subject matter of history is what persons have done in the deliberate exercise of their freedom and in the light of moral consciousness. History is the story of what human beings have made of themselves within the context of their physical and social environments. It is the account of the moral adventure of mankind, of decisions for good and for evil, and of the judgments revealed in the consequences. Collingwood holds that the value of history is self-understanding. "Knowing yourself means knowing, first, what it is to be a man; secondly, knowing what it is to be the kind of man you are; and thirdly, knowing what it is to be the man *you* are and nobody else

[1] *The Meaning of History*, Meridian Books, Inc., New York, 1962.
[2] *History as the Story of Liberty*, Meridian Books, Inc., New York, 1955.
[3] Oxford University Press, Fair Lawn, N.J., 1946, p. 9. Reprinted by permission of the publisher.

is . . . The value of history, then, is that it teaches us what man has done and thus what man is." [4]

We are now in a better position to understand what an event, the basic historical unit, really is. An event, as the etymology of the word suggests, is an *outcome*. An outcome of what? An event is what comes out of human deliberation. It is a decision to act in a certain way. The object of historical inquiry is therefore to understand particular decisions that people have made in the past.

It is clear that history is not the same as *chronicle*, that is, the relating of observable acts in temporal sequence. The elements of chronicle are not events at all, in the sense indicated above, but simply outward behavior. Events, on the other hand, are consequences of inner deliberation. Chronicle is the skeleton of history, history without any animating principle, history without any personal significance. The confusion of history with chronicle is one of the chief sources of distaste for history on the part of students. They can hardly be expected to be interested in a recital of dead "facts" that have no apparent relevance to them as persons in search of meaning.

The goal of historical inquiry is to attain an understanding of past human events *from the inside*. This requires an imaginative identification by the historian (and by those who read his works correctly) with the persons whose decisions have caused the happenings of the past. Historical understanding thus consists in a re-creation of the past through participation, in thought, in the lives of those who made the past what it was. History from this standpoint is making the past come alive in the present.

The concreteness of history is consistent with this analysis of the inner meaning of events. As explained in Chapter 16, personal knowledge is concrete and existential rather than concerned with abstract essences. Actuality described as a chronicle of observable phenomena is not history because it is not personal. Actuality as the personal reenactment of the past in the present is the object of historical understanding, and since it is personal, it is concrete.

Is history, then, merely a subdivision within the synnoetic realm? No, history is an autonomous and distinctive field whose

[4] *Ibid.*, p. 10. Reprinted by permission of the publisher.

special office is to integrate meanings from the other realms primarily in the mode of temporal relation. *Historical understanding is personal insight expressed in ordinary language, informed by scientific knowledge, transformed by esthetic imagination, and infused by moral consciousness.*

The aim of historical inquiry is to ascertain the *facts* about the human past. The word "fact" is especially appropriate to history since in its derivation a "fact" is something *made* or *done.* Now history is about things done by persons; it concerns acts or deeds. Also history is something which is made by the historian. These two sets of acts are related in that the making of history is the redoing of what was done in the past. Thus, history is factual in a double sense. A third sense is also relevant, namely, that a fact is something done, finished, past.

The problem of understanding the past is quite different from that of immediate perception, as in art and personal knowledge, or of prediction on the basis of repeatable observations, as in science. The past is gone, leaving only traces of itself, and the task of the historian is to restore that past as faithfully as may be, and make it live again as though it were present.

Writing history does not consist in taking certain given happenings, arranging them in chronological order, and weaving them into an interesting tale. The historian has no ready-made events to relate, except as he uses the results of some other historian's labors. He has to *make his own events;* his facts are not given, but made. The whole point of historical study is to find out what really did happen by reconstructing it in imagination.

The making of history is a process of drawing *inferences* from available *evidence.* What evidence does the historian use? He may use anything at all that he finds relevant to the reconstruction of the past. Included are the accounts of eyewitnesses to past events, written documents, monuments, artifacts, and (perhaps most important of all) the whole present world of things and people, since the present state of the world is largely a consequence of the past actions of men. History may then be defined as *that imaginative re-creation of past human events that best accords with the evidence of the present,* or more briefly, as *the best possible explanation of the present in terms of the past.*

Historical constructions are made by the *interpretation* of evidence, separating relevant from irrelevant factors, reliable from unreliable reports, and *primary sources* from *secondary, tertiary* and *higher* orders of sources (the latter referring to sources that are themselves historical interpretations or interpretations of interpretations rather than original records or artifacts). Each interpretation is a historical *hypothesis,* a statement of what might have happened, and the consequences of each such hypothesis are developed to see how well they agree with the available evidence.

As pointed out above, an event may be inwardly understood only as an outcome of deliberate human decision. Many factors enter into the outcome, in that each decision concerns what to do given certain material and social circumstances, personal goals, and moral principles. The reconstruction of the past therefore requires a considerable fund of knowledge. The more the historian knows of the empirical, personal, moral and even esthetic factors that went into the making of the decisions to be reconstructed the better will be his hypotheses about what occurred in the past.

Particularly important in such historical analysis and explanation are psychology and the social sciences. From political science, for example, generalizations are available concerning the various modes of exercising power. Every decision is made within the context of certain influences, pressures, and forces, about which political science yields valuable information. In psychology generalizations may be found regarding such factors as drives, unconscious motivation, developmental stages, and character types, all of which may aid greatly in the formation of fruitful hypotheses about how past decisions were reached. Sociology can contribute relevant knowledge of possible formative elements such as social structure, roles, norms, and social class, and anthropology can help in the formation of hypotheses from the standpoint of cultural patterns. Economic and geographic influences may also be of great importance in the formation of the events which the historian endeavors to recapture.

Valuable as the generalizations of the various sciences are in framing historical hypotheses, they are not sufficient to account for the unique particulars of history. Here is where the arts become relevant, particularly drama, which is a fictional presentation of persons making decisions affecting their destiny. The novelist's or playwright's convincing portrayal of life in fictional form can provide helpful suggestions to the historian as he seeks to present his convincing portrayal of life, answerable to the conditions and evidences of actuality.

The reenactment of the past is achieved when unique events are imaginatively concretized as personal decisions in the light of the claims of conscience. The past as human events cannot be understood simply as a description of objects or even as an artistic presentation. What is required is an active personal engagement with people in the past regarded as moral subjects involved in the struggle to fulfill their destiny. Interpretations on this basis are certain to reflect the predispositions and personal biases of the historian more than would be the case with knowledge in the empirical realm. Nevertheless, history is not merely a record of the historian's personal reactions, for the historian is obliged to show that his interpretations and explanations best account for the available evidence. This obligation puts a check on subjectivity and opens the way to the progressive criticism and improvement of historical knowledge.

Although the event is the basic unit of historical knowledge, a "history" in the usual sense is an account involving many events in their mutual interrelations in time. The events selected may fall within a given time span (say, 1900 to 1950), and they may be limited to a certain class or type (such as military, economic, or scientific events), or to happenings taking place within a given area (such as the United States or Africa) or in connection with a particular institution or person.

A further method of simplifying historical analysis is through *periodization,* that is, the grouping of events into periods for which certain general characterizations may be made. For example, the "Renaissance," the "Colonial Period," the "Age of Reason," and the "Jacksonian Era" are names for historical periods about which certain statements can be made regarding typical styles of thought, movements, social structures, dominant personalities, and the like. While these periods in effect constitute generalizations about events, they may themselves be regarded as concrete macroevents requiring the same kind of explanation as happenings resulting from individual decisions. The historian tries to project himself imaginatively into an age, reaching for an awareness of what it must have been like to live in that period. He then considers how people living at that time might be expected to have behaved, and he checks his predictions by whatever evidence of their actual behavior has been preserved to the present time.

Going beyond the generalization effected by periodizing, some historians attempt to describe certain general principles or laws of historical development by which the past may be explained and the future course of events to some extent predicted. In this manner comprehensive theories of history are developed in which particular events are seen as examples of universal laws. While theorizing of this kind may possibly have some value, it does not properly belong to history since it swallows the singular event up in generality. "Laws of history" belong to the social sciences rather than to history proper, since their logic is that of empirical inquiry and not of distinctively historical study. Laws are timeless, abstract, and impersonal, unlike the personal concretions in time that are the proper subject matter of history. "History never repeats itself" is a true saying, in the sense that events as history treats them are unique happenings. While analogies between events may be of scientific interest and may even enter into the reconstruction of events by the historian, these regularities are not themselves the goal of historical understanding.

Summing up, history is the study of what human beings have deliberately done in the past. Its content is not, as in science, generalizations about observable occurrences, but particular events ordered temporally. These events are conceived as outcomes of personal existential decisions at particular times. Hypotheses about what happened are formed by the imaginative re-creation of the past, using relevant empirical knowledge from every field, together with personal understanding and ethical insight. Finally, these hypotheses are tested and progressively improved by checking them with effects of the past in the form of present evidence.

19

RELIGION

Like history, religion as a synoptic field integrates all the realms of meaning. Integration in history is achieved by the consideration of events in time. The reenactment of these events requires meanings from all the realms. In religion the common element uniting all the realms is *ultimacy*. The term "ultimacy" is a general designation for such ideas as infinitude, absoluteness, the un-limited, transcendence, perfection, completeness, all-inclusiveness, the supreme, and many others. It stands in contrast to concepts of finitude, the relative, limitation, partiality, and the like.

The content of religious meanings may be anything at all, provided it is regarded from an ultimate perspective. Or it might better be said that religious meanings comprehend or include all things, and that a religious attitude with respect to any given thing is to consider it in the light of all that is, i.e., from the standpoint of the Whole.

The methods of gaining religious understanding are many and varied, including prayer, meditation, active commitment, and ritual practices. One element is, however, essential in all methods of pursuing religious meanings, and this may be described as "going to the limits." This means proceeding to the point where ordinary finite experience is exhausted and where the significance of proximate and limited meanings is called into question.

Not everyone agrees that this "going to the limits" is a meaningful process. Those who do not agree think that finite experience is all that people can have and that concepts of ultimacy are therefore empty and their objects illusory. Generally they hold that no question ever need arise beyond the pursuit of finite meanings, that human life consists simply in the sum total of particular happenings, and that while various coordinations and interrelations can be established, the concept of understanding anything in the light of the Whole is meaningless.

Those who affirm the meaningfulness of religion believe that in "going to the limits" in prayer and other religious practices a new and essential perspective is gained on everything particular and that in some sense this new perspective is an illumination from the Whole, constituting what is generally referred to as *revelation*. Moreover, people who accept the religious view usually hold that those who deny any ultimacy implicitly affirm it in the vigor of their denial and that their clinging to finitude is an effort to escape the overwhelmingness of an ultimate that can neither be encompassed nor controlled.

The idea of "the limits" may be somewhat misleading, since in the approach to ultimacy there is no question of reaching a dividing line between two domains of experience. The "limits of the finite" symbolizes the way to the infinite, but the infinite is not simply another kind of finitude on the other side of the limits. That is why in the religious sphere the basis of understanding is said to be *faith* and not the forms of understanding that characterize the finite realms. Faith is the illumination that comes in going to the limits. It is the light that shines from the Whole, where the Whole is not simply the sum of everything within the finite realms, but the Comprehensive that comprehends or holds together all things in a transcendent unity, and is itself not comprehensible within any finite entity.

The realm of ultimacy is frequently designated as the "supernatural," which is another way of speaking of infinitude. The supernatural is what is beyond the limits of the finite or natural. This mode of speech is likely to be misleading too, for the supernatural, the Kingdom of God, Heaven, and other such terms are not meant to be interpreted geographically, as separate realms. Religion means nothing apart from a relation of natural and supernatural, finite and infinite, the latter being another order of reality from the former. The relation is that of creature to Creator, of beings to Being-Itself, and of the temporal to the Eternal. The disclosure of this relation is revelation, and its mode of apprehension is faith.

Each of the realms of meaning hitherto described is necessary to the Comprehensive that is apprehended by faith. From the symbolic realm *religious symbols* are required. In ultimate perspective, language is seen as the primordial creative Word, which was in the beginning, and from which all things were made. The ultimate word is the link binding together finite and infinite, time and eternity. It is the ordering principle in all things, the bond of community among disparate entities.

Many different symbolic forms are used as the vehicles of faith. Some of these are based on ordinary language, including common words like love, anger, and power. In these cases the meanings are generally to be understood figuratively and not literally, experiences from finite existence being used to point to faith analogues. When the symbols of faith are understood in their ordinary language sense, the religious meaning is missed and religious utterances are regarded as meaningless or at most as anthropomorphic projections. Actually, a degree of anthropomorphism is inherent in symbolic usage and is the basis on which the infinite becomes intelligible within finite existence.

In addition to ordinary language used extraordinarily, religious symbols include many other nondiscursive forms. Especially important are *rituals,* by which relations to the ultimate are regulated. For these purposes the religious community may designate special times and places (holy days, shrines, temples) and special persons (priests) and may consecrate certain objects as *sacramental.* Even more important in ritual are the symbolic acts, including postures, gestures, and other bodily movements regarded as symbolizing the approach to the divine. The various symbolic patterns thus employed belong to the language of religion.

One more especially significant aspect of religious expression is the use of *silence*. Silence is a mode of expression which symbolizes the boundary situation from which faith springs. In the silence one bears witness to the infinitude that cannot be contained in any finite act or utterance. Silence is the expression of the ineffability of the ultimate, which religious mystics have always acknowledged. From the standpoint of faith the atheist is in a sense correct: the divine is literally *nothing*, that is, not a thing which can be set alongside other things, put into categories, and named. The Comprehensive cannot be comprehended; it is nameless. For these reasons the symbolism of silence is an essential one in religion.

In the realm of scientific meanings, the ultimate appears as the *Truth*. The "Truth" in the religious sense does not mean simply the sum of all the true propositions known and yet to be known. It means the one Source and Ground of all partial truths and the Light that shines within every particular illumination of intelligence. These capitalized terms are symbols of ultimacy in relation to the enterprise of empirical inquiry.

The religious consciousness seeks to affirm a Reality from which the phenomenal world is derived, a Being whose intelligence is revealed in the laws and theories of empirical science. The man of faith affirms an explanation in which all particular explanations are comprehended, and a First Cause (not in order of time, but of being) in which all proximate causes are grounded.

This Source, Ground, Light, Being, Reality, First Cause, is named by many names, and all are names of the *divine* or of *God*, the term most commonly applied to the ultimate Truth. By faith this God is held to be the primal Fact, whose being and nature are expressed in theological propositions and credal formulas. These statements of faith are not regarded as empirical propositions in the same class as other such propositions referring to the finite realm. Yet they are stated in empirical form to express the conviction that the God of faith is actual fact and not a fiction of the imagination. Theology is regarded as the supreme science, providing systematic generalizations and theories about the ultimate Reality.

With respect to the esthetic realm, the man of faith believes that the God of the creative word and of ultimate truth is also the

Source of all beauty. Whatever excellence a work of art has he believes to be due to its participation in the divine excellence. He regards every finite perfection as a reflection of the infinite perfection of God. Hence, in the perception of a work of art, or of any other object esthetically regarded, the eye of faith also perceives pure, unalloyed Beauty. This is not a sense perception, but a faith perception that is believed in, though not actualized in experience. Through this perception the finite instances of beauty serve as symbols of the divine.

From an ultimate perspective, the activity of the artist may be regarded as an analogue of the divine creative activity. God is sometimes symbolized by the figure of the Master Craftsman. In his dialogue *Timaeus* Plato represents the creation of the world as the work of the divine Demiurge shaping formless substance according to the pattern of the ideal forms. Similarly, the God of one of the versions of the creation in the Book of Genesis is portrayed as a plastic artist. Dorothy Sayers, in *The Mind of the Maker* [1] beautifully develops the analogy between the work of the creative writer and the divine life, using as her basis the Christian doctrine of the Trinity. She sees the Father as the creative Idea, the Son as the material Incarnation of the idea, and the Holy Ghost as the communicative Power of the incarnate idea, and she shows how the doctrine of the Trinity and the knowledge of good literary craftsmanship mutually reinforce one another.

The religious significance of the esthetic realm is especially evident in the abundant use made of all the arts in providing religious symbols. Much of the greatest music, painting, and architecture has been inspired by religious faith and has served to inspire others to a similar devotion. From the earliest times the dance has been intimately connected with sacred rites, and as Francis Fergusson shows, [2] the classic drama, which had its roots in the festivals connected with the mystery religions, came to its most complete fulfillment in the cosmic vision of Dante's *Divine Comedy*.

Ultimacy in the realm of personal knowledge is expressed in

[1] Meridian Books, Inc., New York, 1956.

[2] *The Idea of a Theater,* Princeton University Press, Princeton, N.J., 1949.

the conviction that God is *personal*. The creative Word, the supreme Truth, and the divine Harmony are understood by faith
as not only objective abstractions, not merely impersonal cosmic
principles and powers, but as One with Whom each person may be
in direct personal relation. As Buber says, God is the eternal Thou
and He is known in every I-Thou encounter. Wherever a
person meets another in awareness, acceptance, and acknowledge-
ment of his unique being, the eternal Thou is present. God is
affirmed to be Love, and He is known wherever love is found.
Every act of devotion in the finite realm is regarded by the faithful
as a partial manifestation of that primal divine love shown forth
in the creation of all things and in God's abiding solicitude for
their redemption and fulfillment.

The personal God is believed to be the source and ground
of created persons. The traditional term for the person regarded
from an ultimate perspective is the "soul," by which is meant the
real core of a person's being, as contrasted with the empirical self
whose characteristics can be described in the categories of finitude.
The soul is the mysterious depth in persons, in which are hidden
the inexhaustible possibilities of being. In the inwardness of the
soul reside the springs of freedom, whereby the person shares with
the divine in creative activity. There reside the powers of limitless
self-transcendence, the ground for self-awareness, imagination, self-
determination, and participation in real time, including the ability
to remember and to anticipate. In the light of faith these latter
capacities betoken the union in the soul of the temporal and
the eternal, and from this joining spring intimations, hopes, and
expectations of a destiny of the soul beyond the mortal span, as
symbolized in doctrines of preexistence, reincarnation, immortality, and resurrection—the various beliefs differing in the matter
of the relation between the body and soul in the person.

Above all, God, the ultimate Being, is believed to be disclosed in the innermost life of the soul. He is not a Person to be
sought in the far reaches of the cosmos. This is, again, why the
faithful agree with the atheist, that the God who is merely an
object of empirical inquiry—a supreme object—does not exist. He
is known in the Love made manifest in the inwardly accepted
gift of personal existence.

The divine is further known to the faithful as the Holy One. He is supremely righteous, the ultimate source of all good. He is the Judge of all, and in Him the final justification of moral principles resides. These concepts are, however, to be understood metaphorically. God as the righteous judge is not to be conceived as an objective supernatural sovereign issuing commands and rendering judgments. The images used are intended to point to the ultimate Rightness in which all finite principles and achievements of right participate. The divine Goodness, likewise, is a symbol for the ultimate perfection discerned by faith in every particular good.

From a religious standpoint the right and the good are not conceived as impersonal principles and qualities, but as rooted in the personal divine Ground. Right and good have no moral quality apart from personal freedom, which entails the power to act according to the right or contrary to it. Because of freedom persons may choose evil instead of good and thus may become guilty of *sin*. Sin is wrongdoing from the standpoint of relation to the divine.

But since not all evil can reasonably be traced to deliberate disobedience to the moral law, the category of the *demonic* plays a role in religious thought. Various symbols of the antisacred have been developed, including devils as personifications of evil powers, and hells as destinations for unredeemed souls and for the demonic agencies.

The goal of the religious life is *salvation,* which consists in final deliverance from sin and from the ultimate evil, death, and in the realization of union with God Himself in an eternity of love.

The *problem of evil* is perhaps the greatest of all difficulties to religious faith. No satisfactory rational solution to the apparent contradiction between the reality of a loving creator and the actuality of evil (whether as sin or otherwise) has been offered, and it is regarded as the duty of the faithful to affirm the love and the power of God in spite of the mystery of evil, and to make good their faith by taking an active part in the conquest of evil.

Religious meanings incorporate all the realms of meaning in a comprehensive orientation. Religious understanding presupposes a common ground of all meanings. The Word, the Truth, Perfection, Love, the Holy—all refer to one and the same Being. They are the faces of God, in Whom the faithful see things united. Within the finite sphere things are separate and distinct. From the perspective of the infinite all things spring from a single source. In faith realms that are different and distinct are seen as aspects of one Whole.

The foregoing treatment of meanings in the field of religion has necessarily been general and has done little justice to the great variety of actual religious forms in the traditions of mankind. The pursuit of ultimacy may occur through many different symbols, beliefs, rites, codes and institutions. Some groups emphasize the sacred word, and have a religion of the Book. Some groups seek the divine primarily through ritual practices. Other religions are intellectual, centering in creeds and theologies, or esthetic, offering fulfillment in the heavenly vision, while still others stress the way of love and devotion, expressed in the life of prayer and worship. Finally, some show their concern mainly through the deed, believing that salvation comes through obedience to the absolute moral command and through working for the creation of a community conceived in righteousness. No major historical religion has been exclusively of one type; each contains a mixture of elements.

Despite this multiplicity, certain common concerns can be discerned within the religious life of man, and these have been indicated in the foregoing analysis of the fundamental religious ideas. To those who reject religion as an illusion, the diversity of religious forms appears as evidence of the relativity and subjectivity of religion and of the objective meaninglessness of religious symbols. On the other hand, the proponents of religion may claim that the plurality of forms is a consequence of the insufficiency of any finite formulation to do justice to the infinite and that the literal inadequacy of religious symbols, which leads to the search for better ones and hence to multiplicity, is not a defect in relation to the ultimate, but a necessary virtue.

Whether or not the claim of the religious believer is affirmed, the type of meaning intended by the faithful should be clear. Regardless of the results of the search, religious inquiry is directed toward ultimacy, in the sense of the most comprehensive, most profound, most unified meanings obtainable. At the very least, faith refers to an ideal and a hope for maximum completeness, depth, and integrity of vision. On these minimal terms, in which no transcendent realities are posited, everyone should be able to acknowledge some religious meanings. Others do not find that such modest meanings do justice to their most compelling insights, and they bear witness to a faith, mediated by any of a great variety of symbols, in a divine reality that they believe is at once the ground of their own being, the law of their life, the foundation of their hopes, and the creative source of all things.

20
PHILOSOPHY

Like the other two synoptic fields already treated, philosophy is comprehensive in scope. It is concerned with every kind of human experience and not with any one domain. No claim about past, present, or future, actual or ideal, real or possible is beyond the limits of philosophic scrutiny. Philosophy is not even limited, as history and religion are, to certain dimensions of experience, such as the past or the ultimate. All dimensions of all kinds of experience come within its purview. It is thus the most inclusive of the synoptic disciplines.

Still, philosophy has its distinctive ways and ends which mark it as a recognizable and autonomous field of inquiry. It is not inclusive in the sense of being a mere summation of meanings from all the other fields. The distinctive function of philosophy is the *interpretation of meaning*. It is the function of the various other fields to *express* meanings of various sorts: symbolic, empirical, esthetic, synnoetic, ethical, historical, and religious. It is the business of the philosopher to interpret these meanings. Thus the meanings expressed in philosophy are *meanings of meanings,* or what might be termed "meta-meanings."

The present study is an example of such philosophic inquiry, in that its method is to interpret the several fundamental patterns of meaning, with the aim of understanding the curriculum in the light of this interpretation. Since the intention in the fifteen preceding chapters has been to inquire about the meaning of the main classes of human meanings, they should afford some sense of the scope and methods of philosophic inquiry.

It is evident, then, that philosophy draws upon knowledge from all the other fields. It is not a primary and independent field of study in the same way as physics, music, and even religion are. Philosophy presupposes a fund of expressed meanings from other fields of human experience, and it is these meanings developed directly elsewhere that philosophers take as their point of departure and subject of inquiry. Although in its methods it is autonomous, philosophy is dependent and derivative in respect to subject matter.

The method of philosophy is essentially that of *dialectic*. By this is meant a process of conceptual examination by raising questions, proposing answers, and developing implications of those answers in continuing cycles. For the philosopher no expression of meaning is taken at face value. It is his function to ask such questions as: What does this *really* mean? How is this expression of meaning to be interpreted? What type of meaning is here expressed? How can this meaning be justified? How does this meaning compare with other meanings? In philosophic inquiry the question is more important than the answer, for the answer, if accepted as beyond question, stops inquiry. The philosopher is committed to continued inquiry, and experience has shown that the problems of meaning are sufficiently profound to provide ample material for sustained dialectical investigation.

One may speculate as to whether or not the perennial questions of philosophy will ever be finally answered. Some hold that they can be settled by careful attention to the logic of language. Others believe that the persistence of the questions is due to the fact that the available means of expression are never sufficient to communicate the depth and richness of reality. Still others maintain that the questions persist because of the differing personal commitments presupposed in the various answers and that because these commitments express man's freedom they cannot be resolved on any objective basis of agreement.

The medium of philosophical inquiry is discursive language, regardless of the symbolic forms in which the meanings interpreted are expressed. For example, the philosophical examination of art, of personal knowledge, and of religion is carried out with discursive language, even though the meanings in these realms are not usually expressed discursively. While the language of philosophy is to some degree that of ordinary discourse, a technical philosophical vocabulary is also employed. Some philosophers have even tried to develop a completely new symbolism for their inquiries, in which the imprecision and ambiguity of everyday discourse are eliminated. The pioneer effort in this direction was made by Alfred North Whitehead and Bertrand Russell in their celebrated *Principia Mathematica,* [1] which became the inspiration for a variety of systems of *symbolic logic* using special mathematical symbolisms for expressing the meta-meanings of philosophy.

Even when ordinary language is used in philosophy, many terms are employed in unusual and specifically philosophical ways, making them in effect special technical terms. Much confusion and difficulty in philosophy have been occasioned by this practice, and one of the main directions of modern philosophic effort, in what is called "ordinary language analysis," is to show that many philosophic puzzles and perplexities have been caused by twisting ordinary language meanings out of their proper ordinary senses. Some philosophical analysts believe that the careful scrutiny of ordinary language usages can lead to the final settlement of many of the perennial questions of philosophy.

If philosophy as a synoptic discipline is to provide a common basis for interpreting the several realms of meaning, then a single language system must be applied to the entire range of meanings to be interpreted. For this purpose discursive language is the natural choice. It then becomes a question, however, whether or not justice can be done in philosophy to the realms of meaning that are not expressible in discursive form, and whether or not

[1] Cambridge University Press, New York, 1915.

philosophical discourse is by its expressive structure biased in favor of discursive meanings to the detriment of nondiscursive ones. These considerations suggest that philosophical commitment to the method of conceptual dialectic may impose substantial limitations on the adequacy of philosophy as an interpretive discipline. Yet this limitation seems unavoidable, for dialectical examination is inherently discursive. The process of comparison, correction, and generalization of ideas that is the essence of interpretive inquiry could not be carried out by presentational forms, the essence of which is their uniqueness and incomparability. Discursive language therefore seems to be the only means available for the work of reflective thought about the meaning of meanings.

The concepts used in philosophical discourse are of a high order of *abstraction*. Concepts like energy, field, organism, and evolution are stretched to their utmost generality and are used in philosophy to interpret a much wider range of experience than they do in the special fields from which they have been derived. The goal of philosophic inquiry is to frame principles and laws of great generality relating widely diverse fields of experience through some common conceptual scheme. For example, changes of all kinds whatsoever are covered by the Aristotelian principle that change is the actualization of potentiality. Again, the Kantian principle that all empirical knowledge of the world is produced by the innate structures of the mind, organizing the materials of sense, supplies an abstract conceptual interpretation of all possible descriptive meanings. Again, in the present study, the concept of meaning is intended to encompass all the realms of meaning within a common conceptual framework, and the principle that each field may be characterized by a distinctive mode of symbolic expression provides a basis for comparison and contrast of fields and thus for synoptic philosophic interpretation.

In the interpretive activity of the philosopher three main components may be distinguished. The first is *analysis*. This term does not refer only to the process of dividing complex wholes into constituent elements. More often it consists in making distinctions between the various possible meanings of concepts and between the various ways in which meanings may be expressed. Where meanings are ambiguous, analysis serves to clarify them. Where expressions of meaning are misleading—the typical mode of one domain of meaning being used in another domain—analysis serves to call attention to the resulting confusion and to show how expressions can be transformed so as to be appropriate to the kind of meaning expressed.

The second component in philosophic interpretation is *evaluation*. Analysis answers questions such as: What does this expression mean? Evaluation is concerned with the problem of justification. More precisely, in evaluation the philosopher is concerned with how the validity of any given expression of meaning may be established. Clearly, evaluation and analysis are closely interconnected, not only because before one can determine the validity of an expression one needs to know what is being expressed, but also because the method of validation is an important clue to what an expression really means.

The third component is *synthesis*. Meanings are not isolated and totally independent. They have similarities and interconnections. As stated earlier, it is the task of the philosopher to develop concepts general enough to establish connections between diverse experiences, some of these concepts being sufficiently abstract to permit the formulation of a single comprehensive theory of meaning in which the possible types of meaning may be distinguished and the relationships among them may be exhibited. In this manner the entire range of human experiences in their typical expressions may be organized into a single pattern of meanings with appropriate departments and subdivisions. The analytic and evaluative work is, of course, essential to the development of such a philosophic synthesis, since the quality of the whole depends upon that of its parts. Meanings cannot be organized unless it is known what they are, and the validity of the total structure of meanings presupposes the validity of its constituents.

Thus, by a coordinated effort of analysis, evaluation, and synthesis, philosophers seek to construct a synoptic view of the entire range of expressible human experiences, insofar as they can be interpreted within the categories of rational discourse. This comprehensive enterprise has traditionally been divided into a number of specialized fields of inquiry, generally corresponding to the realms of meaning described in the foregoing chapters. In fact, the structure of the discipline of philosophy supports the position taken in this study with regard to the fundamental patterns of meaning. Furthermore, the analysis of meaning in each realm has drawn upon insights from the corresponding branch of philosophy. The following brief description of the main departments of philosophic inquiry will therefore at the same time provide a summary review of the fundamental patterns of meaning.

Philosophy of language or *philosophy of symbolic forms* deals with such questions as the nature and functions of language, the relation of language to reality, the possible types of symbolic systems, and the basis for evaluating language systems. One of the classic (and continuing) problems of the philosophy of language concerns the status of *universals,* that is, of the general ideas represented by symbols. According to one position (realism), the universals have a reality independent of the human mind and intention, while according to the opposing view (nominalism), universals are names or categories invented for purposes of organizing human thought and for guiding human activity. A satisfactory philosophy of language clearly has to account for the existence of a great variety of symbolic systems (as emphasized by the nominalists) and for the fact that the forms of language are devised to enable man to deal effectively with a real world that is to a large degree *given* (as the realists emphasize) and not arbitrarily constructed.

Philosophy of mathematics concerns the foundations of mathematical knowledge, in which questions such as the following arise: What are the general structure and function of the propositions and theories of pure mathematics? How and why is mathematics capable of being applied to the actual world? What is the meaning of the concept of infinity and how can its use be justified? Answers to these and similar questions give rise to several different positions in the philosophy of mathematics, among which the three most important contemporary ones are *logicism* (in which pure mathematics is considered to be a part of the science of deductive logic), *formalism* (in which mathematics is regarded as comprised of systems of consistently applied rules for the production of empirically perceptible formal objects), and *intuitionism* (in which mathematical objects are held to be nonperceptual introspectively self-evident intuited entities).

The field of *logic,* as a formal discipline, is concerned with the principles of valid discursive reasoning, that is, with the criteria for making correct inferences from one or more *propositions* to another, where a proposition means anything of which truth or falsity can properly be predicated. Logic deals with the *forms* of argument from premises to conclusions, the former being regarded as *evidence* for the latter, the essential formal requirement being *consistency*. Inferences are *deductive* when the conclusions follow from the premises by necessary implication. When the premises are only partial evidence for the conclusions, the inference is *probable* rather than necessary.

Formal logic is of special interest for the philosophy of language because it supplies the basis for distinguishing discursive from nondiscursive symbolic forms. It contains general rules for determining the validity of reasoning processes in ordinary language, in mathematics, and in the sciences—in fact, wherever meanings are expressed in propositional form. Also, in some fields, such as drama, which mainly use symbols nondiscursively, discursive forms, obedient to the canons of logic, may still apply to many utterances as constituent parts of the total presentational form. Similarly, if it is assumed that moral judgments may be either true or false, moral statements can be expressed as propositions and moral arguments can be carried out and evaluated formally according to the rules of logic.

Philosophy of science provides critical analyses of empirical meanings. This field is sometimes considered as a branch of applied logic, with particular emphasis on the methods of probable inference. The philosopher of science examines the presuppositions of scientific inquiry and analyzes the meanings of such general scientific categories as fact, hypothesis, principle, generalization, law, explanation, theory, and model. He attempts to describe the patterns of experimental inquiry, showing the role of *deductive* and *inductive processes,* the function of *imagination,* the nature of *measurement,* and the differences between methods of *discovery* and methods of *verification*. In addition to this analysis of scientific concepts and methods in general, philosophy of science deals with the differences between the several branches of science, investigating how the nature of their subject matter affects the categories and procedures required.

The critical analysis of esthetic experience comprises the field of philosophical *esthetics* and the related field of the *philosophy of art*. Three central terms are analyzed, namely, the *esthetic attitude* or *experience* (the perception of intrinsically interesting objects, whether man-made or natural), *art* (the creation of objects through human agency), and *beauty* (the attractiveness or value of an object). Various theories of what constitutes a work of fine art are examined, such as representationalism, formalism, and emotionalism. Categories for analyzing works of art, including matter, form, and expression are clarified and illustrated. Various criteria for judging the value of works of art are critically studied, including appeal to rules, context, the artist's intention, the observer's impressions, and the individual work as containing its own norms. Finally, the basis for any method of esthetic criticism is discussed, in the light of such possible positions as *objectivism* (value is inherent in the work), *subjectivism* (value is in the perceiving subject), and *objective relativism* (value is a relational property).

The interpretation of meanings in the synnoetic realm belongs to the fields of *philosophical psychology*, or *philosophical anthropology*, and *social philosophy*. The philosophy of man is concerned with the problem of defining precisely what is meant by the term "man." What is uniquely human? Does man's essence reside in his reason, his culture, his freedom, his spirituality? Is man essentially good or evil, neither or both? Is he a functional unity or a duality of body and mind? Is he essentially solitary or social, and how is his individuality related to his social nature? Respondents to such questions range from *materialists* who hold that a human being is nothing but a completely determined material system to *personalists* who regard each person as a unique, divinely created free agent.

Meanings in the ethical realm are the subject matter of *ethics*. In this field the philosopher analyzes the meanings of such basic terms as good, right, obligation, and duty. He investigates the methods of moral inquiry, especially as they may bear upon the settlement of moral disputes. Positions on the import of moral statements divide between those who affirm their *cognitive* significance and those who regard them as *emotive* or *persuasive* utterances. The cognitivists divide between those who affirm a *naturalistic* basis for moral knowledge and those who take a *nonnaturalistic* or *intuitionist* position. Both of these divide between the *formalists* or *deontologists,* who hold that *right* is the ultimate category, and the *teleologists,* who hold that *good* is the ultimate category, with *right* dependent on it. On the substantive question of what things are good and what actions are right, detailed answers differ widely, yet with substantial agreement on certain basic goods, such as survival, absence of pain, love, and freedom, and on certain basic principles such as telling the truth and keeping promises.

In the synoptic realm, historical meanings are interpreted in the *philosophy of history.* In practice there are two different meanings of philosophy of history. One is mainly analytic and deals with questions about the nature of historical knowledge and the methods of historical inquiry. Is knowledge of the past possible? Is history a science? What is the value of historical knowledge? Positions range from the *positivistic* view that pure objective facts about the past can be established to the *historicist* emphasis on the particular cultural, personal, and temporal factors influencing every historical judgment. Intermediate positions reject these extremes, recognizing both the personal creative element in historiography and the possibility and obligation of critical and responsible checking of historical reconstructions against available objective evidence.

The second type of philosophy of history is primarily synthetic and aims at a comprehensive interpretation of the whole course of history. Interpretation of history here has reference to such questions as these: What is the lesson of history? Where did mankind come from and whither is it destined? Are there any laws of historical development, and if so, what are they? Many different theories have been proposed. One ancient position is that history reveals a more or less steady decline from a primordial *Golden Age.* The opposite, *progressive,* view is that history is a steady march forward from savagery to a future utopia. Some advance a *cyclic* theory that history consists in an endless repetition of similar patterns. Others combine the cyclic and linear theories in a *spiral* conception of history. In *deterministic* positions history is held to be governed by material necessity, in *voluntaristic* theories by human free will, and in *theocratic* philosophies by divine providence. Finally, some philosophers of history see no grand pattern in the sweep of human events. They are skeptical about the possibility of finding any meaning in history beyond the intrinsic significance of individual events and certain related event-sequences, and they adopt the view that history is *ironic* and *paradoxical,* full of surprises and contradictions, and that its main lesson is that the final word on the meaning of history can probably never be said.

Philosophy of religion is concerned with the critical analysis, evaluation, and synthesis of meanings in the domain of religion. It provides interpretations of such leading religious concepts as God, the soul, the supernatural, omnipotence, immortality, and transcendence. Particular attention is given to the beliefs held in the major historic religions of mankind, including Hinduism, Buddhism, Taoism, Confucianism, Judaism, Christianity, and Islam, as well as to the religious practices and ideas of primitive societies. Besides undertaking the philosophical analysis of traditional religious ideas, philosophers of religion have worked out systematic views on such principal religious questions as these: Where did the universe come from and where is it going? Is this world all there is, or is there another world beyond this one? What is the destiny of the individual person? Why are there evil and suffering and how may they be overcome or accepted? Answers are of many kinds and may be classified in such contrasting categories as supernaturalism and naturalism; theism, atheism, and agnosticism; orthodoxy, conservatism, and liberalism (or modernism). These positions range from the literal acceptance of traditional expressions of religious belief, through reinterpretations of them as metaphorical terms, to outright rejection of religious ideas as outmoded superstitions, as in the philosophies of naturalistic humanism and of atheistic existentialism.

Of all the branches of philosophy the two which are the most comprehensive in scope and hence the primary basis for the synoptic function of philosophy as a whole are the *theory of knowledge* (or *epistemology*) and *metaphysics*. Theory of knowledge concerns the problem of knowledge in its most general form. What does it mean to know? What are the conditions and limitations of knowledge? How can knowledge be validated? What kinds of knowledge are there, and how are they related to one another? The main types of answers to these questions include those of *idealism* (knower and object known belong to a single interdependent and coherent system), *realism* (the object of knowledge is independent of the knower and the knowing process, and true knowledge is measured by correspondence with reality), *constructionism* (knowledge is a construction by the knower using elemental sense data), *intuitionism* (true knowledge consists in pure intuition of a reality more fundamental than the split between subject and object), *organicism* (the components of cognition are events, or "actual occasions," and "eternal objects" organized according to certain principles of mutual relevance), *pragmatism* (the validation of knowledge is determined by criteria of satisfactory adjustment, whether emotional, active, or conceptual), *logical empiricism* (empirical statements and tautologies are the only kinds of meaningful expressions; scientific methods are the only basis for cognitive inquiry), *linguistic analysis* (there are many functions of language and many significant modes of human inquiry, and these functions and modes must be distinguished by patient analysis of symbolic forms as actually used), *phenomenology* (knowledge is intuition of the inherent essences, forms, or structures of things, as revealed by a critical analysis of conscious experience), and *Existentialism* (existence is prior to essence, and the most significant truth for man is found in subjective concrete decision rather than in abstraction, objectivity, and systematic reflection).

Metaphysics, the other inherently synoptic philosophic field, is concerned with questions about the nature of reality. What is really real? What is the ultimate nature of things? What can be affirmed about everything that is? The answers to these questions are closely related to those offered in connection with the problem of knowledge, for views on the content and ways of knowing clearly depend on what is believed about the nature of things, and conversely, what is believed about reality depends on convictions about knowledge. Metaphysical positions fall into such categories as *monism* (reality is ultimately of one kind or substance), *dualism* (there are two kinds of reality), and *pluralism* (reality is a manifold of different but interdependent entities). Views on the nature of the ultimate stuff of things include *idealism* (reality is mental), *materialism* (reality is material), *naturalism* (reality consists in the whole spatiotemporal order revealed by science), and *organicism* (reality is a network of interacting elemental organisms, each with both mental and physical aspects).

Thus philosophy, the discipline devoted to the interpretation of meanings, comprises within itself fields in which the nature and structure of each of the possible realms of meaning is analyzed, and fields that effect a critical synopsis of the entire spectrum of meanings. On this account philosophy provides the appropriate summary conclusion of the inquiry into the fundamental patterns of meaning that has occupied us during Part Two of the present study. With this inquiry complete, the way is prepared to consider applications to the curriculum for general education.

The Curriculum
for General Education

21

THE SCOPE OF
THE CURRICULUM

In Part One it was argued that human beings are distinguished by their capacity for meanings and that there are six basic realms of meaning that are characteristically human. In Part Two the fundamental patterns of meaning in these six realms were set forth. In Part Three an attempt will be made to draw some conclusions regarding curriculum on the basis of these considerations about human nature and the patterns of meaning.

We begin by asking: What does a person need to know? What is the appropriate scope of the course of study that ought to be provided? The answers to such questions depend upon many factors, including the unique personality of the student, the social and cultural context in which he lives, and the available resources for teaching and learning. More important than all of these, however, is the end to which education is directed. For example, the recommended curriculum aimed at technical efficiency differs from one that considers the delights of contemplation to be the highest good.

The premise of the present argument is that the highest good to be served by education is the fullest possible realization of the distinctively human capacities and that these capacities consist in the life of meaning. Hence, the course of study should be such as to maximize meanings.

Then the question becomes: What should be taught in order to maximize meanings? What provides for the fulfillment of the life of meaning? There are five principal answers to such questions, and each has certain merits. The first answer is that fulfillment consists in *mastery*. The meaningful life is that in which the person finds *one thing* to do and learns to do it very well. The realization of existence lies in *depth* of understanding. The wealth of possible meanings is so great that a person has to choose the one channel into which he can pour his energies with maximum effect. People who scatter themselves in many directions dissipate their powers and never transcend superficiality. Most of the outstanding achievements of mankind have been made by people who have developed a single line of competence to a point sufficient to yield something really new. The all-around person can only follow the paths laid out by the single-minded pioneers.

According to this view, the scope of the curriculum for any given person should be narrow rather than broad. Each person should be highly trained in a specialty instead of comprehensively as a generalist. Depth of knowledge and skill should be the goal, rather than superficial acquaintance with a variety of fields.

A second position is that fulfillment consists in *belonging to a community* in which the various meanings are realized. The significance of each person's life results from participation in the meaning of the social whole. The good life is not conceived as depth of mastery, as in the first view, but in loyal membership in the social body.

From this standpoint the course of study to be followed depends upon a person's place within the social complex. Each individual plays his part and is required to develop competences that best equip him to contribute to the whole. Unless his function is that of comprehensive social planning, he does not need to cultivate meanings in other than the special sphere in which he serves the community. Nor does he need to plumb more deeply in any given field than his social position requires. This view results in specialized curricula for most students, usually with less depth than the first position entails and with particular provision for understanding the nature of the social enterprise as a whole.

A third answer to the question about fulfillment is that it consists in *many-sidedness*. The desirable goal is well-roundedness and variety of interests, and the curriculum should be correspondingly broad and diverse. Instead of specializing in one field, it is said, the student should gain some understanding of many different fields. Rather than developing one skill to a high degree, he should be encouraged to gain some competence in a number of different types of activity.

A fourth position is that the fulfillment of meaning consists in the *integrity* of the person. The main objective is to secure a coordination of whatever meanings are acquired into a coherent whole. The evil to be avoided is inner division and partiality. Each person should possess a sufficient range of meanings in his own self without depending for the significance of his life upon his position in the social whole. That is, he should become relatively independent, with rich inner resources for meeting a variety of situations and exigencies. From this standpoint the most important consideration in the curriculum is that the studies form an interrelated whole and not a collection of unrelated pieces. The materials of learning also need to be capable of assimilation by the particular person so that they may contribute to his integral selfhood.

A fifth and final view is that fulfillment consists in gaining a certain *quality* of understanding, that the ideal of life has to do with quality rather than with depth, participation, extensiveness, or coherence. According to this position, there are certain esssentials which need to be learned, and beyond them everything else is unimportant. In this case the breadth of the curriculum depends upon what it is deemed essential to know, whether a few things or many.

Fortunately, the foregoing positions are not mutually exclusive. It is not necessary to choose one and reject the others. Since in modern civilization study extends over many years, sometimes for the greater part of a lifetime, it is possible to achieve fulfillment of meaning in more than one way. Indeed, in the long run it is possible to achieve fulfillment in all the ways suggested above. A person can attain high mastery of one field and good understanding of many other fields. He can achieve both inner integrity and satisfaction in belonging to a larger whole. He can pursue essential understandings without minimizing the significance of less than essential ones.

The analysis in Part One suggests that human nature itself supplies the clue to the minimal scope of the curriculum. Human beings are characterized by a few basic types of functioning. They use symbols, they abstract and generalize, they create and perceive interesting objects, they relate to each other personally, they make judgments of good and evil, they reenact the past, they seek the ultimate, and they comprehensively analyze, evaluate, and synthesize. These are the universal, pervasive, and perennial forms of distinctively human behavior. They are the foundation for all civilized existence. All of them are deeply woven into the texture of life whenever it transcends the level of biological and social survival.

Furthermore, the analysis of Part Two shows that these fundamental types of human understanding are interdependent. No one realm of meaning can be perfected without the aid of the others. All six realms form a complex unity of interrelated yet relatively autonomous domains.

It follows that the curriculum should at least provide for learnings in all six of the realms of meaning: symbolics, empirics, esthetics, synnoetics, ethics, and synoptics. Without these a person cannot realize his essential humanness. If any one of the six is missing, the person lacks a basic ingredient in experience. They are to the fulfillment of human meanings something like what basic nutrients are to the health of an organism. Each makes possible a particular mode of functioning without which the person cannot live according to his own true nature.

This sixfold curriculum answers to the fifth or qualitative criterion of fulfillment. Since the six realms form a whole integrated by the synoptic meanings, it also satisfies the fourth criterion, of wholeness. Similarly, it indicates the need for a varied curriculum with at least the six fundamental components. What of the other two criteria—of mastery and belonging? Is the six-realm curriculum consistent with them? It might seem at first that concentration on mastering one field would exclude concern for anything else. Such is not the case, because *the basic realms are such that all of them are required if a person is to achieve the highest excellence in anything at all.* They are essential in the sense that a person cannot do his best in any human undertaking without some understanding of all the realms.

For example, a person cannot attain maximum mastery in any scientific field without having some competence in language, the arts, personal relations, morals, and synoptics, since scientific activity in its own structure includes symbolic, esthetic, personal, ethical, and integrative factors. Again, a person cannot attain the highest mastery in the arts unless he knows how to communicate, understands facts and generalizations, relates insightfully with others and with himself, has a sensitive conscience, and has achieved a certain perspective on the whole. Similar conclusions hold for the mastery of any of the other departments of human activity.

It follows that learning in the six realms is necessary even when the goal of specialized mastery guides the construction of the curriculum. Concentration should not proceed to the point of neglecting any of the essential human capacities, since the fullest mastery itself requires all these abilities. The same is true of the curriculum based on fulfillment through communal participation. A person cannot understand his place in the whole and behave accordingly unless he is aware of the basic functions of civilized man. He must possess the powers of speech, description, creation, relation, choice, and integration if he is to play a significant part in the human commonwealth. In other words, he has to become essentially human himself if he is to participate in a meaningful civilized order.

The foregoing concept of the six essential domains in which every person needs to develop understanding and skill is the basis for the idea of *general education*. The curriculum of general education contains those provisions for learning that are necessary for the development of the person in his essential humanity. General education is contrasted with *specialized* education, which includes provisions for the development of particular competences for other purposes than the becoming of a person as a person.

The distinction between general and specialized education

is admittedly vague and imprecise. It is difficult in any given case to make a clear-cut and unequivocal judgment between the two. But it is not necessary to do so. The significant distinction is between studies intended to develop *kinds* of understanding (not *particular* understandings) that *everybody* needs simply because he is human and studies intended to develop kinds of understanding that only *some* people need in order to fulfill certain particular individual or social ends. Evidently the judgment as to whether a study is general or special does not apply to content as such, but to the relation between content and purpose for the given person and situation. An item of knowledge that is an essential ingredient in the humanizing of one person may be used by another for special purposes.

The importance of specialized education lies in fulfilling meaning in the first two senses indicated above, namely, mastery and belonging. To become an expert in any field of learning a person needs to go far beyond what one needs to know to achieve human stature. In fact, some other way of gaining the *kind* of understanding required by everyone can always be found as an alternative to any particular specialty, while there is no substitute for particular specialized study if one wishes to gain mastery in that field. For example, to become an expert in physics one must study a great deal of physics to an advanced level, while for purposes of general education one does not need to study physics at all, since there are many other scientific disciplines that can just as well yield the basic understanding of empirical meanings.

Specialized study is likewise requisite for the common good in a complex civilization. The basis for advanced society is specialization of function, in which each person concentrates his energies upon doing a few things well rather than many things poorly. The gain in social efficiency through such specialization is spectacular. To make it possible, specialized education is required. Such an education gives knowledge and skill to people in any given field of specialization far beyond the general understanding that everyone should acquire in the realm of meaning to which that field of learning belongs.

The distinction between general and specialized studies is quite different from another distinction that is important for curricular purposes, namely, the distinction between the *funda-mental* and the *derivative* or *applied* fields of learning. The term "fundamental" refers to fields that are concerned with the delib-erate and direct pursuit of one of the six possible kinds of mean-ing. All the disciplines discussed in Part Two are fundamental in this sense, and others not included for want of space could be added. Derivative or applied fields, on the other hand, result from the utilization of meanings from the fundamental disciplines in the solution of problems arising out of biological and social exigencies. The fundamental studies focus on the pure types of meaning, having regard for their distinctive forms. Derivative studies grow out of practical considerations, and workers in them seek solutions to problems without regard to purity of logical type.

The skilled crafts are derivative fields, drawing in various degrees upon the arts and the sciences for the requisite under-standings. The same is true of engineering, with major emphasis on the natural sciences. Law is concerned with problems of social control, and draws chiefly upon the social sciences, ethics, and the synoptic disciplines (particularly history and philosophy). Business is compounded of empirical knowledge and ability in personal relations, with an occasional admixture of ethics. Educa-tion as a field of learning draws upon all the fundamental fields. Social work combines social science with personal knowledge and, to some extent, ethics. In all the applied fields, of course, language also plays an important part.

As mentioned above, the distinction between fundamental and applied studies is independent of the distinction between general and specialized studies. Work in a fundamental discipline, such as pure mathematics, may be used either for general educa-tion or for specialized education, depending on the person and the situation. Again, applied studies may be used either for general or specialized education. Thus, the practical field of ceramics may be a means either for general education in the esthetic realm or for the training of an expert in that craft. The study of law may also be used either for the ethical component of general education (among other goals) or for the preparation of professional lawyers.

Whether specialists concentrate on fundamental or applied studies depends on what their specialties are. A linguist, an artist, or a philosopher specializes in advanced fundamental studies. An engineer, a businessman, or a doctor specializes in applied studies, together with such fundamental studies as are needed to support his special applied field (e.g., mathematics and physics for the engineer, the social sciences for the businessman, and biological science for the doctor).

The decision as to whether fundamental or derived studies shall be used in general education is not as easy as it is for specialized education. Derived studies may have a more immediate appeal to the interests of the student, and on that account may prove more instructive in the basic meanings than would fundamental studies, in which these meanings are developed directly. For example, a student might learn more mathematics and physics by studying them in the context of automobile mechanics and electronics than as pure disciplines. On the other hand, it should be possible to teach fundamental studies in such a way as to capture the interest of the student, particularly if ample use is made of examples of application, thus in effect incorporating materials from the applied fields into the teaching of the fundamental disciplines. Using the fundamental disciplines for general education also has the major advantage of keeping the various distinct ways of understanding clear and of helping the student to avoid the confusions of meaning that are all too prevalent in ordinary life and practical affairs.

The present work is concerned with the curriculum of general education and not with specialized studies. It is also concerned with the fundamental disciplines and not with the applied fields. The foregoing discussion of specialized and derived studies is included to make it clear that the scope of the curriculum as a whole extends beyond the provisions made for general education using the fundamental disciplines and to suggest briefly some of the relations between general and special education and between fundamental and applied studies.

Having said this much about the total curriculum, in all that follows we shall be concerned only with that part of the curriculum which is devoted to general education using fundamental studies. It will be assumed that insofar as derivative materials are employed, they will be introduced as auxiliary to the teaching of the fundamental disciplines.

The scope of the *school* curriculum depends in part upon whether or not other agencies besides the school take responsibility for certain aspects of education. No general rules can be laid down to decide this question, since the agencies of education and their assigned responsibilities differ from one social system to another. It is conceivable, for example, that esthetic learning might take place mainly through museums, theaters, and the mass media, making instruction in the arts unnecessary in the schools. Religious and moral instruction might be assigned to the home and the church, and personal relations could be regarded as everybody's province and therefore not in need of explicit care in schools. Nevertheless, it is desirable to include some provision for all six realms of meaning in the school curriculum, in order to provide the requisite consistency and unity in the experience of learning. Provisions made in other institutions can then be supplemented and corrected by the corresponding studies within the school curriculum.

Because people differ, no one curriculum suffices for everybody. Some people are abler than others, and their abilities are of different kinds. One person has unusual facility with language, another in artistic creation, and a third in human relations. Interests and dispositions also differ and these differences affect progress in learning. The conclusion to be drawn from individual differences is that for most effective learning curricula need to be designed as far as practicable to take account of each person's particular aptitudes and enthusiasms.

However, the consequences for general education are not necessarily the same as for specialized education. Normally a person's special interests and abilities are an important clue to what he should specialize in, indicating the fields in which it would be most profitable for him to take the most advanced work. By contrast, in the case of general education, which is concerned with what everyone should understand, less study rather than more is indicated for those fields in which a person has unusual ability, since he can be expected to gain competence in them more easily and quickly than in studies where his abilities are of a lower order. In general education the lesson of individual differences is mainly that particular attention needs to be given to devising materials and methods designed to awaken the interest of those who do not respond easily and naturally to certain of the fundamental disciplines. In so doing, the educator takes responsibility for seeing to it that each person develops all the types of understanding required to become fully human.

Since the task of realizing one's humanity is never really completed, general education is not simply a matter of developing certain minimum competences in the fundamental disciplines. General education need not be elementary and introductory. One can be as advanced in general studies as in specialized ones. As stated earlier, the difference between the two is one of purpose and function rather than of the subject itself. Every person should continue throughout life in the cultivation of his humanness. In fact, a major goal of general education in school should be to establish habits of study that will lead one to continue general learning regularly after completing his formal education. The measure of the success of the school curriculum is the degree to which graduates voluntarily and zestfully go on learning in later life, and the measure of its failure is the lack of interest of its graduates in further study of the kind done in school.

The number of years devoted to general education in schools is determined in large part by economic factors and by the dedication of the public to humane values as contrasted with efficiency in organization and production. If economic conditions are poor, it is necessary to turn every effort toward increased production and better distribution of goods, with corresponding emphasis on specialized studies and the applied fields. Even so, since certain basic human competences are required for success in practical endeavors, a minimum of general education is important even in a relatively poor society.

When resources are ample, a society can afford to allow considerable time for general education. It seems likely that everything necessary to prepare a person in the general competences and for lifelong continued general education can well be done in a period of from ten to sixteen years of school. It should thus be possible to complete formal general education sometime during the high school or college period. The usual pattern in the United States is for the least able students to complete general studies after eight or ten years and for the most able students to continue general studies at least through the second year of college, and often for the entire four college years.

A program for the curriculum of general education in schools may then be conceived as providing for instruction in all six of the fundamental types of meaning—in language, science, art, personal knowledge, ethics, and synoptics—over a period, say, of fourteen years, with some opportunity for concurrent specialization where individual abilities and interests and social needs indicate its desirability. To achieve a well-balanced program it may further be recommended that the program be divided approximately equally among the six realms. In this way considerable variety within each type of meaning can be offered, and the criterion of fulfillment as richness and breadth of understanding can be satisfied, along with the other criteria earlier discussed.

For example, during fourteen years of general education a student could study not only his own everyday language, but also mathematics and one or two foreign languages. He could study several of the sciences—physical, biological, psychological, and social—and, among the arts at least the four groups of disciplines treated in Part Two—music, the visual arts, the arts of movement (in physical education), and literature. He could have regular opportunities for gaining personal insight, through a program of social activities and of work with skilled guidance counselors. He could have instruction and practice in making moral decisions, through the study of moral problems and the methods of ethical inquiry consummated by responsible participation in decision making where the common good is at stake. Finally, he could be given a thorough grounding in history and a basic understanding of religious commitment and philosophic interpretation.

Within the broad recommendation of a sixfold program of general education through instruction in the fundamental meanings a great variety of particular curricula can be conceived. No one curriculum is the best for all people and for every culture and situation. The course actually chosen in a particular school will depend upon the circumstances of the case, including the character, traditions, and history of the community and the predispositions of its students. A general philosophy for the curriculum can only indicate the large design of the curriculum and certain principles for making decisions about the sequence of studies and the selection and organization of materials for instruction.

22

THE LOGIC OF
SEQUENCE IN STUDIES

Since learning takes place over time, the materials of instruction
have to be arranged in temporal sequence. Not everything can be
studied at once; hence, decisions must be made about the order
of instruction. How are these decisions to be made? What principles of sequence are available?

It should be granted at once that to a degree the order of
studies is arbitrary. There is no law of sequence that, if it were
known, would prescribe exactly the succession of learning events.
Education is in this respect like many of the affairs of ordinary
life, in which the order of activities may be a matter of indifference. If one plans both to read a magazine and to run an
errand, there may be no reason at all for doing one rather than
the other first. Similarly, if it is decided that the curriculum is
to include both music and painting, it may be a matter of indifference which comes first. It follows that, to some degree, accidental factors relating to historical traditions, personal inclina-
tions, and available resources may properly be used to determine
the sequence of studies and that many different, equally satisfactory orders can be devised.

Granted this limited arbitrariness, it is still necessary to study the principles of sequence that govern a desirable curriculum. There are two kinds of sequence factors to be considered. One kind has to do with the psychological factors in learning, by which the order of studies is related to the order of human growth and development. These considerations will be taken up in the next chapter. The other kind of sequence factors relate to the logic of what is to be learned. This is the subject of the present chapter.

Temporal sequence is arbitrary from a logical standpoint only if the materials to be learned are logically independent. If they are logically interdependent, then the order of studying them is significant. If one subject logically depends upon the conclusions of another subject, then clearly the former subject must follow the latter subject in the course of study.

In Part Two attention was directed to the logical characteristics of the six realms of meaning and of certain disciplines within these realms. These analyses provide the basis for some conclusions about the logical order of studies in the curriculum of general education. There are three levels of logical sequence requiring consideration. First, the logical relations among the six realms will be examined. Next, the relations between disciplines within a given realm will be considered. Finally, the logic of sequence within a particular discipline will be discussed.

Logically the realm of symbolics has priority over all the other realms of meaning, because they all depend on symbolisms as means of expression. One cannot express empirical meanings without discursive symbolisms. Understanding of the sciences beyond the qualitative descriptive stage depends on a knowledge of the language of mathematics. Esthetic perception requires the use of presentational symbols. Personal and moral knowledge are mediated by ordinary language or by nondiscursive symbols, and history, religion, and philosophy have their characteristic patterns of words and symbolic acts. Thus, there is abundant justification in the logic of meaning for the traditional practice of concentrating upon reading, writing, speaking, and computation in the early years of school. The further practice of beginning early with the nondiscursive modes of expression is also indicated. Exclusive preoccupation with discursive symbolisms in the first years of school may lead to a serious imbalance in expressive power, inhibiting esthetic, personal, historical, and religious growth in favor of one-sided development of literal ways of thinking.

The empirical and esthetic realms may be introduced as soon as language becomes available. Since neither science nor art is to any large degree logically dependent on the other, neither is pre-requisite to the other in the curriculum. In their essential logic, personal knowledge and ethics are independent of empirical and esthetic meanings and therefore can be introduced as soon as communicative means have begun to develop. However, since factual knowledge is an important resource in the improvement of understanding in both personal relations and morals, the full development of these meanings depends upon the prior acquisition of a considerable fund of empirical knowledge. Such knowledge is necessary in making wise decisions, based on the consideration of alternatives and the prediction of consequences. As between personal relations and ethics, neither has logical priority, the two being in reciprocal relation. Moral decision presupposes a free and integral self-in-relation, and becoming a person depends upon making moral choices. The logic of the two realms thus indicates their contemporary rather than sequential development.

The logic of the synoptic disciplines places them last in order, because they depend upon all the other realms for their materials. History requires a knowledge of symbols, empirical data, dramatic methods, decision making, and moral judgments, to be welded together into a reenactment of the past. Religion depends upon experience of language, truth, beauty, being, and goodness, as elements in a vision of ultimacy. Philosophy requires a comprehensive world of meanings to analyze, evaluate, and synthesize.

It is evident that the sequence of topics in Part Two reflects the logical order of the realms outlined above. First is symbolics, then empirics and esthetics (here there is no preference as to precedence), next personal knowledge and ethics (these are reciprocally related and, although distinctive in their essence, are dependent for their development upon empirical knowledge and, to some extent, esthetic understanding; hence, they are subsequent to science and art in logical sequence), and finally synoptics.

It does not follow from the foregoing conclusions that the

study of language and mathematics must be *completed* before any of the other studies can begin, and that the synoptic disciplines cannot be begun until work in all the other realms has been finished. Since there is no limit to what can be learned in any realm, it is impossible to complete one kind of study before starting the next. All that logic requires is that enough learning take place in one subject to enable work to proceed in other subjects that are logically dependent on it.

The usual curricular program provides for several different kinds of studies to be pursued concurrently. This is desirable for the sake of the interrelationships of the various kinds of meaning and the integration of meanings into the person as a whole. The ideal curriculum is one in which the maximum coherence is achieved, and segmentation is minimized. To this end, the curriculum of general education may be planned so as to provide concurrent study in all six of the realms of meaning, subject to the logical condition that each topic be introduced only after the prerequisites to its proper understanding have been mastered.

In many cases logical prerequisites can be offered directly in association with the topics for which they are needed. For example, instruction in certain phases of mathematics may be given in connection with the study of the science topics for which these particular mathematical formulas are required. Similarly, in learning to think historically a student may be introduced to the prerequisite empirical, personal, and moral understandings. Moreover, as pointed out in the chapters on the arts, the connection between the nondiscursive symbolic forms comprising the symbolism of the arts and the particular works of art in which they are used is so intimate that it is not practicable to separate instruction in art from the study of the prerequisite symbolic forms, as can be done for ordinary language and mathematics, which are formally separable from their specific expressive uses.

Balancing the twin factors of integration and sequential logic, the optimum curriculum for general education would appear to consist of concurrent studies in all six realms of meaning, with early major emphasis on mathematics and languages (both discursive and nondiscursive), and later major emphasis on synoptic studies. From the very first years of school, while concentrating on powers of expression, the student should acquire factual knowledge, learn to make and to understand things of perceptual significance, gain in understanding of himself and others, grow in moral sensitivity, and begin to integrate his understandings. In the later years, in high school and college, he should concentrate on understanding the past, on achieving ultimate perspective, and on interpreting critically all phases of his experience.

A balance is also desirable between subjects studied explicitly for themselves and those undertaken as preparation for learning in another discipline. Some language and mathematics should be learned as such in their own domains in order to gain insight into the distinctive qualities of symbolics as a kind of meaning. Some symbolic forms should also be learned in connection with other types of inquiry, in order to make evident how symbolism functions in the various other realms of meaning. In the later years, while it would seem desirable to teach a good deal of science, art, personal knowledge, and ethics within the context of historical, religious, and philosophic studies—these being the consummatory disciplines in general education—some work should also be taken, concurrently, in the separate subjects, in addition to the synoptics, in order to ensure thorough understanding of the distinctive characteristics of these other disciplines. Without such understanding, the synoptic meanings themselves are likely to be confused and distorted.

Besides the sequence of realms it is necessary to consider the logical factors in the sequences of disciplines within each realm. Within the realm of symbolics ordinary speech is logically prior both to mathematics and to the nondiscursive symbolic forms, since the import of mathematical symbolisms, gestures, rituals, and other presented forms is normally explicated by means of common discourse.

Among the sciences, a logical hierarchy also exists. Physics is the most fundamental science because it is concerned with certain aspects of all things whatsoever. The biological, psychological, and social sciences are less fundamental in the sense that they deal with more limited classes of things. This logic is, however, challenged by those who regard the categories of life, or even of mind and society, as more fundamental than those of matter and energy. Furthermore, regardless of which discipline proves to be the most fundamental in providing the ultimate explanatory models, each has its own relative autonomy and may be studied largely independently of the others. This statement must be qualified with respect to certain disciplines that make substantial use of other disciplines. For example, astronomy makes much use of the principles of physics, and experimental psychology depends to a considerable extent upon biology.

Among the arts no clear order of precedence is discernible, except that a case can be made for the logical priority of the arts of movement, on the grounds that sensitivity to bodily movement is a prerequisite to full understanding of rhythms in music and drama and of tensions and balances in the visual arts. For the most part, however, it appears that each art may be developed largely independently of the others.

The three synoptic disciplines are by and large logically independent. If any one were to be assigned priority in sequence, history should be chosen, for both religious and philosophical understanding make use of knowledge of the past. Hence, of the synoptic studies, history should have temporal priority.

The third and most important aspect of logical sequence concerns the order of learning within particular disciplines. From the standpoint of logic, in what order should the various topics and phases of a given field of study be presented? Which topics and phases are prerequisite to which others? Such questions can be effectively answered only by reference to the logical structure of each discipline. If a subject of study is regarded simply as a collection of isolated items, there is no reason to prefer one arrangement over any other. If, on the other hand, the subject is seen as an orderly pattern of interconnected items, then the sequence of study becomes of great importance. For this reason, in making decisions about logical order the teacher needs to be familiar with the patterns of meaning in his field of instruction.

In practice, the problem of deciding sequence on the basis of structure is not easy to solve, for at least three reasons. First, there is no single logical pattern that must be used for any given field of inquiry. Any number of different (though not ordinarily inconsistent) conceptual schemes may be devised for the interpretation of a discipline. The continuing discussion concerning fundamental concepts and methods, by practitioners of every field of study, is evidence of the plurality of possible structures.

Second, logical structure only provides a set of relationships among the various components of a discipline. It does not in itself dictate order in time. For example, in language one may designate phonemes and morphemes as basic structural elements, of which words and sentences are composed. It does not follow that a student must first learn phonemes, then morphemes, and then rules of morphology and syntax. Normally it is better to begin with sentences and proceed to analyze them into their constituent elements.

This distinction between logical and temporal priority requires special emphasis. From the fact that a concept is an elemental or basic idea in a discipline, it does not follow that that concept should necessarily be taught first in time, as an explicit topic. Even though measurement is a ruling concept in natural science, it is probably not wise to begin the study of science with a deliberate study of the idea and meaning of measurement. Similarly, although the idea of ultimacy is fundamental to religion, it would not be desirable to begin a study of religion with an explicit study of that idea.

The third reason is an elaboration and specification of the first two. A distinction should be made between two types of logical patterns. One type is an order of discovery, the other an order of analysis. The former refers to creation and synthesis, the latter to dissection and critical evaluation. Both reflect the structure of the discipline, and each is consistent with the other. They differ in their respective points of departure and their temporal progressions. The order of discovery moves from the unknown to the known; the order of analysis moves from knowledge toward a more critical perspective on the known. Many descriptions of the structure of science, for example, are derived from an analysis of the results of scientific inquiry. These descriptions do not disclose much about the ways in which the results were discovered. Similarly, the art critic may analyze the structure of a work of art without revealing the way in which the artist created his work.

The clue to curricular sequence consists in combining the two types of order in such a way that discovery is aided by analysis. The student, who is in the position of the discoverer, needs the help of the teacher. From his more advanced analytical perspective, the teacher can direct the student's inquiry into the most profitable channels. Thus, the order of instruction within a given field of study is given by a judicious alliance of the logics of creation and analysis.

Another way of stating the problem of sequence within a subject is in terms of the progression from elementary to advanced levels. It is a truism, if not a tautology, to say that instruction should begin with the elementary and proceed to the advanced levels. [1] The question for any discipline is: What *are* the elements, and how are the advanced stages built up from the elementary ones? No general answer to this question can be given. For any subject of study the answer depends upon the possibility of organizing the field into some consistent hierarchical pattern. If no such hierarchy can be found, because the various items to be learned are unrelated to each other, then no progression in learning is possible, and no distinction between elementary and advanced levels can be made. Any subject for which the distinction is possible is one in which the components are organizable into certain orders of mutual interdependence.

The progression from elementary to advanced levels is not merely a passage from the simple to the complex or from the particular to the general. It is, rather, a cyclic process of successive differentiations and integrations, the nature of which differs from discipline to discipline. Naïve experience is largely undifferentiated, and learning consists in making discriminations by means of conceptual abstractions. These abstractions afford a great simplification of experience, enabling an inchoate mass of impressions to be organized into a system of manageable categories. In one sense, the most advanced phases of a subject are the simplest, because they make use of the most powerful organizing concepts. In another sense, the advanced levels are the most complex, in that

---

[1] It is true, if at first glance paradoxical, that instruction at all levels, from elementary to advanced, should be *elemental*. This is the theme elaborated in Chapter 26 below.

a greater range and variety of apparently disparate factors are integrated by these concepts.

In the languages the advanced stage consists in skill with syntactical rules. In the sciences the aim is understanding of generalizations and theoretical models. In the arts the objectives are significant particular esthetic constructions. In personal relations the goal is concrete existential understanding of self and others. In ethics it is knowledge of the good and practice of the right. In synoptics the aim is comprehensiveness of vision. In each of these realms the end in view influences the nature of the rhythmic process of differentiation and integration by which the movement is made from elementary to advanced stages of understanding.

As noted earlier, there are many possible logical sequences for instruction in any given discipline. A picture puzzle can be put together starting with any piece. However, once that piece is in position, the logic of the puzzle begins to unfold, as each added piece gives hints about neighboring pieces that must be integrated into the total pattern. While each of the many possible sequences is consistent with the structure of the puzzle as a whole, there is no single preferred order of development.

The picture puzzle analogy applies only to some kinds of subjects, particularly those fields, such as the sciences, which are discursive and additively cumulative in character, being built up by the juxtaposition of separate units. It is not satisfactory to think in this way about progress in the arts, in personal knowledge, or in the synoptic disciplines. In such studies the analogy of the developing organism with its cycles of differentiation and integration is preferable.

Whatever analogy is used to describe the sequential organization of a discipline, two principles always hold. The first is the previously discussed principle of multiple possible orders. The second is the principle that the best routes are those that lead most directly to the goals of the discipline. It follows that the pattern of the whole should always govern the choice of progression. In the picture puzzle analogy the directness of solution is greatly enhanced by imagining how the completed picture will appear. Similarly, in the organic analogy each cycle of differentiation and integration takes place under the direction of the genetic pattern, in which the plan of the whole developed organism is contained. Accordingly, a logical sequence of study in a discipline is any succession of experiences that are consistent with the internal patterns of meaning in that discipline and that are conceived in relation to the goals of the discipline as a whole.

In speaking of the goals of the disciplines, a note of caution is in order. Fields of study easily become standardized and thus fall behind significant developments in knowledge and method. The radical revisions in the mathematics and physical science curricula recommended (among others) by the influential School Mathematics Study Group and by the Physical Science Study Committee in the 1950s were necessary to break the outmoded patterns that had become traditional in those subjects. Important revisions have likewise been planned for other disciplines. That the earlier curricular revisions that had occurred in the 1920s proved insufficient for the 1950s suggests that current formulations should not be expected to stand forever. Disciplines undergo modification, and corresponding changes are appropriate in the patterns of instruction based on those disciplines. This is why the study of pedagogy needs to be carried on in continuous relation to the work of the scholarly community and why schools of education should be closely linked with the arts and sciences divisions in the university.

Provision for carefully controlled sequences underlies the development of programmed instruction, which is a rapidly growing feature of modern educational practice. Attention has chiefly been focused on the psychological aspects of such instruction, supported by the doctrine of reinforcement in learning theory. Perhaps even more important is the impetus provided by the programming movement to the careful examination of the logical patterns of the subjects of instruction. A good program from a logical standpoint is one in which the sequence of items is in accordance with the inherent logic of the subject and is designed so as to bring the learner in the minimum number of steps to the kinds of meaning which characterize the discipline in its mature expressions.

Programmed instruction is simply the regularization (and, in some of its phases, the mechanization) of what has always characterized effective teaching, namely, the organization of learning experiences in accordance with the logical nature of what is to be learned. Every discipline has its distinctive patterns of meaning, which must be respected in constructing an effective order of instruction. While the logic of meanings is not the only clue to sequence, it is by all odds the most important one.

23

DEVELOPMENTAL
FACTORS IN THE
SEQUENCE OF STUDIES

In addition to logical factors, the findings of developmental psychology can be used to help decide the order of studies. The logic of sequence is not a sufficient guide because education is not a process of constructing a complex of disembodied meanings, but of facilitating learning in real people. Meanings grow in active, developing persons. Hence, if instruction is to be effective, consideration must be given to the patterns of human growth and development.

One elementary fact to be noted at the start is that of all the animals man is the learner par excellence. In contrast with many of the lower animals, a human being's behavior patterns are only to a very minor degree instinctive. They are learned through interaction with the environment; they do not emerge simply from internal growth processes. Human nature is plastic. It is capable of being shaped by external influences so as to produce any of many different kinds of behavior.

On the other hand, a human being is not solely a product of his environment. There are limits to how one can be molded by environmental influences. A person is not simply a sum of the forces which have acted upon him.

If a person were entirely governed by instinct, education would have no meaning and the order of personal development would be wholly dictated by genetic factors in the organism. If a person were exclusively determined by his environment, then the sequence of learning could be decided entirely on the basis of the logic of the subject fields without regard to psychological factors.

The pertinence of developmental psychology arises from the fact that a person is neither purely a creature of instinct nor of environment, but develops by a complicated series of interactions between the growing self and various surrounding entities. At every stage of development the nature of the person affects what can and what cannot be learned, and how easily anything can be learned.

In part, the possibilities of learning depend on the *maturation* of the biological organism. No behavior pattern can be learned unless a suitable physical and neural basis exists for it. All instructional efforts that are not consistent with the empirical facts of maturation are certain to fail. Thus, knowledge of maturational sequences provides one type of clue to the sequence of studies. Maturation fixes the limit of expected achievement and to a considerable extent determines the speed of learning.

Besides maturation, the possibilities of learning are influenced by previous learning. The combination of maturation and earlier learning determines what a person is capable of learning at any given time. The developmental concept of *readiness* refers to the condition of being optimally prepared for some particular learning experience. The ideal order of studies is one in which each experience is introduced at the most propitious time in the person's development. If some experience comes too early, it cannot be grasped at all or only at the price of excessive strain and frustration. If it comes too late, other learning dependent upon it will be postponed and the whole development of the person will be retarded. The best curriculum for any student is one that makes each learning experience available to him as soon as he is ready for it.

The readiness concept, like any other idea applied mechanically or interpreted rigidly, can become a blinder, reflecting traditional prejudices. Human beings are extraordinarily adaptable, and by appropriate preparation may be *made ready* for learning that does not fit any standard readiness schedule. The principle of readiness is really an aspect of the more fundamental principle of maximum *economy* in learning.

How well a person learns is also greatly affected by the factor of *motivation*. If one has powerful needs to fill, one quickly learns how to satisfy them. If one's goals are clear and urgent, one learns more readily how to reach them than he would if he had weak purposes. A person is not really ready to learn anything unless he has strong motivation in relation to it. Motives are often a result of temporary conditions, and they may well be controlled to some degree by external factors, such as rewards and punishments. More deeply rooted in the personality are those motives that reflect the basic orientation of the developing person. These basic goals of the self are of great importance to the teacher, for they determine the direction in which effective learning can occur in the student. They represent an inner hospitality to certain kinds of experience, making the person ripe for development in the indicated directions.

In planning the sequence of studies a basic developmental principle is that of *continuity*. The growing person is an organism and not simply an aggregation. This means that each step in development must fit into previous steps so as to form a consistent whole. The organism is an "open system" seeking to maintain itself with stability amid change. To ensure this, whatever new influences are brought to bear must be such as not to threaten the continuing integrity of the person. The successive experiences in learning should therefore be sufficiently different to provide stimulus for growth but not so strange as to set up self-protecting reactions in the student. They should also be such as to form a coherent succession rather than a miscellaneous and random collection. The experiences of the student should be consistent both among themselves and with the basic orientation of the learner as revealed in his enduring motivations.

In planning curricula in the light of studies in human development use may be made of certain generalizations about patterns of growth. It is possible to predict in broad terms what kinds of experience will be appropriate to children and young people at successive periods in their development. However, these generalizations are useful only as a first approximation, as an estimate of probable average conditions within a particular culture. In reality every person is different, and in principle a different curriculum is needed for every person to take account of the way he uniquely develops. In practice, ways can be found to effect a reasonable compromise between a curriculum that is the same for all within a given society and individual courses of study. Examples of such compromises are the various systems of grouping students by age and ability and the methods of organizing instruction to permit each individual student to proceed at his own pace, independently or with individual guidance, and to make his own special contributions to group efforts.

Because environment is such a large factor in human development, the patterns of growth vary not only from person to person, but also from culture to culture. There is no single universal average developmental sequence. Each social group exerts influences upon its members that they internalize and that become important factors in learning. Accordingly, the teacher should be aware of the cultural patterns influencing his students, and he should take account of these patterns in planning the sequence of studies.

In using knowledge from the field of human development for planning the curriculum, a threefold distinction should be kept in mind, namely, the distinction between actuality, possibility, and ideality. Developmental inquiries yield knowledge of how certain persons have actually developed. This knowledge is not necessarily an appropriate direct basis for making curriculum decisions because the conditions of growth may have been neither optimal nor comparable to the situation of the students for whom the curriculum is being planned. The inquiries may show that under certain conditions specified learnings are possible. But the demonstration of possibility is no guarantee of ideality, for it does not follow from the fact that a person *can* learn something at a given stage in his growth that he *ought* to learn it then. Thus, the educator should use the facts of developmental psychology critically, ordering instruction so as not to expect the impossible of students and choosing from among the possible learnings those that will lead most directly to the fulfillment of meaning.

From the developmental standpoint the earliest and most fundamental experiences are those of personal relations. From the moment of birth, or even earlier, the child lives in relation, first to his mother, then to other persons in the family, and as he grows older, to wider and wider circles of persons and things. The entire course of a person's life may be analyzed in terms of the development of personal meanings. For example, the psychoanalyst Erik Erikson in *Childhood and Society* [1] describes eight stages in the personal career. He says that in the first period the task is to establish a basic sense of *trust,* or confidence in the goodness of existence and in the reliability of those on whom one depends. The second stage is that of *autonomy,* in which the child learns to "stand on his own feet," without shame or doubt. The third stage, *initiative,* marks the ability to do and to make, as the waxing powers of movement and manipulation appear. Fourth comes the period of *industry* and the use of tools, in which the child discovers the wider world of things into which he sees he can enter as an active producer. In the fifth period, adolescence, the main task is achieving a sense of *identity,* by internalizing and integrating the various social roles in which one is cast. The sixth stage is that of *intimacy,* in which the person learns to find fulfillment by losing himself in loving others. The seventh period is that of *generativity,* where the person assumes responsibility for bringing into being and guiding the next generation, whether as parent or otherwise. Finally, the eighth stage is that of achieving *integrity,* including an assurance of order and meaning, a feeling of personal dignity, and absence of the fear of death.

This is only one scheme among many that have been devised to chart the general pattern of growth of the self-in-relation. Nevertheless, it may serve as the focus for discussing several important points about the sequence of learning experiences. The first point is that the appropriate lessons in the realm of personal relations vary according to the stage in life. One should not expect to teach a child industry when he is concentrating on autonomy

[1] W. W. Norton & Company, Inc., New York, 1950.

or identity. Teaching should be planned so as to take account of the particular tasks confronting the person at the stage in life in which he is living.

Second, the several tasks of personal growth are hierarchically ordered. Each stage presupposes the successful completion of the earlier stages. Until one has attained the initial capacity for trust, he cannot enjoy a secure autonomy. Without autonomy he cannot well exercise initiative, and so on from stage to stage. The educator needs to understand the sources of failure at any stage in the light of possible failures of achievement at earlier stages, and be prepared to make available such remedial reeducation as may be necessary to shore up the weak foundations.

Third, the stages of life are not separate and independent ways of functioning. They are continuous with each other, interrelated, and overlapping. At every stage all the ego goals of the other stages are present to some degree. Even in the very young child the integration of maturity is in some measure an aim, and in the mature adult the trust of the infant is still in need of perfecting. Hence, the stages represent functional emphases in various periods of life rather than discrete lessons to be mastered once and for all.

Fourth, the development of personal relations is intimately connected with the development of other kinds of meanings. The first appearance of language may be regarded as one evidence of growing autonomy, as the child feels the need to communicate with others across a separating difference. The stage of initiative may relate to the beginnings of esthetic creativeness, and the period of industry may correspond to the exploration of rational and empirical meanings. Clearly the stages of identity and intimacy pertain most directly to personal meanings as such. The stage of generativity, with its emphasis on responsibility, is concerned with moral meanings, and the stage of integration corresponds to the synoptic realm.

This developmental analysis in some measure confirms the earlier conclusions as to the relative priority of the realms based on logical considerations. Developmentally, language clearly comes first and integrative studies last. Moral meanings appear relatively late, after a firm sense of oneself and of one's relationships with others has been established. As between science and art, the priority developmentally seems to rest with art, this being the more immediate and intuitive ground from which the rationalistic and generalizing scientific meanings subsequently develop.

What a life-span sequence like Erikson's suggests is that persons may not ordinarily be ready for mature understanding of self and others, for moral insight, and for integrative perspectives until they have passed beyond the usual period of formal general education. Such a conclusion points to the need for continuing general education throughout life, particularly in the fields of applied psychology (especially guidance and counseling on an individual or group basis with an existential emphasis), morals, history, religion, and philosophy. It may be that the average person can profit most fully from such studies after assuming adult roles. From a developmental standpoint, it can then be argued that during the years of formal schooling through adolescence the major emphasis in general education should be on the languages, arts, and sciences, all of which can be learned effectively within the developmental framework of childhood and youth, and that the remaining three realms of meaning should be the chief concerns of adult general education.

Developmental considerations thus suggest that general education can profitably extend beyond the usual period of twelve to sixteen years of formal schooling. If economic and social factors limit the period of formal education, then it is important to make provision for continuing education on an informal basis. The mass media of communication can play a significant role in this respect. It is clear that in such informal education special attention should be given to personal knowledge, ethics, and the synoptic disciplines, these being the domains in which adults can especially benefit from continuing opportunities to learn. Opportunities for continuing education in the other realms of meaning should also be provided.

On the other hand, the principle of the unity and interrelations of meanings in the education of a whole person argues for *some* study of all of the six realms throughout education, as recommended in Chapter 21. This fundamental principle should not be nullified by attending exclusively to the emphases indicated by developmental considerations. Personal knowledge, ethics, morals, and integrative studies have pertinence to every stage of education, even if they may not come fully into their own until adult life. These studies can be of particular importance in providing a basis for the intelligent use of informal educational resources in later years. On these grounds it is still reasonable to affirm the position taken earlier that all six realms of meaning belong within the curriculum of formal general education and that particular emphasis should be given in the latter years of the curriculum to the ethical and synoptic realms—to which the realm of personal knowledge may now be added as a further culminating emphasis.

The consideration of education from a developmental standpoint indicates that meanings in the fourth realm, personal knowledge, play a pivotal role in all the other meanings. As pointed out in Chapter 16, personal knowledge may be regarded as the primordial basis for all understanding, prior even to language. "In the beginning was the relation." At the same time, there is a distinctive logic of personal meanings that allows them to be arranged alongside empirical, esthetic, and ethical meanings as a relatively autonomous type. This dual role is evident in the developmental analysis, which is concerned with the person at every stage in development, even though the characteristic synnoetic meanings (existential awareness of self and others) first appear fully in the period between adolescence and adulthood.

This unique role of personal knowledge in all the realms of meaning is of great importance both to the teacher and to the student. Every linguistic attainment, every empirical insight, every esthetic perception, every moral judgment, every integrative perspective belongs to a developing person and is colored by the quality of his relations to himself and others. Since a meaning in any realm is a meaning to a person, the value of that meaning depends on personal well-being. In more familiar terms, though one speak many tongues, know all the secrets of nature, create things of beauty, perform deeds of the highest virtue, and have the combined wisdom of Socrates and Solomon, if he has no love, these profit him nothing.

This is not to say that love is the one thing needful and that all education should be solely directed toward personal understanding. Love is not enough. Indeed, love cannot be fulfilled apart from language, science, creative activity, morality, and integrative vision. But these without love have no human worth. It is for this reason that intelligent and sensitive concern for persons is the one essential ingredient in good education.

The findings of developmental psychology are not only of value in suggesting the general sequence of study emphases, as discussed above, but also in indicating for particular fields of study the kinds of learning experiences that are likely to be appropriate to learners of various levels of maturity.

For example, knowledge about language development, of which numerous studies have been made, can save the teacher both from starting a child to read before he is ready for it and from delaying reading instruction too long. Such knowledge can also aid in selecting materials that fall within the vocabulary capability of the student, neither being so far beyond him as to frustrate understanding nor so familiar to him as to provide no challenge to new understanding. Language development studies show the great importance of skill in communication for the general well-being of the child. They make clear the close relation between the language habits, social environment, and emotional life of the child, and they suggest ways of diagnosing and correcting language deficiencies in individual children.

The growth of mathematical ideas in children has also been intensively investigated. Some studies show, for example, that geometric ideas develop prior to arithmetical concepts and that nonnumerical concepts of quantity precede numerical ones. It is generally agreed that the high abstraction and rigor of pure mathematics are beyond the comprehension of young children and that they must begin with simple instances, only gradually moving on to generalized concepts. When the normal patterns of cognitive growth are ignored and adult mathematical conceptions are introduced too early, the child may develop an aversion to mathematics that will handicap him throughout life. On the other hand, modern research in the teaching of mathematics suggests that with proper methods of instruction many important mathematical ideas can successfully be taught much earlier than was once thought possible or desirable.

Scientific ideas, like those of language and mathematics, show a developmental progression. The generalization and theorizing goals of scientific thought cannot be attained at once. As the child grows, he has an increasing body of memories upon which to draw, providing a basis for generalization and discrimination, both of which are necessary for the formation of scientific abstractions. The leading investigator of the development of children's concepts is Jean Piaget, who has studied, among other things, the growth of the idea of physical causality. [2] Piaget holds that conceptual growth occurs in discrete stages. Up to the age of three, he says, the child believes things happen by magic. From three to seven or eight he thinks in egocentric and animistic terms, and from then on his thought becomes mechanistic and logical. Other investigators disagree with Piaget's results, holding that ideas of physical causation in space and time grow gradually and are not necessarily preceded by magical and animistic stages. Regardless of how the matter is resolved, the point to be made here is that since the meaningfulness of scientific ideas is affected by the child's development, the teacher needs to know what can and what cannot usefully be introduced at any given level of maturity.

In the esthetic realm, the same gradual maturing of understanding occurs. The child begins with simple geometric forms, colors, melodies, rhythms, and tales, and step by step becomes capable of enjoying more complex designs in pictures, sounds, bodily movements, and words. At each level of growth new expressive interests appear, together with new skills in execution and perception. It is the teacher's function to provide a rich esthetic environment and ample encouragement for creative expression in the manner appropriate to the child's physical, emotional, and intellectual attainment, giving special consideration in this domain to the particular interests and capabilities of the individual child rather than relying on standardized expectations. This concern for the individual does not negate the value of esthetic standards and of instruction in esthetic principles by demonstration and critical evaluation when the student has reached a sufficiently advanced stage of esthetic maturity.

[2] Jean Piaget, *The Child's Conception of Physical Causality,* tr. by M. Gabain, Harcourt Brace & World, Inc., New York, 1930.

Social and moral values are acquired largely through participation in the life of family, peer groups, and community. The young child tends to accept the value orientations of his parents and then as his horizons widen he takes on values from other significant associations. If the teacher is aware of the source of moral values in the whole personal-social development process, he will be prepared to interpret students' conduct intelligently and to introduce kinds of decision-making situations in which moral growth may occur. It has been amply demonstrated that mere verbal indoctrination of moral ideas is not effective in the improvement of conduct and that a person is not ripe for moral learning until he is confronted with situations in which he must make personal choices. The wise provision of such experiences requires an understanding of the personal maturity level of the students involved.

Finally, inquiries into the growth of religious consciousness may be of great value in determining the desirable sequence of studies in religion. Advanced theological ideas are unintelligible to a child. Only gradually does he succeed in grasping the more profound meanings of faith. He begins with concepts derived from his experiences in the home, where love, trust, and the goodness of existence, mediated by human relationships, are first disclosed to him. Later, these meanings may be generalized and deepened to provide the basis for a mature religious faith. Premature introduction of certain religious ideas may cause permanent distortion of beliefs, and neglect of religious instruction may deprive the person of needed resources for his personal growth. Here, as in all the other domains of meaning, developmental factors may be decisive in determining the order of instruction.

The foregoing brief comments about the growth of ideas in language, mathematics, science, art, morals, and religion are intended to illustrate the significance of knowledge of human development for the ordering of instruction. Some of the main subjects of school instruction have been analyzed by scholars in relation to such problems as maturation, readiness, and motivation, and to some extent psychologically justifiable sequence patterns have been determined. However, far too little is known about developmental factors in learning, and in every field much further research remains to be done.

In this and the preceding chapters it has been shown that both logical and developmental factors are relevant to decisions about the order of instruction. These factors do not wholly determine the content of what should be taught. They do, however, set certain limits to the selection of materials and provide one kind of pattern for their organization.

24

THE PROBLEM
OF SELECTION IN
THE CURRICULUM

Up to this point the range of meanings to be included within the curriculum of general education has been considered and some observations regarding the sequence of instruction have been offered. Yet even with these indications of scope and sequence of studies, the content of the curriculum is far from being determined. Further principles of selection are required to guide the choice of materials within the bounds set by the considerations of the three preceding chapters.

The problem of choosing what to teach is generated by the conditions of modern advanced civilization. In primitive societies the store of traditional wisdom is very limited. In fact, knowledge is so rare in these cultures that the function of the man of knowledge is to guard his wisdom as a secret to be disclosed only on appropriate occasions and to certain favored persons. Even in the great civilized societies, knowledge for the most part has been regarded as concentrated in a limited number of traditional sources. Examples are the Judaic culture centered in Torah and Talmud, Christians who regard their Bible as a final and sufficient rule of faith and practice, Muslims with their infallible Koran and authoritative Traditions, and traditional Chinese civilization based on the Classics. One does not need to go back many decades in American life to reach times in which it was assumed that the necessary content of learning was embodied in a few standard works and that all other knowledge was superfluous. Even today there are defenders of the position that the best source of a liberal education is comprised in one hundred Great Books.

The modern problem of selection in the curriculum is due to the fact that the earlier conditions of limited knowledge have given way before an avalanche of new knowledge. All prior ages have been ones of relative scarcity in materials for instruction. The present age is one of cultural superabundance. Cultural want has given way to affluence. The picture of an Abraham Lincoln eagerly appropriating the few reading materials available to him is replaced by that of the modern student perplexed at which, if any, of the thousands of works at his disposal he shall read and how much of his limited time he shall spend using other means of enriching his understanding, such as newspapers, magazines, radio, television, and motion pictures.

Not only has available knowledge greatly increased, it is continuing to increase at an accelerating rate. Each accession of understanding is the basis for new explorations that bring even greater increase. Inquiry does not so much yield settled answers as open up fresh avenues for investigation. Every problem solved generates a set of further problems to be solved.

These conditions of cultural abundance are accentuated by a number of factors. One factor is economic and technical. The vast programs of research and development that produce the new knowledge are possible only because of ample machine power and large concentrations of capital. Human energies have been released for cultural creation by machines that take the burdens from man's shoulders. Culture grows only when men have leisure to make and to inquire, free from the necessities of winning daily sustenance.

A related factor is the rapid increase in the number of people engaged in the creation of new knowledge. As the world's population grows, many more minds are at work finding problems to solve and by their solutions setting more problems for others to attack. Moreover, because of modern facilities for travel and communication, the fruits of creative effort are not localized, but quickly become widely disseminated. Whatever anyone discovers anywhere in the world, no matter how remote, is available almost immediately everywhere else. It is for this reason that the critical factor in the production of knowledge is not the *proportion* of workers available to develop it, but the *absolute number* so engaged.

Not only has machine power released many people to engage in productive scholarship, but machines now directly contribute to the work of investigation. Most research requires tools. There is a limit to what man can find out simply by reflection. He needs instruments to extend his powers of inquiry. These indispensable aids to research have been provided by modern technical developments and they have greatly accelerated the rates of cultural growth. The electronic revolution has been especially significant in this respect. With the development of automatic data processing equipment, problems that formerly were practically insoluble, or soluble only at the cost of great intellectual effort, are now easily resolved.

Furthermore, great advances have been made in the storage and retrieval of knowledge. Vast resources of information can be preserved on tapes, films, discs, and other devices, as well as in the more conventional forms of books and artifacts, and they may quickly and inexpensively be reproduced for wide distribution. Effective new methods of indexing, cataloguing, abstracting, and cross-referencing have also been developed, so that whatever is known will not be lost from sight and so that the relevance of any given item to many other items of knowledge may be kept in view.

A common designation for the situation arising from the conditions described above is the "explosion of knowledge." The condition is not one of a quiet accumulation of information, but such a rapid expansion as to cause a shattering effect upon the modern mentality. A revolution of quantity has taken place, demanding a wholly different orientation to learning. The gradual assimilation of a relatively fixed body of knowledge can no longer be the goal of education. Contemporary man somehow has to learn to accommodate himself to a world whose transformations proceed at a rate even more rapid than any one person's possible rate of growth. Today everyone is presented with the frustrating situation of falling farther and farther behind the advancing edge of knowledge, no matter how fast he runs to keep up with it. His present challenge is to find a way of winning the fight for understanding, even while quantitatively he is losing it to a culture expanding explosively.

This multiplication of knowledge in modern times is accompanied by a growing need for understanding. As life becomes more complicated, the demands made upon each person increase, and the insights required to deal successfully with the problems of living are much greater. This increased demand applies to all aspects of human understanding. One needs greater skill in communication to cope with the closer interconnectedness of society. More scientific knowledge is needed to be secure and successful in a culture increasingly fashioned and managed on a scientific basis. To balance the rational and technical side of life and to make profitable use of growing leisure, more refined esthetic perceptions are necessary. As modern civilization makes larger and more highly controlled social mechanisms necessary, threatening intimate personal relations and the sense of authentic selfhood, greater emphasis on the personal dimensions of understanding is urgently needed, and with enlarged powers and wider possibilities of choice, the importance of moral concern increases. Finally, as people are swept on by the stream of change, they more than ever require the perspectives of history, the larger vision of faith, and the critical comprehension afforded by philosophical reflection.

Thus, a person living in the contemporary world is confronted both with an explosion of knowledge and with greatly increased need for understanding. This convergence of enlarged resources and heightened demands creates unprecedented problems and opportunities for education. The great question is: How can the needed resources be made available to the learner?

The difficulty of the problem arises from the fact that, while the outer conditions of life and culture have radically changed in the ways described above, the learning abilities of human beings have remained substantially the same. No mutation in the human species has occurred to parallel the outward transformations of the natural and cultural world man inhabits. People with the same potentialities as before are required to live in a radically new kind of world, chiefly of their own making.

Contributions to the solution of the unparalleled educational problem of modern man are being made from a number of different directions. Each of these approaches is designed to deal with the growing gap between what people need to know and what they are able to learn in the limited time available for education. Each is concerned with the problem of how to cope with the alarming disparity between the relatively limited human learning capacity and the virtually limitless abundance of things that can and need to be learned. Five main kinds of contribution to the problem may be noted.

One way to ameliorate the effects of the rapid expansion of knowledge is through increasing specialization. Since no one can keep abreast of all areas of knowledge, it is said, let each person specialize in one field in which he can become an expert. Every person will then be able to speak and act authoritatively in his own domain, and he may rely upon authorities in other fields for whatever he needs to know about their subjects of special competence.

This increase in specialization has become a dominant feature of modern higher education. For the most part it has not yet greatly influenced the elementary and secondary curriculum in the United States. Nevertheless, it is increasingly recognized that a person must be highly trained in a particular field if he is to make a significant contribution in a complex and interdependent society, and this awareness has affected the concerns of students and teachers at all levels.

Necessary though specialization is, it does not offer a satisfactory solution to the contemporary dilemma. It turns out that a specialist cannot even keep pace with the expanding knowledge in his own field, let alone try to master other fields. Hence, he does not really solve the modern problem by retreating to a specialty. But that is not the most serious difficulty. As pointed out in Chapter 21, for his own fulfillment a person needs more than depth in one area. He requires a many-sided general education. Even to be a really good specialist he needs such education, because fields enrich each other, and to know the limitations and boundaries of one subject a person must be aware of other subjects. In a world of interconnection the requirement is even more urgent that each specialist know how he fits into the whole scheme of things and how to take his appropriate responsibility for the well-being of the entire civilized endeavor. Such understanding cannot be gained by specialized education alone. It depends upon general education.

Thus, the educational problem of modern civilization is to devise a program of *general* education that will meet the needs for greater general understanding in a time of mounting responsibilities and resources.

A second kind of contribution is through administrative and organizational procedures. Many improvements have been made in the design of schools and colleges, making learning conditions more satisfactory, and providing light, fresh air, convenient working spaces, and access to instructional resources. Classes have been organized in new ways, with ability groupings and independent study programs to accelerate learning, with team teaching to make use of specialized competences, and with teacher aides to enable the professionally trained teacher to give full attention to the main task of teaching. Many have urged the lengthening of the school day and the elimination of the long summer holiday—as an unnecessary relic of the agrarian society—because it substantially reduces the time available during any calendar year for instruction.

Some of these organizational changes have proved their value under certain conditions. Others have drawbacks that are not present in the systems displaced. In any event, it appears unlikely that any large increase in learning can be effected by such measures. Certainly whatever improvements may occur will be of a different order of magnitude than those that are necessary to meet the critical problems described above.

A third type of contribution to the crisis in learning is to use for educational purposes the very technology from which the crisis stems. If people need to be taught more, it is suggested, let us turn to the machine for help in teaching. From this proposal has sprung a rapidly growing new educational industry, turning out devices of many kinds to accelerate learning. Among the most widely used are the aids to language instruction, by means of which students can rapidly learn to understand and speak foreign languages, using the oral-aural method, with recording and playback mechanisms. Various sorts of teaching machines have also been devised for instruction in many subjects. The major values of such devices are these: They make it possible for each student to proceed at his own rate without having to adjust his learning to the different rates of others. They permit each student to learn continuously, not waiting for his turn in a recitation group. The built-in feedback mechanisms enable the learner to get immediate reinforcement for correct responses and immediate correction of incorrect responses.

Technology further provides the basis for the extremely important educational potentialities of the mass media of communication. Never before could so many be taught so much by so few. Using television with a relatively small number of highly gifted teachers, it is now possible to provide a high quality of mass instruction at very lost cost per pupil. Inexpensive paperback books are also greatly expanding the materials available for instruction, and a wealth of motion pictures, filmstrips, slides, and other audio-visual materials exists to enrich the students' experience.

Impressive as these educational devices are, it is evident that they do not in themselves solve the problem of the learner. In fact, they may accentuate his frustrations. Machines are educationally neutral. They only channel information to the student. They do not and cannot do what only he can do, namely, learn. The main effect of educational technology has been to bring more things to the student to learn, and in this sense the new technology aggravates his difficulties. It loads him with still more tasks within his limited time, energy, and interest.

The justification, if any, for educational technology rests not in the mechanisms themselves, but in the content of what is put into the machines. Insofar as the new devices merely communicate old materials more quickly, they only add to the sum of what has to be mastered by the learner. No doubt some machines do enable a student to learn substantially more than he could with less advanced techniques. But as in the case of the other attempts, these gains hardly begin to solve the critical problem. The machines make a radical difference only when they occasion a complete revision of the materials of instruction, along the lines to be set forth in Chapters 25 to 28. It should be added, however, that the radical solution is also available, using the same revised content, without benefit of the machines.

A fourth approach to the problem is through the psychology of learning. If the need of the student is for greater learning capacity, then by investigating how learning occurs it may be possible to increase its efficiency. For example, if it turns out that emotional factors play a major part in aiding or inhibiting learning, then provision for optimum emotional conditions is a way to improve learning ability. Psychological tests may add further information regarding a person's special capabilities, enabling him to be given opportunities that make fullest use of his learning powers.

It appears, too, that such psychological techniques are only of limited use in closing the gap between the demand and the need for learning. Some much more powerful means of attack on the problem of modern education is necessary if more than minor alleviation is to be found.

A fifth possibility of solution to the crisis in learning exists, and this is the one that appears to have the best chance of succeeding. The essence of this approach is in the judicious selection of materials for the curriculum. The modern educational problem is caused by the overwhelming volume of available knowledge. It does not seem likely that human learning capacity can be proportionately increased. Therefore, some means are required for reducing to human size the volume of what has to be learned. The aim is to discover ways of making sense of the entire vast and expanding domain of human culture consistent with the strict limitations of human learning power. The goal is to find a solution to the problem posed by *quantity* by means of a principle of *quality* in curricular materials. This is the meaning of the statement that the solution lies in the judicious selection of the materials of instruction. Chapters 25 to 28 will set forth some principles for such judicious selection of curriculum content, within the framework of scope and sequence of studies outlined in Chapters 21 to 23.

The educational problem described above, to which the selection principles to follow are proposed as a solution, is part of the larger problems of modern civilization giving rise to the sense of meaninglessness discussed in Chapter 3. When a person is faced with a huge mass of bewildering material that he cannot master, his frustration begets a feeling of hopelessness and despair. He comes to doubt his own powers, he may develop a cynical attitude, and he may project his self-doubt onto life and the world generally, holding them to be absurd and valueless. He loses his sense of the interrelations of things and contents himself with disconnected fragments of experience. He is constantly oppressed by the surfeit of things to be coped with and deeply anxious at the ceaseless change in which he is immersed.

The four sources of the life-denying sense of meaninglessness —cynical doubt, fragmentation, surfeit, and pervasive transience— are thus implicit in the crisis of learning created by the conditions of advanced industrial civilization. If a solution can be found to this fundamental educational problem, it will contribute to modern man's search for meaning, and thus to his fulfillment as a person. The principles of selection now to be set forth are therefore offered as a further basis for the realization of meaning in human life.

25

THE USE OF
THE DISCIPLINES

The first principle for the selection of the material for instruction is that all of it should be drawn from the organized scholarly disciplines. The present chapter will be devoted to explaining and justifying this recommendation.

It will be recalled that the central problem of the modern educator is to make the best use of limited learning capacity and that the most promising way to do this is to select the qualitatively most significant materials from the totality of what is known. It is important then to know where these most significant materials are to be found and how to distinguish the consequential from the trivial.

The clue to the desired method of discrimination may be found through an analysis of the social sources of knowledge in advanced civilization. As pointed out earlier, the basis for social efficiency is specialization of function. If each person were forced to be self-sufficient, the standard of living of all would be very low, for few people can do a great variety of tasks well. The common welfare is best served when each person performs a few specialized functions for the benefit of others and in turn receives a share in the fruits of their labor. The quality of civilized achievement is dependent upon such cooperative endeavor among groups of specialized workers.

This interdependence of specialists is the basis for the advancement of all knowledge and skill. A high level of culture in a society is a direct consequence of the work of dedicated specialists who possess competences in their fields far above the capabilities of the average person. These specialists are the creators and guardians of the cultural treasure of the society. They are the responsible agents for maintaining the qualitative level of civilization.

These specialists are of two kinds. The first comprises persons of skill who are able to perform specialized functions with great efficiency and precision, and who do so by habit. They do not work by reflection and deliberation, but automatically, according to predetermined patterns of their skill specialty. The other kind comprises persons whose performance is also highly skilled but who act with comprehension of the meaning of their actions. They function in a reflective manner, conscious of their behavior and able to give good reasons for what they do.

The first kind of person is a *skilled worker,* regardless of whether his activity is ostensibly manual or mental. (One's work in every case is a way of behaving as a complete person, with psychophysical unity.) The second is a *man of knowledge,* again no matter whether he appears to work with his hands or with his mind. The skilled worker merely *acts.* The man of knowledge *understands.* While skilled workers and men of knowledge may both contribute much to the civilized enterprise, the latter are the creative sources of culture. The former help to sustain society and to put into practice what men of knowledge discover. The qualitative level of civilization is determined by those who understand.

An organized field of inquiry, pursued by a particular group of men of knowledge, may be called a *scholarly discipline.* These disciplines are the sources for what one can claim to understand with some measure of authority. The disciplines are sources of authoritative knowledge only in the sense that the specialists in the various fields of inquiry are, as a group, originators or authors of what they profess. They are not authorities in the sense either that what they affirm is to be accepted without question or that what they believe is necessarily true. It is quite in order to question such authorities, especially so that they may show the grounds for their conclusions—a practice in which by definition a man of knowledge is well versed. It is also not unusual for authorities to disagree among themselves (giving good reasons for doing so) and to revise their findings as further disciplined inquiry directs.

The men of knowledge within the disciplines comprise *public* communities of scholars, transcending all sectional, national, racial, religious, economic, and social differences. Derek Price's reference to the "invisible colleges" of scholars [1] is reminiscent of the Christian idea of the "invisible Church"—that communion in which there is neither Jew nor Greek, bond nor free, male nor female. In like manner, scholars are united in obedience to a common discipline and not by reference to any factors other than the public standards of knowledge and inquiry within their discipline.

The concept of a scholarly discipline (hereafter referred to simply as "discipline") enables us to distinguish between knowledge and mere opinion. Everyone has opinions about all sorts of topics. These opinions derive from many sources—traditions, hearsay, personal experiences, wish projections, and the like. They are ordinarily not subjected to any critical examination and are accepted with scant justification, if any. Knowledge, on the other hand, is an outcome of disciplined inquiry. It is tested by criteria of justification developed by organized companies of specialists.

The idea of a discipline also presupposes the distinction previously made between automatic skill and meaningful understanding. The excellence inherent in a skill is of a higher order than mere opinions. But it is lower in value than disciplined understanding, upon which skills depend for their justification and orderly improvement.

The essential task of education is to foster the growth of real understanding. There is no end of opinions that can be learned. There are also many skills that can be acquired. The educator's function is to direct the student toward authoritative knowledge rather than toward the lower forms of learning. Such knowledge is

[1] See his *Little Science, Big Science,* Columbia University Press, New York, 1963.

found within the disciplines. Hence, it is to the disciplines that the teacher should turn for the content of instruction.

Furthermore, if learning time is to be economized, *all* material should come from the disciplines, and *none* from other sources. Since there are specialists whose social function is to develop justifiable understandings in their several fields, the teacher has an obligation to give the students the benefit of this best available knowledge, selecting this and nothing else. If anything is used from sources outside of the disciplines, the students are to that extent deprived of their due as members of a civilized order.

The principle of disciplined knowledge excludes commonsense approaches to learning, in which teachers and students try to understand their world naively and directly, without making use of the findings of the dedicated specialists whose labors have been devoted to saving others from the frustrations and losses occasioned by ignorance. Education is justified only if it makes it unnecessary for every generation to begin the long climb to civilization from the beginning. It is justified by providing a long head start, in fact, by having the new generation begin as nearly as possible at the end. This does *not* mean beginning at the level of everyday, commonsense opinion nor even at the level of skills that have proved their usefulness in the past. It means introducing the child to understandings that derive from experts whose specific task is to know with authority and with conscious justification.

If all materials for the curriculum are to be derived from the disciplines, and if the disciplines are fields of inquiry pursued by specialists, does it follow that the content of education should be only specialized knowledge? If so, what becomes of general education? Is it excluded along with commonsense opinion? The answer is that the principle of disciplined understanding in no way contradicts the idea of general education. In fact, the former is the foundation of the latter. The appropriate content of general education is not the kind of "knowledge in general" that everybody has and that is only another way of describing opinion. The proper content of general education is authentic disciplined knowledge. It is "general" only in the sense that it is of general human relevance and is not confined to the members of a special group. The appropriate content of general education is therefore to be secured from specialists in the several disciplines. The function of the man of knowledge is not primarily to enjoy his own treasures of meaning, but to create and conserve them for the benefit of all.

The special office of the teacher in the work of general education is to *mediate* the knowledge of the specialists in the disciplines so as to reveal the general human relevance of this knowledge. The teacher is to be a *humanizer of knowledge.* In this capacity he does not act as an authority himself (though he may also be a specialist in this sense), but as one whose task is to make available and vital to the student the understandings developed within the disciplines. The special work of teaching, in general education, is thus functionally distinct from the special work of those who accept responsibility for the production and justification of knowledge in particular fields of scholarship.

The teacher's mediation is essential because the thought of the beginner is necessarily rudimentary in comparison with that of the specialist. The child studying arithmetic is certainly not capable of understanding what the seasoned mathematician does. Nevertheless, if the discipline principle holds, it must be possible to assert that what the beginner is taught belongs just as truly within the discipline as what occupies the attention of the most advanced scholar in the field. Disciplines contain knowledge of all degrees of difficulty, from the simplest beginnings of the subject to the most complex elaborations. What qualifies any item as belonging within a discipline is not its level of difficulty but its authenticity. The mediative and humanizing task of the teacher is to select materials from the disciplines that are also within the ability of his particular students to understand.

It is especially to be noted that authentic simplicities (*elemental* ideas) suitable as disciplined content for beginners are not necessarily obvious matters of common sense. If they were, the entire case for the use of the disciplines for the content of general education would fall to the ground and general education could be equated with teaching what thoughtful, observant people generally know from their own experience. In fact, what seems to be obvious often turns out to be wrong on careful examination. The advance of civilization rests mainly upon uncommon sense.

The aim of education is to draw students away from reliance on the illusions of the obvious. To be effective this emancipation ought to begin as early as possible. It is a waste of valuable educational resources to use advanced specialized studies to correct the errors occasioned by an *undisciplined* general education. Advanced specialized work should rather build on a foundation of disciplined knowledge laid from the very beginning.

At every level of difficulty, from the most elementary to the most advanced, disciplined knowledge differs *in quality* from undisciplined opinion. If anything, the difference in kind is most evident at the elementary levels, for there the contrasting patterns of meaning appear in clearest form, uncomplicated by the special approximations, assumptions, and compromises that may be necessary on higher levels. For example, the treatment of elementary science by a teacher using materials from such disciplines as physics and biology would differ radically from that of a teacher approaching the subject from a commonsense nature-study standpoint, and the difference would probably be more radical than between disciplined and undisciplined approaches to the study of jet propulsion by a group of high school students.

The most impressive claim the disciplines have upon the educator is that they are the outcome of learning that has actually been successful. A discipline is a field of inquiry in which learning has been achieved in an unusually productive way. Most human efforts at understanding fail. A very few succeed, and these fruitful ways of thought are conserved and developed in the disciplines. Every discipline is simply a pattern of investigation that has proved to be a fertile field for the growth of understanding.

It is for this reason that all curriculum materials should come from the disciplines. Disciplined understanding leads to further insight; undisciplined thought does not. Impressions and opinions confuse and obscure rather than open up new perspectives. The scholar in a discipline can speak with authority because he stands within an enterprise in which the participants have learned, with maximum economy of effort, eliminating the false starts and circuitous paths that would be taken by anyone not having the benefit of the discipline.

Understanding the disciplines is therefore essential to good teaching, for the disciplines are the key to knowledge and methods of inquiry that have demonstrated their fruitfulness in learning. Without the disciplines the teacher is cast adrift on a sea of arbitrary opinion. This is not to assert that knowledge from the disciplines is *sufficient* for good teaching, for the teacher is a mediator and not primarily a specialized scholar. A specialist in a discipline can be a failure as a teacher because he lacks ability or concern for mediation.

Yet these two functions—disciplined knowing and mediation—are not unrelated, because the way of the discipline is a way of learning, a mode of inquiry in which understanding grows. For that reason the form of the discipline is inextricably connected with what and how the teacher as mediator teaches. That is to say, many clues to effective mediation may be found within the disciplines themselves, as successful enterprises of teaching and learning. Other factors, such as those derived from child psychology, may also aid in the mediating process. But these others alone are not sufficient for good teaching. Accordingly, the teaching of material from any discipline should always be considered specifically in relation to the character of that discipline and not from some supposed principles of teaching in general.

If all curriculum content is to be derived from the disciplines, it is evidently important to identify them. Yet it would be unwise to attempt an exhaustive listing of the disciplines, or even to offer criteria by which any given field of study could be positively designated a discipline. The general test for a discipline is that it be the characteristic activity of an identifiable organized tradition of men of knowledge, that is, of persons who are skilled in certain specified functions that they are able to justify by a set of intelligible standards. Each discipline has distinctive concepts and methods that set it off from other disciplines. In each case these characteristic ways of inquiry have proved their power to increase knowledge and to economize learning effort.

A number of disciplines have been identified and analyzed in Part Two of the present book. Fields of study such as mathematics, psychology, music, and history are generally acknowledged as disciplines. Some of the fields discussed in Part Two might not be so regarded—for example, personal knowledge and religion.

One might even question whether the arts can properly be designated as scholarly fields. The best response to such doubts and queries is to refer to the analyses of the fields in question, such as those in the foregoing chapters, which are intended to exhibit the characteristic features of the fields as disciplines.

A major purpose of this book has been to mark out a wide range of disciplines rather than to restrict the designation to certain traditional academic fields of scholarship universally acknowledged as disciplines. It has been presupposed in the previous chapters that each of the six realms of meaning is a source of disciplined understanding. The expositions of those realms have been designed in each case to show certain patterns of ideas that have proved productive of human understanding in the development of the disciplines discussed.

The disciplines charted in Part Two do not, however, exhaust the possibilities. They are only illustrative of the great families of fundamental disciplines at one period in time. Some disciplines are compound, such as biochemistry and astrophysics, and these have distinctive concepts and methods differing from those of the component disciplines. New disciplines may arise and established ones may change or fall into neglect for lack of continued generative power. Accordingly, it would be hazardous in the extreme to offer any definitive catalogue and description of disciplines.

However, it has been suggested in the present work that all meanings may be classified into six fundamental types, each having certain basic logical features. Each fundamental type may contain any number of disciplines, all of which have the same general logic but differ in subject matter and in the detailed methods and concepts used.

In Chapter 21 a distinction was made between fundamental disciplines and derived or applied studies. Thus, the discipline of physics is fundamental, while mechanical engineering is an applied field. The discipline of personal knowledge (as worked out, for example, in existential psychology) is fundamental, while guidance counseling is an applied field. Since it appears that the applied studies always refer back to fundamental disciplines, the latter seem to be the ultimate sources for all curricular materials. Some subjects of inquiry are not disciplines as such, but *areas* of study. For example, science and art are not separate disciplines, but groups of related disciplines. Business and engineering are applied areas, each making use of a number of fundamental disciplines and derived studies. Similarly, education is an area of study composed of many interrelated applied fields. The teaching of mathematics is an applied field combining materials from the fundamental discipline of mathematics and to some extent from psychology. Curriculum is an applied field dependent upon such fundamental disciplines as sociology, philosophy, psychology, and political science, together with the various subject disciplines studied in schools.

From the principle that the content of the curriculum shall come entirely from the disciplines, it is not to be concluded that the materials of instruction ought necessarily to be organized into separate courses each of which pertains to one of the disciplines. The discipline principle is not an argument, for example, for a departmentalized curriculum in the elementary school—or, for that matter, in the high school or college. It is possible to use knowledge from the disciplines in connection with studies that cut across several disciplines. Thus, a social studies course might draw upon authoritative materials from the disciplines of history, economics, sociology, political science, and literature. Similarly, a course in general science or in the arts and modern civilization could make use of disciplined knowledge from the relevant sciences and arts, respectively.

The difficulty with cross-disciplinary studies is that they offer a temptation to shallow, nondisciplined thinking because of the mixture of methods and concepts involved. They require more knowledge and skill, greater care, and better mastery of materials than do studies within a particular discipline, where the lines of productive thought may be kept more directly and continually in view. It must be granted, then, that the discipline principle in practice tends to favor studies along the lines of disciplines or in groups of related disciplines (such as the arts or the sciences).

On the other hand, students engaging in a variety of concurrent studies are constantly crossing discipline lines. To learn to do so easily and intelligently is part of becoming educated in a balanced and integral way. Hence, there can be no objection to organizing studies along lines that make it necessary to shift from discipline to discipline, provided *some* reasonable pattern of organization is adopted. It is not desirable to teach a disorganized miscellany of materials, even though they may all be drawn from the disciplines. Any reasonable pattern of organization is in essence disciplined and corresponds to one or more of the fundamental patterns of meaning.

For example, it would be perfectly legitimate to organize a course or a unit in a course around the topic "The American Indian." It would not be satisfactory to teach such a course by simply presenting an odd assortment of facts about the American Indians without any plan or purpose in mind. The study could be made from the standpoint of some one discipline, such as anthropology, geography, history, art, or religion. Or the course could be organized in such a way as to bring into play insights from all of these, and other disciplines, without the course itself being organized according to the canons of any one discipline. It might be particularly helpful for a class to be set up with some students working on the anthropology of the Indians, others working on their history, others on the geography, and so on, the entire class then coming together in a kind of miniature body politic to share what they had learned from their various authoritative sources. In such a class the implicit organizing principle might be esthetic or even personal.

Furthermore, every discipline is to some degree integrative in nature. Every discipline makes use of materials from other disciplines. They do not exist in water-tight compartments. Some disciplines by their very logic are strongly integrative. This is true of the synoptic disciplines, but also of others, such as geography and literature. Hence, practice in crossing discipline lines is available even in the study of individual disciplines.

In considering the organization of knowledge it should be remembered that the disciplines of personal knowledge and moral knowledge are legitimate and important modes of thought that can serve as the basis for organizing studies. For example, a course in the problems of democracy might be organized on the basis of moral standards in responsible decision making. Or a course on the principles of human relations could be set up on the basis of disciplined personal knowledge, taking materials from many other disciplines, such as sociology, psychology, history, and religion.

Apart from these considerations no definitive guidance can be offered for organizing the subject matter for instruction. [2] No one plan is best for every teacher and for all students in all situations. If a teacher is enthusiastic about his way of organizing the materials, his interest will often inspire the students. If he follows a plan that is not meaningful to him, it is likely that the students will not respond well to his teaching. Authentic knowledge from the disciplines can be arranged in many forms and combined in many intelligible ways for purposes of instruction. To choose among these ways the ones that will best interest and serve particular persons is part of the art of teaching for which no general rules suffice. It is an art governed by canons of fitness in particular situations, motivated by concern for students, and sustained by knowledge and love of what is to be learned.

Thus, the first principle of selection, with which this chapter has been concerned, does not prescribe any mode of organizing the materials of instruction. It prescribes only that whatever is taught, in whatever manner it may be arranged, be drawn from the scholarly disciplines. This principle in itself is the basis for a drastic restriction in the content of what should be taught. It excludes a large part of common experience and understanding and directs attention to sources of knowledge that by comparison are qualitatively of very special and limited kinds.

---

[2] See pp. 340–341, for further discussion of the organization of content, based on a consideration of methods of inquiry.

26

REPRESENTATIVE IDEAS

The first principle for the selection of curriculum content discriminates between disciplined and undisciplined materials. Other principles are required to guide the choice of materials within the disciplines. The need for such guidance has been occasioned by the explosion of knowledge—an explosion due largely to the activity of workers within the disciplines themselves. The educator not only has to choose authentic knowledge in place of commonsense opinion; he has the even more difficult task of selecting from the rich resources of authentic knowledge that comparatively small portion that will best serve his students. The second, third, and fourth principles of curricular selection, which will be explained in the present and the following two chapters, are designed to guide this choice within the disciplines.

The second principle is that content should be chosen so as to exemplify the representative ideas of the disciplines.

As the term suggests, a "representative idea" is an idea that represents the discipline in which it occurs. It is a typical idea in the sense that it reveals the type or kind of the discipline. It is a characteristic idea in the sense that it manifests the character of the discipline. Representative ideas are concepts that afford an understanding of the main features of the discipline. They are not minor or subordinate ideas; they disclose the essence of the discipline. They are elements of the subject that stand for the whole or important aspects of it. They are aspects within which the image of the complete discipline or major portions of it is contained. They are epitomes of the subject.

Representative ideas exist because disciplines have form, pattern, or structure. A representative concept represents the pattern of the discipline. It characterizes the structure of that field of inquiry. It is an idea that enables one to distinguish one discipline from another. The assertion that disciplines have form means that their various components fit together according to some scheme of coordination. They cohere in some systematic fashion. A discipline is not merely a collection of various and sundry ideas. It has a characteristic logic that provides a standard for judging whether or not any given item belongs to the discipline, and if it does, how it fits together with the other components of the field. Representative ideas are the organizing principles of the discipline. They exhibit its distinctive logic.

Representative ideas are clearly of great importance in economizing learning effort. If there are certain characteristic concepts of a discipline that represent it, then a thorough understanding of these ideas is equivalent to a knowledge of the entire discipline. If knowledge within a discipline is organized according to certain patterns, then a full comprehension of those patterns goes far toward making intelligible the host of particular elements that fit into the design of the subject.

From the existence of consistent patterns within disciplines it follows that the metaphor of an explosion of knowledge is not really an apt one. For an explosion normally suggests uncontrolled, chaotic expansion. If knowledge is developing within organized disciplines according to specified patterns, then an organic metaphor would seem more appropriate for the increase in knowledge. It might be better to say, for example, that knowledge is showing exuberant healthy growth. The reason for its growth is that certain fruitful concepts have been discovered which enable continuous, productive learning to take place. These fruitful concepts are simply the representative ideas described above.

Representative ideas are therefore at one and the same time principles of growth and principles of simplification. They are principles of growth because the patterns they reveal prove to be productive of further insight, yielding more and more particular exemplifications of what they typify. They are principles of simplification because they provide a kind of map of the discipline that keeps one from getting lost in the details. This is a surprising fact, that an understanding of the very ideas that make a discipline fertile, causing knowledge in it to expand rapidly, is also the basis for simplifying the task of learning the discipline.

The use of representative ideas is one way of solving the problem of quantity in knowledge by means of qualitative principles of selection. Representative ideas are not components of a discipline chosen at random. They are very special elements within it, selected for their representative qualities. They are of such a quality that they stand for large quantities of material. They are elements the understanding of which makes it unnecessary to learn large numbers of particular items of knowledge.

What has been said thus far may have given the impression that a discipline is made up of two kinds of ideas—representative and unrepresentative ones—and that the recommended principle of selection is to teach the former rather than the latter. Such a view is misleading. It is not actually possible to divide the contents of a discipline into two compartments on the basis of representativeness. There is a sense in which any item of knowledge belonging within a discipline represents that discipline; if it is properly placed in one discipline rather than in another, it may be said to represent that discipline. Representativeness is actually a matter of degree. Some components within a subject are more representative than others in that they more clearly reveal its pervasive essential features. The less representative components are those that draw attention to particular aspects of the subject rather than to the essential patterns of the whole.

Thus, the ideas comprising a discipline may be arranged in a hierarchical order. At the top (first in representative quality) belong those few concepts that characterize the discipline in all its parts. Next come certain corollary ideas suggested by the primary ones. On the next lower level appear certain important concepts that serve as organizing principles for large subdivisions of the discipline, and below these are ranked many more particular ideas that prove useful in the detailed development of the various special problems and areas of the subject. At the bottom of the hierarchy appear the host of individual results of inquiry in the discipline, reflecting applications of the general concepts to particular cases and holding within specified conditions.

The analyses of the various fundamental patterns of meaning in Chapters 5 to 20 above were intended to identify certain representative ideas in the disciplines, showing both the most essential ones and some with lower orders of representative power. At the highest level are the ideas that characterize the general logical type of a discipline. For example, at the most general level, a language is characterized as a conventional symbolic structure, and this distinguishes language knowledge from empirical, esthetic, personal, moral, and synoptic knowledge. Each of these other realms is characterized by representative concepts of the same high order of generality.

In the general realm of symbolics different representative ideas typify the several constituent disciplines. The concepts of phoneme, morpheme, and syntactical classes, for example, apply to ordinary language but not to mathematics or to the nondiscursive symbolic forms. The fundamental ideas of set, complete abstraction, and logical consistency are typical of mathematics but not necessarily of the other symbolic fields. Similarly, the ideas of presentational form and of figurative meaning pertain characteristically to the nondiscursive symbolic forms.

At a lower order of representativeness in the symbolics are such important ideas as inflection in ordinary language, variable in mathematics, and gesture in nondiscursive symbolic forms. At the bottom of the representative hierarchy are particular words and word sequences, particular mathematical propositions, and particular presentational symbols.

In this manner a hierarchy of concepts can be constructed for each of the fields discussed in Part Two. At the top appear those ideas that are shown to be fundamental to the entire realm of meaning. Next come the characteristic features of the constituent disciplines, followed by ranks of important organizing concepts in the various divisions and subdivisions of each subject. Probably no single order of precedence of concepts can be defended as the right one. Different points of view can be taken regarding organizing principles. For example, mathematicians are not agreed as to whether number or set is the more characteristic idea for mathematics; a satisfactory hierarchy of concepts can be arranged either way. The main objective is that *some* defensible organization of ideas in each discipline be achieved. It is hoped that the analyses of the disciplines in Part Two may illustrate in a general and tentative way the lines along which such organization can proceed.

The working out of patterns of representative ideas within the several disciplines is a task that only specialists in the disciplines themselves can really satisfactorily accomplish. Only experts with intimate understanding of their disciplines can make dependable judgments concerning the relative precedence of concepts and the ways in which ideas fit together in the pattern of the entire discipline. The specialists who undertake this work also need a degree of philosophical interest and competence. They need to become critically aware of their enterprise as a whole and to be capable of developing interpretive categories in which to express the inter-relationships of ideas within the subject.

If it is granted that disciplines have characteristic features and that it is possible to construct hierarchies of representative ideas, it still remains to be explained how these qualitatively special concepts are to be used by the teacher. It might appear that the answer to the crisis in learning is to select and teach first the most representative ideas, that is, the ones at the top of the hierarchy, then to move on to the next lower level, and so on down toward the particularity and detail of the lowest level, as far as time permits. Such a view of the principle of representative ideas in teaching is quite mistaken. Instruction on such a basis would prove completely ineffective.

The principle as stated early in this chapter was that content should be chosen so as to *exemplify* the representative ideas of the disciplines. The italics are important. It was not said that the representative ideas themselves should be taught as explicit concepts. These ideas are of a highly abstract nature. They belong to the philosophical analysis of the disciplines. They have no place in the actual content of instruction at the introductory stages. For example, the representative idea of the principle of conservation is not an appropriate topic for explicit abstract treatment in the early stages of physical science. The analytical concept of the musical idea is not a suitable way to begin the study of music. The idea of personal knowledge as being concrete, existential, and intersubjective is not of direct value for beginning instruction in that field, any more than the idea of the logical distinction between fact and obligation would be appropriate as an explicit topic in elementary moral teaching. The representative ideas of history as the reenactment of unique events, of religion as ultimate commitment, and of philosophy as interpretation of meanings are likewise not helpful as specific material for basic instruction in the synoptic disciplines.

The most fundamental ideas are usually not appropriate as explicit content until a fairly advanced stage of understanding has been reached. They are high abstractions that are not meaningful except to persons who possess a considerable fund of knowledge in the subject to which they apply. The less comprehensive ideas are, the more easily they can be understood by the beginning student.

What, then, is the use of the representative ideas if they are not suitable from the beginning as curriculum content? Their function is to guide the selection of learnable content so that it will exemplify the characteristic features of the disciplines. The place of the representative ideas is not in the first instance on the lips of the teacher, but in his mind, to direct him in the choice of learning experiences that will illustrate the ideas he has in mind. In the arts, for example, not much would be learned if the teacher talked about individual perceptual forms. What is required is a series of experiences all of which exemplify concern for the unique perceptual object. In the study of history the student would not be helped very much initially by talk about relevant evidence or about history being the best possible explanation of the present. He would be assisted by specific experiences judicially chosen to illustrate the meaning of relevance and the manner of using present data as the evidence for the construction of history.

Thus, in the beginning stages representative ideas are for the guidance of the teacher (or the curriculum maker) and not directly for the student. Later they may be made explicit for the student and may prove as useful to him in advancing and epitomizing his own understanding as they are for the teacher. The essential point is that at every stage of instruction the representative ideas should govern what is taught. Every particular should manifest the larger concept that it illustrates. The poor teacher piles item upon item of information and experience, only making certain that each contribution falls within the subject being pursued. The good teacher, by contrast, chooses each item or experience with the deliberate purpose of giving substance to certain basic concepts that are distinctive of the discipline studied.

The manner in which representative ideas should be used in teaching is summed up in Alfred North Whitehead's dictum that "the problem of education is to make the pupil see the wood by means of the trees." [1] The wood is the subject as a whole. The trees are the particular instances chosen to exemplify the whole. This is the approach to teaching through the use of representative ideas, as advocated in the foregoing pages.

By way of contrast, three other common approaches to teaching may be noted. The first is to teach by using the trees only. This is the method of simple accumulation of knowledge, piece by piece, without any consideration for the relationships among the parts or for the structure of the whole. This is the way resorted to by those who are confused about the meaning of the multiplicity of experiences presented by modern life. They take refuge in particularity, heaping up fragments of existence without regard to their coherence or direction. While students may become absorbed in this flow of miscellaneous experience, they sooner or later feel its emptiness, finding in the arbitrary juxtaposition of ideas no satisfactory basis for personal fulfillment.

A second type of teaching is in direct contrast with the first. This is the way of teaching by using the wood only. Such teaching is concerned only with general principles. It is the way of the theoretically minded person, who loves abstractions above all.

[1] *The Aims of Education*, New American Library of World Literature, Inc., New York, 1949, p. 18.

Concrete instances he regards as beneath his notice, for he dwells in the lofty atmosphere of pure idea. This kind of teaching would be tolerated, if at all, only at the higher academic levels. Children and young people would gain nothing from it and would properly react strongly against it, because it is too remote from their concrete experience.

This unsatisfactory second type is one that might readily be confused with the method of teaching by the use of representative ideas. These ideas are general concepts that represent the wood— the discipline as a whole. To economize learning effort it might be urged that these representative ideas be taught, leaving out all unnecessary details. As pointed out earlier, such teaching would be vacuous. The students would learn nothing from it. They would at most learn how to repeat certain philosophical generalities about the various fields of study. They would have no real understanding either of the disciplines or of the general ideas they had learned to utter.

For example, a student of mathematics might know that the discipline has to do with abstraction, sets, deductive inference, and postulational method and yet not really understand the subject at all, because he had never *seen* and *savored* these elemental ideas through specific illustrations. Again, a student who knew history in the abstract sense that he could describe the subject as the re-enactment of unique past events, using relevant evidence, would not really understand history unless these abstractions had first been brought to life for him by particular illuminating illustrations.

A third approach to instruction is to help the student see the trees by means of the wood. Here the emphasis is on the particular instance, and the generalizations are used to make the individual case intelligible. For instance, music may be studied with the ultimate objective of understanding particular musical compositions, and representative concepts, such as rhythm and harmonic texture, may be introduced only when needed to render certain features of the individual works intelligible, but there may be no attempt to comprehend the larger meaning of music as a significant human activity. Again, language may be studied purely for the sake of speaking it, and representative ideas like morpheme and paradigmatic class (regardless of whether or not such technical terms are used) may be introduced only to clarify certain meanings or constructions that prove difficult in the course of studying the language, rather than to afford an understanding of the significance of the language enterprise as a whole.

The distinctively human goal in learning is to expand meanings beyond particulars to the larger patterns of understanding. Human fulfillment consists in enriching and deepening comprehension through the ever-expanding integration of experience. Hence, seeing the trees is not appropriate as an ultimate goal of learning.

Furthermore, it is doubtful that one could understand the wood by which to see the trees if he had not first been shown the wood by means of the trees. In the music instance above, it is doubtful that the general concepts of rhythm and harmonic texture would have any clarifying power when applied to particular compositions unless these ideas had earlier become meaningful in themselves through vivid particular exemplifications. In the language instance it is doubtful that the general ideas of morpheme and paradigmatic class would be of any help in particular situations unless these concepts had already become significant through carefully chosen illustrations directed at illuminating their meaning.

Thus, we return to the proposition that the aim of teaching is comprehensive understanding and that the way to achieve it is to choose particular materials for instruction that in an unusual degree exemplify the pattern of the subject as a whole. Another way of stating this is to say that the particulars of instruction should be representative, typical, or paradigmatic materials, their representativeness being measured by how well they show the typical features of the discipline they are supposed to illuminate.

Accordingly, a drastic reduction in the amount of what has to be learned can be effected by the use of representative materials. The student comes to an *implicit* understanding of the characteristic features of the disciplines step by step. By the consistent nature of his experiences in connection with a given discipline he gains an intimate sense of its basic patterns, so that he can make sound judgments regarding materials in it and can readily familiarize himself with new knowledge as it develops in the field. Of greatest importance, however, is the consequence that a student taught by the use of representative ideas understands *meaningfully*. He possesses a power of inner appropriation, by which he feels himself at home in the universe of meanings.

Teaching by the use of representative materials is not a recent innovation. Good teachers have always practiced the art of communicating the essence of their subject by means of unusually illuminating specific examples. What is required in the contemporary situation is a deliberate cultivation of such teaching, based on a clear recognition of the close relation between efficiency in learning and knowledge of the characteristic ideas of the disciplines. Some of the best new instructional materials, particularly in mathematics and the sciences, have been prepared by the cooperative efforts of scholars in the disciplines and teachers at the various grade levels affected. The value of these materials is due in large measure to the fact that they unite the necessary pedagogical specificity with a high degree of discipline representativeness. More such materials for the teacher's use are urgently needed in all areas of the curriculum. Since the individual teacher seldom has the time or ingenuity to create his own representative materials, he must normally make use of published guides. Great opportunities exist today for the advancement of education through the joint efforts of experienced classroom teachers, curriculum experts, and scholars in the disciplines in providing study materials constructed on sound principles from both pedagogy and the theory of knowledge.

27

METHODS OF INQUIRY

The third principle for the selection of curriculum content is really a corollary of the principle of representative ideas treated in the preceding chapter. The general term "representative ideas" refers to any aspect of a discipline that discloses its essential features. One especially significant set of such ideas are the *methods of inquiry* used in the discipline. Each discipline has characteristic methods of investigation that distinguish it from other disciplines. By describing the way men of knowledge in a particular field of scholarship go about their professional task, these methods in fact define the discipline. The right of a scholar to speak as an authority in his field rests on his acceptance of the canons of inquiry by which knowledge is created and validated in it.

While the discussion of representative ideas in the preceding chapter gave some implicit consideration to methods, most attention was directed to basic concepts, examples of which are *phoneme* in ordinary language, *set* in mathematics, *organism* in biology, *mediating process* in psychology, *movement* in the dance, *self* in personal knowledge, *right* in ethics, and *ultimacy* in religion. However, such ideas, which are part of the intellectual apparatus used to express meanings in the various disciplines, may be understood fully only in relation to the processes of inquiry. Hence, our discussion of representative ideas needs to be rounded out with an explicit treatment of the methods of inquiry.

Our third principle for economizing learning effort is that materials should be selected so as to exemplify the methods of inquiry in the disciplines. Centering attention on methods has the effect of ameliorating all four of the main threats to meaning earlier described—cynicism, fragmentation, surfeit, and transience. First, an understanding of methods overcomes cynicism because it provides clear means for the acquisition of understanding. Frustration and despair are a result of seeing no way to overcome ignorance. They vanish when ways of knowing are available. Thus, knowledge of methods replaces destructive doubt by confidence in the possibility of understanding.

Second, methods are the unifying elements in a discipline, binding together all the separate results of inquiry into one coherent domain of study. Hence, an understanding of methods helps to counteract the fragmentation of modern knowledge. The particular items of knowledge within a field all bear the stamp of a common derivation. All have their source within one set of methodological principles. Moreover, since the methods of the disciplines can be compared and contrasted among themselves, a basis exists for relating one discipline to another, thus further unifying the disparate components of the world of meanings.

It is also clear that understanding of methods helps solve the problem of surfeit in knowledge. If one possesses the tools of inquiry, he is not in need of a large store of accumulated knowledge. He is able to adapt and improvise to meet the needs of particular situations and is less dependent upon the results of others. The methods of a discipline in effect contain all the particular findings that result from inquiry. In that sense knowledge of methods is a kind of surrogate for everything that can be discovered by applying them. This is why their use as a basis for curriculum content can contribute so much to economy in learning.

The study of methods in the disciplines is especially helpful in respect to transience, the fourth of the modern threats to meaning, because methods generally change much more slowly than do the results of applying them. In fact, the overall strategy of inquiry in the several realms of meaning does not change at all. The respective logics of language, science, art, personal understanding, morals, and the synoptic disciplines remain constant. Language usages and empirical facts are justified today in the same general manner as they always were, nor have the basic programs of the artistic, personal, moral, and integrative enterprises changed over the centuries. Even in science, where the transformations have been most striking, substantial similarities unite the empirical inquiry of the ancient Greeks and Babylonians with the outlook and methods of the modern scientific researcher.

At a lower level of generality methods of inquiry do change, more in some fields than others. In physics the methods of Newton differed in important ways from those of Planck and Einstein, and in economics the methods of Ricardo differed greatly from those of Keynes. So also do the procedures of the modern historian differ from those of Herodotus, and Cézanne's approach to painting differs from that of Michelangelo. Less changeable, perhaps, are the particular methods used in arriving at linguistic understanding and in making moral judgments.

Despite these changes, it is still true that the methods of a discipline are generally more stable than are the results of inquiry. Knowledge continually undergoes modification. New discoveries are made, requiring revision of older ideas that may have been developed by essentially the same methods. Therefore, while it may prove impossible for a person to keep pace with the advancing tide of knowledge in a discipline, he may be able quite satisfactorily to remain abreast of the methods of inquiry in it.

These considerations are of paramount importance for the modern educator. In a time of rapid cultural transformation the content of what is learned at any given time is likely to be unusable before many years have passed. The old conception of the school as a place for accumulating knowledge to be used over a lifetime is no longer appropriate, for much of the knowledge that will be needed in the future is not yet discovered at the time the student is in school, and much of what he may acquire there will soon be obsolete. If schooling is not to become an exercise in futility, it is imperative that materials for instruction be selected so as to minimize these effects of cultural change. One promising way of achieving this is by teaching methods of inquiry.

If students in their school years become familiar with basic modes of thought and investigation, they will be better prepared to cope with their changing world than if they merely possess a store of information. Furthermore, by having attention directed to methods, they learn attitudes which will prove useful in adapting not only to changing content but even to changing methods.

These considerations about the changes occurring in modern civilization reinforce the suggestion made in Chapter 23 that education now needs to continue beyond the years traditionally assigned to formal schooling. Adults in contemporary society need periodic "refresher courses" to help them maintain currency in their knowledge. In these continuing studies, as in the work of the earlier school years, the emphasis should fall on the newer methods of inquiry rather than on the latest findings of scholarship. Such renewal of perspective is usually more necessary in specialized education, where advanced and detailed knowledge are needed, than in general education, which is directed toward a broad grasp of types of understanding. Yet even in general education periodic occasions for renewal may be helpful in times when fresh vistas are opening up continuously.

A note of caution is needed at this point. The concern for being up to date should not lead educators to follow the latest fads or to judge the value of knowledge by its recency. There is wisdom in allowing time to sift the worthy from the unworthy. Much of what is newly made or discovered is far inferior in quality to older things. The latest methods are sometimes not as productive in the long run as the older, established procedures. In general education especially, the great enduring ways of thought, which have proved their value in the long experience of mankind, should be emphasized. The novel ways had better be tested by specialists before they are seized upon as desirable elements in general education, the purpose of which is not to keep a person up to the minute, but to impart qualities of experience required to fulfill the life of meaning.

Perhaps the most compelling reason for selecting the materials of instruction in order to exemplify methods of inquiry is that these methods are also ways of learning. They are the methods that long experience has shown are most productive of new understanding by workers in the disciplines. Methods are adopted as working procedures as a result of their demonstrated instructiveness to investigators. They are the modes of thought that experts have found most efficient in promoting understanding in their disciplines.

However, it should not be concluded that the ways of inquiry used by experts in a discipline provide a pattern to be imitated by the teacher and student in general education at all levels. As explained in Chapter 25, disciplines contain materials of all degrees of difficulty. This holds true of methods too. There are elementary methods and advanced methods. Normally the experienced worker uses advanced methods, while elementary methods are appropriate for beginning students.

Moreover, the methods most useful for teaching something that has already been discovered are not likely to be the same as those actually used in discovery. Education would be a very inefficient enterprise if each student had to try to rediscover everything that people usually far more able and experienced had already found out.

Nevertheless, the methods of inquiry in a discipline are still substantially relevant to the methods of teaching that discipline in the curriculum of general education. For example, the essence of learning mathematics is in learning to think like a mathematician. To really learn art is to think the way an artist thinks (in the broad sense of "think," where feeling and form are combined in a unitary significant perception). Gaining personal knowledge is learning to think as an authentic and responsible person thinks (where "think" is here taken in a still different, concrete, existential sense). Learning history similarly depends on thinking like a historian.

One clue to good teaching, then, lies in a program of *guided rediscovery*, in which the student discovers for himself what others before him have found out. His discovery, however, differs from the original in that it is carried out under conditions graded to his level of advancement in the subject and with guidance based upon prior knowledge, saving him from unrewarding errors and frustrations.

But more than the method of discovery is needed. In every discipline there are both ways of acquiring new knowledge and ways of validating knowledge. These two kinds of methods are not the same. The ways of learning a language are not the same as the ways of checking the correctness of language usages. The ways of arriving at moral decisions or historical assertions are different from the ways of justifying them. Both kinds of methods have an important place in teaching. At some times the teacher may wish to lead the student into the experience of discovery, helping him to recapitulate certain aspects of the thought of an original researcher. At other times—probably more frequently—the teacher may wish to instruct the student in ways of checking and evaluating existing knowledge. Thus, to take a difficult case, one may evaluate what a poet expresses in his poem by reading the poem thoughtfully and sympathetically, having respect for the work, allowing for one's own irrelevant associations and biases, and judging in how far the poem is an "authentic reading of life." Teaching such evaluative methods in poetry is not the same as teaching the methods of poetic creation, involving the choice of metaphors, the use of rhythmic patterns, and other methods of the art of composition.

Yet the two types of inquiry—discovery and validation—are not really as disparate as might appear at first sight. The method of discovery in science, for example, involves the formation and testing of hypotheses, the latter operation being identical with the method of verification. Similarly, the method of the painter in constructing his design involves the same kind of repeated observations and critical appraisals that are made by a sensitive viewer of the finished work. The two kinds of methods are related because they both reflect the one logic of the discipline to which they belong. For example, the methods of making moral decisions are congruent with the methods of judging them because both kinds of methods are based upon the same logical pattern of meanings in the ethical realm.

The connection affirmed in the present chapter between

methods of inquiry and methods of instruction has important implications for the theory of teaching. It has been supposed by some adherents of the Experimentalist philosophy of education that thinking follows a single logical pattern—that of the intelligent biological organism solving the problems of adjustment to its environment. The classic source for the description of this pattern is John Dewey's *How We Think.* [1] According to the Experimentalists, thought occurs when the impulses of the organism are blocked and some way is sought to direct its energies into channels where satisfaction is possible. According to this view, problem solving is the sovereign method of thought and the central focus of education. This theory underlies the life-adjustment curriculum, in which the real problems of children and youth are the central concern of teaching and learning, and in which the purpose of instruction is to use the many resources of culture (including the organized bodies of knowledge) to develop effective habits of adjusting to life situations.

The present analysis of the fundamental patterns of meaning indicates that thought does not follow only one logical pattern, such as the supposed method of scientific problem solving advocated by the Experimentalists, and therefore that no single answer can be given to the question of how we think. In the languages thought follows the pattern of arbitrary symbolic construction. In the sciences the methods are those of classification, hypothesis formation, generalization, and explanation by the use of theories and models. In the arts thought proceeds by perceptual abstraction through particular presented forms. In the personal realm thought consists in the existential realization of intersubjective relationships. Moral thought involves deliberate decisions to act in consideration of principles of right or consequences of good. Historical thinking integrates understanding through re-creation of past events in the present. Religious thought unites finite and infinite by means of the symbols of ultimacy. Philosophic thought consists of analytic, synthetic, and critical evaluation of meanings by the use of interpretive concepts.

If human beings think in many ways—in at least the six

[1] D. C. Heath and Company, Boston, 1933.

fundamental ways corresponding to the realms of meaning—and if ways of teaching and learning follow from ways of thinking, then there are correspondingly many ways of teaching and learning. The methods of teaching language are distinctive to the symbolic realm, and similarly, the methods of teaching science, art, personal knowledge, morals, and synoptic understanding are each characteristic of their own realm. There is no identifiable set of principles that define the methods of teaching in general, because there is no one set of principles that describes how we think. There may well be certain principles of classroom management, of child development, and of lesson planning that are applicable to teaching in a great many different disciplines, and in this sense one could properly refer to general teaching methods. However, such methods are not in themselves sufficient to guide instruction. They only describe certain aspects of good teaching. The real substance of method is determined by the structure of what is taught, and, as already indicated, that varies according to the realm of meaning.

Teaching methods also differ within each realm according to the discipline. The methods of ordinary language instruction differ from the methods of teaching mathematics and both differ from the methods of teaching the nondiscursive symbolisms. Methods of teaching physical science differ in important respects from those appropriate to the life sciences, psychology, and the social sciences (which also differ among themselves). Teaching methods in music are unlike those in the visual arts, the arts of movement, and literature, and so on through all the disciplines.

The nature of the appropriate methods of instruction follows from the analyses of the fields in Part Two. The method of teaching for any discipline, according to the principle of the present chapter, is simply to provide experiences that encourage the student to engage actively in inquiry according to the patterns of discovery and validation characteristic of the discipline being studied.

There are also many different methods within each discipline. Like representative ideas, methods appear in hierarchies ranging from the most general to the most particular. In physics, for example, physical measurement is a general method of inquiry. Less general are the distinctive methods of measurement adapted to such different physical phenomena as light, electricity, and heat. More specific still are the methods used to make certain particular measurements, such as the speed of light and the flow of electric current.

Methods of inquiry are most readily taught when studies are organized by disciplines (as in English, biology, or history). In studies organized across disciplines but within the same realm (as in general science or art) the general methods applicable to the realm in question may be taught. Broader interdisciplinary studies, such as programs combining English, history, and social science, and curricula based on the project method, in which resources from many disciplines must be used, are not so favorable to the teaching of methods. This is because each of the several component disciplines has a different method and no clue is provided by the subject matter itself as to the methods appropriate to the composite inquiry. For the interdisciplinary type of course the synoptic disciplines may provide useful suggestions concerning methods of integrating meanings from several different realms.

As pointed out in Chapter 25, the structure of the disciplines does not necessarily dictate the organization of instructional materials. What is required for good teaching is only that some convincing pattern be used to coordinate the materials taught. Yet, in a broad sense, any satisfactory structure for a course must exemplify one or more of the realms of meaning, assuming that those realms cover the entire range of logical possibilities of human signification.

For example, any materials of instruction can be organized *symbolically,* by treating the subject matter, whatever it may be, from the standpoint of the analysis of symbolic systems. Any materials can be organized *empirically,* by treating them descriptively and theoretically. Similarly, any content can be organized as an *esthetic* pattern or in terms of *personal understanding;* it can also be organized *normatively,* or *integratively* from the standpoint of the past, of the ultimate, or of general interpretive categories.

While there are certain advantages of consistency and reinforcement in choosing the method of organization to correspond with the method (or methods) of inquiry in the materials organized, the two need not correspond. Scientific materials can be organized esthetically, the content of language instruction can be organized around the problems of personal understanding (of self and others), and materials from such diverse fields as music and morals can be organized along historical or philosophical lines. The method chosen in any given unit, course, program, or curriculum depends upon the intention of the teacher or curriculum maker—be it to communicate, to describe and explain, to create interesting perceptual forms, to gain direct existential insight, to respond to the claims of conscience, to gain a comprehensive perspective, or to fulfill any combination of these intentions.

Because the realms of meaning and the disciplines represent ways of productive understanding, they also provide suggestions for intelligible modes of organizing the materials of instruction. Effective teaching depends upon the use of some reasonable pattern of organization, so that instruction is not haphazard and so that the course of study is not a series of miscellaneous experiences having no clearly defined plan or purpose.

Finally, in learning the methods of inquiry the student is stimulated to active engagement with the subject. In being concerned with methods, he cannot assume a role as passive recipient of what Alfred North Whitehead called "inert ideas." Methods are ways of *doing* something—modes of active investigation. Therefore, instruction in the characteristic methods of inquiry in the disciplines enlists the vital participation of the student and thus speeds the acquisition of meanings.

28

THE APPEAL
TO IMAGINATION

The first three principles for the selection of materials for instruction relate efficiency in learning to the logical patterns of the organized disciplines. They show how a radical reduction may be effected in the quantity of what needs to be learned, by capitalizing on the fact that authentic knowledge does not consist of isolated bits of experience, but belongs to organized fields with characteristic designs that provide important guides to teaching and learning. The fourth and final principle of selection relates to the quality of the inner life of the teacher and learner rather than to the logic of the fields. It is consequently different in kind and in point of reference from the first three.

The fourth principle is that materials for instruction should always be selected so as to appeal to the imagination of the students. Good teaching is imaginative in quality, and the effective teacher chooses materials that kindle the imagination of the learner. The aim of the present chapter is to explain what is meant by imagination in teaching and why it is so important for learning.

The central problem to which imagination speaks is that of motivation. Teaching avails little unless the student wants to learn. No matter how high the quality of curriculum materials may be, if the student has no interest in them, he will not readily make them his own.

Now what are the sources of motivation? Some are found in biological needs. When people are hungry or thirsty, cold or in pain, they are moved to action that will fulfill their wants. Other sources are social. People are dependent on one another for protection and for the satisfaction of desires that cannot be attained in isolation, and so they are moved to meet their demands by suitable forms of social behavior. Other sources are intellectual curiosity, love of beauty, ethical concern, and hunger for the divine.

Many investigators of human behavior regard the basic biological and social needs as the fundamental sources of motivation and all other alleged higher sources, such as intellectual, esthetic, moral, and religious interests, as secondary and derivative. They consider man's continuity with the lower animals as the most significant clue to his motivation, and they see his distinctiveness in the ways in which he uses the special capacities of intelligence to secure biosocial demands. From this standpoint, the motives of a person are derived from his animal origins, and his higher powers are instruments for the efficient satisfaction of basic organic needs.

But is the foregoing account of motives satisfactory? Do the functions usually designated as "higher" really exist primarily to serve the basic organic needs? There is much evidence for the contrary view, to the effect that the best clues to the motives of man are found in his distinctive human capacities and not in that part of his nature that he shares with the lower animals. In fact, some authorities in the biological sciences affirm that biological drives themselves can best be understood in the light of the psychic life of man. For example, the biologist Edmund W. Sinnott in *Cell and Psyche* [1] argues that organic hungers are identical with conscious purposes, the former being the outside appearance of what is known inwardly to consciousness. Along similar lines the paleontologist Pierre Teilhard de Chardin in *The Phenomenon of Man* [2] shows that the evolution of the cosmos, from the very

[1] Harper & Row, Publishers, Incorporated, New York, 1961.
[2] Harper & Row, Publishers, Incorporated, New York, 1961.

first organizations of energy to form atoms and molecules, on through the various stages of plant and animal emergence, to its culmination in man and society, requires the postulation of omnipresent powers of a kind that we understand directly in our mental and spiritual life. This is to say, again, that the highest powers of man provide the key to understanding the lower levels of motivation rather than the converse.

The contrast between the two views of human motivation is well illuminated in Hannah Arendt's study already referred to in Chapter 3. [3] She says the contemporary condition of man is determined in large part by the necessities of biological and social needs, his higher functions being harnessed to the service of survival and reproductive demands. This condition sharply contrasts with the classical Greek view that the highest good is the life of contemplation within a community of free, equal, and responsible persons in continuous dialogue, having a sense of meaningful relationship with ancestors and posterity in a historic tradition, and engaging in the creation of a cultural treasure of enduring worth. Implicit in Arendt's analysis is the conviction that the present desperate situation of mankind can be traced to the inversion of values evident in the contemporary subordination of the higher human functions to the lower ones.

The thesis of the present book is that the fundamental human motivation is the search for meaning. A human being is a creature whose distinctive life consists in having meanings and whose basic aim is to fulfill them. He can never rest content simply with biological satisfactions. He is forever disturbed by wants that are alien to animal existence. His real longing is for meaning, and whether he recognizes it or not, all his striving, whatever its apparent object, is directed toward the enlargement and deepening of meaning. On this basis we affirm the view that the distinctively human qualities of mind and spirit are the clue to human motivation, in contrast to the position that the basic biosocial needs govern human behavior.

The above view of motivation is directly relevant to the

[3] *The Human Condition,* Doubleday & Company, Inc., Garden City, N.Y., 1959.

understanding of imagination. Imagination belongs to the active inner life of a person. It is the conscious center of his psychic existence. It is the power that renders his experience vitally meaningful. By contrast, unimaginative aspects of experience are routine, dull, and unexciting. They do not grasp one at the core of his personal being. They are essentially meaningless.

Imagination has remarkable power in fulfilling a person's existence. It centers in the depths of his personal being, yet at the same time it releases him from self-preoccupation. Through imagination one is captivated by the vision of new and wider possibilities. Imagination is a form of ecstasy (meaning literally, "standing outside of") in which one is lifted out of himself and transported to a higher level of existence. It is a manifestation of human freedom, in which one is not constrained by the necessities of the natural and social environment or of his own biological drives, but is able to participate in a world of meanings that the human spirit discovers are its native home.

It may be thought that this life of imagination belongs to a certain small class of unusual persons, including intellectuals, artists, and mystics, but not to ordinary people, and surely not to those who are less able than the average. Many human beings and many human experiences *are* unimaginative. But it need not be granted that nothing better is possible for most people most or all of the time. If the fundamental goal of human existence is the fulfillment of meaning, then the life of imagination belongs to everybody as an essential mark of his humanness. Accordingly, there is no person for whom the growth of the inner life of meaning is not the real goal of all his striving, whether or not he is conscious of it as such. It is a fundamental error to regard most people as more or less intelligent beasts among whom live a few unusual souls who happen to enjoy the "higher things of life." All human beings—and perhaps all lower beings too, in an unconscious way—are aiming at the higher things of life, and ultimately at realization of the highest meanings.

These considerations are directly relevant to the problems of education. Students learn best what they most profoundly want to know. Their learning efficiency is in direct relation to their motivation. Hence, the materials of instruction should be selected in the light of students' real interests. If the biosocial concept of motivation is accepted, instructional materials will be selected so as to help the student satisfy his basic organismic wants. If, on the other hand, motivation is believed to spring from the higher human functions, curriculum content will be chosen so as to maximize meanings.

Modern educational practice has been largely governed by the ideal that studies should be meaningful. The traditional academic curriculum was found deficient in meaning for the great majority of students, and in its place a more "functional" curriculum was developed, guided by the principle that the greatest interest (and the most meaning) would attach to studies contributing to the practical concerns of the learner. It is presupposed by the proponents of the functional curriculum that what students care for above all is the successful satisfaction of their desires, the elimination of their frustrations, and the full opportunity to discharge their impulses, and that the aim of education is to maximize these goals as far as possible for as many as possible.

Suppose now that the concept of meaning presupposed by the functionalists is mistaken and that what students really care for, even if for one reason or another they may not acknowledge it, is the awakening of the inner life through the nurture of imagination. Then studies directed toward the satisfaction of organic and social demands will not enlist enthusiasm or induce effective learning. Students *will* respond to and learn readily materials that release them from their ordinary concerns and lift them onto a new plane of meaning.

The principle of appeal to imagination calls for the selection of materials that are drawn from the extraordinary rather than from the experience of everyday life. They should be such as to transform ordinary perspectives rather than to confirm them. Through his studies the student should find himself in a different world from the commonplace one of practical life. He should see more deeply, feel more intensely, and comprehend more fully than he does in his usual experiences.

The principle may be illustrated in all types of studies. Imaginatively conceived, language may be understood as a game with various possible sets of rules. One can play with roots and affixes, experiment with various combinations of sound and meaning elements, and arrange words into sequences according to various actual and possible syntactical patterns. Language so treated becomes a new and fascinating activity transcending the ordinary practices of talking and writing to meet the demands of social exigency. By considering its extraordinary aspects—those realities that lie hidden beneath the mass of common assumptions about human discourse—the inner meaning of language is disclosed. If, instead, language is taught simply as a means of social interaction and adjustment, the student's imagination will not be kindled and he will miss the vision of what language really means, in the deep mystery of symbols as channels for the revelation of the intelligibility of things.

So also, mathematics imaginatively taught transcends such commonplace problem solving as learning how to make change at grocery stores and how to calculate the heights of buildings. Mathematics is a field of wonder and excitement, with strange symbols and endless possibilities for experiments in thought. In recent years a drastic shift has occurred in many of the most thoughtfully conceived mathematics curricula. The newer materials are designed to produce real mathematical insight rather than merely computational skill for practical application. The recasting of elementary mathematics in the light of the ideal of true mathematical understanding is a signal contemporary example of giving precedence to imagination over biosocial adjustment in the selection of the materials of instruction.

An imaginative teacher of science does not treat his field simply as refined common sense, nor is he mainly concerned to teach students to think scientifically in the affairs of everyday life, in the manner of those who believe that thinking is simply problem solving and that the educated person is one who meets his problems successfully by the application of scientific method. Science is in reality a highly imaginative human enterprise, involving a complete transformation of commonsense ways of thinking. Hence, the teacher who wants his students to understand science introduces them to the extraordinary perspectives on things which are afforded by scientific modes of thought. The fascination (and value) of science consists in its transfigured vision of nature and man, transcending the superficial perceptions and unexamined judgments of everyday life.

In the esthetic realm the functional curriculum makes use of the arts as means of self-expression, affording psychological release and better integration of vital energies. The arts are also seen as one solution to the social problems of leisure time in an advanced industrial society. In the imaginative approach to art education, all such considerations of psychological and social utility are rejected and art is presented as an avenue to the exaltation of life through objectifying the mysterious depths of man's creative life. This transforming power of art can be imparted by bringing students into the presence of works that do not at once disclose their meaning and by showing them how to perceive these works sensitively and expectantly.

The contrast between imaginative and unimaginative instruction is particularly vivid in the case of personal knowledge. Depth analysis of the human psyche shows that the world of self and others is far different in reality from what appears to common sight. That is why commonsense approaches to the improvement of human relationships and to self-understanding are so unexciting and uninstructive. Effective teaching in this domain requires extraordinary insight into the profound depths of the human mind and a level of understanding far different from the judgments of practical life. The psychotherapist's use of dreams and the use of projective tests by the skilled counselor are illustrations of what is meant by imaginative materials of instruction in the field of personal knowledge. The extraordinary considerations of the perceptive counselor are more powerful in teaching than are commonsense observations, because they bring the learner closer to the real inner meaning of his personal existence than do the obvious but fundamentally untrue everyday platitudes.

Moral teaching, like instruction in personal relations, is plagued by unimaginative practicality and obviousness. This condition has been accentuated by the wide acceptance of the theory that moral principles are simply rules for promoting social harmony. Authentic moral meanings are reestablished only when the extraordinary mystery of unconditional obligation is recognized and when the secret inward claim of conscience is reinforced by the consideration of moral dilemmas where the easy justifications of prudence and custom do not suffice.

History has been robbed of its proper interest and meaning when, in the name of meaning, it has been pressed into the service of everyday living, being justified on the grounds that one can live more successfully now if he knows what has happened in the past. The essential meaning of history consists in the absolutely unique and therefore completely extraordinary quality of singular events. To understand history is to engage in an imaginative re-creation of the past, the success of which is measured by one's ability to transcend the preoccupations and presuppositions of the practical present. The capacity for such imaginative transcendence of the present is a fair measure of spiritual maturity.

Although religion in its very essence denies subservience to the ordinary, much of what is called religion is in fact interpreted in utilitarian fashion. In religious instruction God is often represented as the all-powerful ruler to whom the faithful resort for benefits that cannot be secured through natural channels. Such cosmic practicalism is likely to appear to students both as untrue and uninteresting. Imaginative religious teaching, on the other hand, emphasizes the profound mystery of the divine. Authentic religious meanings are perhaps best learned by participation in the life of the worshipping community, by meditation on the unfathomable depths of existence, and by the reverent contemplation of sacred symbols, in which the finite and the infinite are wonderfully interfused.

Finally, everyday ideas are not likely to contribute much to philosophic understanding. The essence of philosophy is deep questioning. Its function is to force thought beyond the obvious to the meanings that lie hidden beneath the surface of experience. The appeal of philosophy consists precisely in its imaginative detachment from ordinary practice for the sake of a truer vision of things.

Thus, in every realm of understanding the principle holds that material for instruction should be selected for its power of stimulating imagination. This does not mean that materials should be bizarre, or esoteric, or sensational. Some teachers depend on the appeal of the unusual, no matter what it is, to maintain interest. The appeal to imagination has nothing to do with such romanticism and showmanship. It has everything to do with finding materials that have unusual power to speak to persons in the depth of their being by giving them a vision of a new order of life in which they can participate and by which their ordinary existence can be transfigured.

This cultivation of the life of imagination is the distinctive office and ultimate aim of general education. In fulfilling this aim the fundamental disciplines are particularly relevant, for they are the consequence of the direct pursuit of meanings, without subordination to the necessities of practical life. Although the applied disciplines can also be taught imaginatively, they are perhaps more readily corrupted than are the fundamental fields by a subhuman utilitarian concept of meaning.

In respect to practicality, it turns out that the pursuit of the apparently impractical fundamental studies using ostensibly impractical imaginative materials proves in the long run to yield the richest harvest of practical fruits. Profound understanding is the source of effective practice, and success in solving the problems of life is best achieved by those whose imaginations are kindled. As in so many affairs of human life, it turns out that in the field of practice the best results are obtained by indirect rather than by direct attack. Power to act is not a prize to be directly grasped, but a consequence of deep understanding. Thus, what the educational functionalists struggle to attain deliberately, they may lose because they do not understand human nature well enough. Contrariwise, through concern for the life of imagination persons may be assured a meaningful existence, which will yield rich fruits in practical affairs.

A final critical question about the principle of imagination needs to be considered. Is the imaginative type of general education advocated above really possible for everyone? Is it as applicable to an under-average child in a slum school as to a bright child in a highly favored suburban school? The answer is that imaginative teaching is suitable for everyone and that it is even more essential in the poor school and for the less able child than in the best school and for the gifted child. To hold this as an active working principle requires faith by the teacher in the potentiality for real human fulfillment in every person. It is the consistent witness of those who have labored in such a faith that their confidence was not in vain.

For the fruits of imaginative instruction to appear, three conditions must be fulfilled. First, it needs to be recognized that the means by which imagination may be kindled differ according to the person, his level of maturity, and his cultural context. The teacher has to choose materials to take account of these factors. What will kindle the imagination of a manually oriented child is not the same as for a conceptually oriented child. Imaginative materials for a country child may be different from those for a city child. They will ordinarily be different for adults than for children. There are no standard materials that can be labelled "imaginative" for everyone everywhere always.

The second condition is that the teacher himself exemplify an imaginative quality of mind. Part of his imaginativeness is manifest in his ability to transcend his own subjectivity and to enter so sympathetically into the lives of his students that he is able to create or select materials that will speak to their inner being. His own imagination must also be alive in respect to his own existence. If it is, he communicates a quality of authentic life—of having been grasped at the core of his personality by the power of meaning—and the students apprehend this quality of reality even if they do not share in the particular meanings that the teacher experiences.

The third condition for successful imaginative teaching is an unconditional faith in the possibility of realizing meaning through awakened imagination in any and every student, no matter what appearances may indicate to the contrary. This faith is not to be confused with a blind optimism in the goodness and indefinite perfectibility of every person. It is rather a working conviction about the essential nature of persons and of the highest human good by which persons are ultimately constrained, namely, the fulfillment of meaning.

Selected Bibliography

Selected Bibliography

1. The Argument

Association for Supervision and Curriculum Development: *New Insights and the Curriculum,* 1963 Yearbook, Washington.

Boulding, Kenneth: *The Image,* The University of Michigan Press, Ann Arbor, Mich., 1956.

Bryson, Lyman (ed.): *An Outline of Man's Knowledge of the Modern World,* Doubleday & Company, Inc., Garden City, N.Y., 1960.

Cassidy, Harold Gomes: *The Sciences and the Arts,* Harper & Row, Publishers, Incorporated, New York, 1962.

Cassirer, Ernst: *Philosophy of Symbolic Forms,* tr. by Ralph Manheim, Yale University Press, New Haven, Conn., vol. 1, 1953; vol. 2, 1955; vol. 3, 1957.

Jeffreys, M. V. C.: *Glaucon: An Inquiry into the Aims of Education,* Sir Isaac Pitman & Sons, Ltd., London, 1950.

Leary, Lewis (ed.): *The Unity of Knowledge,* Doubleday & Company, Garden City, N.Y., 1955.

Maritain, Jacques: *Education at the Crossroads,* Yale University Press, New Haven, Conn., 1943.

Northrop, Filmer S. C.: *The Logic of the Sciences and the Humanities,* The Macmillan Company, New York, 1947.

Perry, Ralph Barton: *Realms of Value,* Harvard University Press, Cambridge, Mass., 1954.

Pryce-Jones, Alan (ed.): *The New Outline of Modern Knowledge,* Simon and Schuster, Inc., New York, 1956.

Reid, Louis Arnaud: *Ways of Knowledge and Experience,* Oxford University Press, Fair Lawn, N.J., 1961.

Robinson, James Harvey: *The Humanizing of Knowledge,* 2d rev. ed., George H. Doran Company, New York, 1926.

Russell, Bertrand: *Human Knowledge, Its Scope and Limits,* Simon & Schuster, Inc., New York, 1948.

Smith, Vincent Edward: *The School Examined: Its Aim and Content,*

The Bruce Publishing Company, Milwaukee, 1960.

Temple, William: *Mens Creatrix,* St. Martin's Press, Inc., New York, 1923.

Tennant, Frederick R.: *Philosophy of the Sciences,* Cambridge University Press, New York, 1932.

Whitehead, Alfred North: *The Aims of Education, and Other Essays,* The Macmillan Company, New York, 1929.

————: *Modes of Thought,* The Macmillan Company, New York, 1938.

2. Human Nature

Bidney, David: *Theoretical Anthropology,* Columbia University Press, New York, 1953.

Cassirer, Ernst: *An Essay on Man,* Yale University Press, New Haven, Conn., 1944.

Dewey, John: *Human Nature and Conduct,* Modern Library, Inc., New York, 1922.

Eiseley, Loren: *Immense Journey,* Random House, Inc., New York, 1957.

Frank, Lawrence K.: *Nature and Human Nature,* Rutgers University Press, New Brunswick, N.J., 1951.

Klubertanz, George P.: *The Philosophy of Human Nature,* Appleton-Century-Crofts, Inc., New York, 1953.

Niebuhr, Reinhold: *The Nature and Destiny of Man,* Charles Scribner's Sons, New York, 1941.

Progroff, Ira: *Depth Psychology and Modern Man,* The Julian Press, Inc., New York, 1959.

Ulich, Robert: *The Human Career,* Harper & Row, Publishers, Incorporated, New York, 1955.

White, Lynn (ed.): *Frontiers of Knowledge in the Study of Man,* Harper & Row, Publishers, Incorporated, New York, 1956.

3. Meaninglessness and Modern Man

Arendt, Hannah: *The Human Condition,* The University of Chicago Press, Chicago, 1958.

Barrett, William: *Irrational Man,* Doubleday & Company, Inc., Garden City, N.Y., 1958.

Dixon, W. Macneile: *The Human Situation,* Longmans, Green & Company, Inc., New York, 1938.

Heinemann, F. H.: *Existentialism and the Modern Predicament,* Harper & Row, Publishers, Incorporated, New York, 1958.

May, Rollo: *The Meaning of Anxiety,* The Ronald Press Company, New York, 1950.

Tillich, Paul: *The Courage to Be,* Yale University Press, New Haven, Conn., 1952.

4. The Search for Meaning

Berdyaev, Nicholas: *The Meaning of History,* The World Publishing Company, Cleveland, 1962.

Chase, Stuart: *The Tyranny of Words,* Harcourt, Brace & World, Inc., New York, 1938.

Feifel, Herman (ed.): *The Meaning of Death,* McGraw-Hill Book Company, Inc., New York, 1959.

Frankel, Charles: *The Case for Modern Man,* Harper & Row, Publishers, Incorporated, New York, 1955.

Jaspers, Karl: *Man in the Modern Age,* Doubleday & Company, Inc., Garden City, N.Y., 1957.

Macmurray, John: *The Self as Agent,* Harper & Row, Publishers, Incorporated, New York, 1957.

May, Rollo: *Man's Search for Himself,* W. W. Norton & Company, Inc., New York, 1953.

Ogden, C. K., and I. A. Richards: *The Meaning of Meaning,* Harcourt, Brace & World, Inc., New York, 1923.

Schneer, Cecil J.: *The Search for Order,* Doubleday & Company, Inc., Garden City, N.Y., 1962.

Walpole, Hugh R.: *Semantics,* W. W. Norton & Company, Inc., New York, 1941.

5. Ordinary Language

Black, Max (ed.): *The Importance of Language,* Prentice-Hall, Inc., Englewood Cliffs, N.J., 1962.

Gleason, H. A., Jr.: *An Introduction to Descriptive Linguistics,* rev. ed., Holt, Rinehart & Winston, Inc., New York, 1961.

Hall, Robert A., Jr.: *Linguistics and Your Language,* Doubleday & Company, Inc., Garden City, N.Y., 1960.

Jesperson, Otto: *Growth and Structure of the English Language,* Doubleday & Company, Inc., Garden City, N.Y., 1955.

Laird, Charlton: *Thinking about Language,* Holt, Rinehart and Winston, Inc., New York, 1960.

Potter, Simeon: *Modern Linguistics,* Oxford University Press, Fair Lawn, N.J., 1957.

Sapir, Edward: *Language,* Harcourt, Brace & World, Inc., New York, 1921.

Schlauch, Margaret: *The Gift of Language,* Dover Publications, Inc., New York, 1955.

Urban, Wilbur Marshall: *Language and Reality,* The Macmillan Company, New York, 1939.

Whatmough, Joshua: *Language: A Modern Synthesis,* New American Library of World Literature, Inc., New York, 1956.

6. Mathematics

Adler, Irving: *The New Mathematics,* New American Library of World Literature, Inc., New York, 1960.

Bell, Eric Temple: *Mathematics, Queen and Servant of Science,* McGraw-Hill Book Company, Inc., New York, 1951.

Courant, Richard, and Herbert Robbins: *What Is Mathematics?* Oxford University Press, Fair Lawn, N.J., 1941.

Dantzig, Tobias: *Number, the Language of Science,* The Macmillan Company, New York, 1954.

Eves, Howard, and Carroll V. Newsom: *Introduction to the Foundations and Fundamental Concepts of Mathematics,* Holt, Rinehart and Winston, Inc., New York, 1957.

Kershner, R. B., and L. R. Wilcox: *The Anatomy of Mathematics,* The Ronald Press Company, New York, 1950.

Körner, Stephan: *The Philosophy of Mathematics,* Harper & Row, Publishers, Incorporated, New York, 1962.

May, Kenneth O.: *Elements of Modern Mathematics,* Addison-Wesley Publishing Company, Inc., Reading, Mass., 1959.

School Mathematics Study Group: *Mathematics for Junior High Schools,* Yale University Press, New Haven, Conn., 1961.

Waismann, Friedrich: *Introduction to Mathematical Thinking,* Harper & Row, Publishers, Incorporated, New York, 1959.

Weyl, Hermann: *Philosophy of Mathematics and Natural Science,* Princeton University Press, Princeton, N.J., 1949.

Whitehead, Alfred North: *An Introduction to Mathematics,* Oxford University Press, Fair Lawn, N.J., 1948.

7. Nondiscursive Symbolic Forms

Cassirer, Ernst: *Language and Myth,* Harper & Row, Publishers, Incorporated, New York, 1946.

Eliade, Mircea: *Images and Symbols,* Sheed & Ward, Inc., New York, 1961.

Fromm, Erich: *The Forgotten Language,* Grove Press, Inc., New York, 1951.

Hall, Edward T.: *The Silent Language,* Doubleday & Company, Inc., Garden City, N.Y., 1959.

Jung, Carl Gustav: *Psyche and Symbol,* Doubleday & Company, Inc., Garden City, N.Y., 1958.

Koch, Rudolph: *The Book of Signs,* Dover Publications, Inc., New York, 1930.

Langer, Susanne K.: *Feeling and Form,* Charles Scribner's Sons, New York, 1953.

————: *Philosophy in a New Key,* Penguin Books, Baltimore, 1948.

Lasswell, Harold D., and others: *A Comparative Study of Symbols,* Stanford University Press, Stanford, Calif., 1952.

Murray, Henry A. (ed.): *Myth and Mythmaking,* George Braziller, Inc., New York, 1960.

Wheelwright, Philip: *The Burning Fountain,* Indiana University Press, Bloomington, Ind., 1954.

Whitehead, Alfred North: *Symbolism,* The Macmillan Company, New York, 1958.

Wicker, Frances G.: *The Inner World of Man,* Holt, Rinehart and Winston, Inc., New York, 1948.

8. Physical Science
Bridgman, Percy W.: *The Logic of Modern Physics,* The Macmillan Company, New York, 1960.

Campbell, Norman R.: *What Is Science?* Dover Publications, Inc., New York, 1952.

Cohen, Morris R., and Ernest Nagel: *An Introduction to Logic and Scientific Method,* Harcourt, Brace & World, Inc., New York, 1934.

Conant, James Bryant: *Science and Common Sense,* Yale University Press, New Haven, Conn., 1951.

Frank, Philipp: *Philosophy of Science,* Prentice-Hall, Inc., Englewood Cliffs, N.J., 1957.

Hanson, Norwood Russell: *Patterns of Discovery,* Cambridge University Press, New York, 1958.

Holton, Gerald, and Duane H. D. Roller: *Foundations of Modern Physical Science,* Addison-Wesley Publishing Company, Inc., Reading, Mass., 1958.

Madden, Edward H.: *The Structure of Scientific Thought,* Houghton Mifflin Company, Boston, 1960.

Pap, Arthur: *An Introduction to the Philosophy of Science,* The Free Press of Glencoe, New York, 1962.

Ritchie, A. D.: *Scientific Method,* Littlefield, Adams & Co., Paterson, N.J., 1960.

Toulmin, Stephen: *The Philosophy of Science,* Harper & Row, Publishers, Incorporated, New York, 1960.

Whitehead, Alfred North: *Science and the Modern World,* The Macmillan Company, New York, 1948.

9. Biology

Bates, Marston: *The Nature of Natural History,* rev. ed., Charles Scribner's Sons, New York, 1962.

Bertalanffy, Ludwig von: *Problems of Life,* Harper & Row, Publishers, Incorporated, New York, 1960.

Bonner, John T.: *The Ideas of Biology,* Harper & Row, Publishers, Incorporated, New York, 1962.

Graubard, Mark: *Foundations of Life Science,* D. Van Nostrand Company, Inc., Princeton, N.J., 1958.

Simpson, George Gaylord, and others: *Life: An Introduction to Biology,* Harcourt, Brace & World, Inc., New York, 1957.

Waddington, C. H.: *Biology: Introduction,* Barnes & Noble, Inc., New York, 1962.

Weisz, Paul B.: *The Science of Biology,* McGraw-Hill Book Company, Inc., New York, 1959.

Woodger, J. H.: *Biology and Language,* Cambridge University Press, New York, 1952.

10. Psychology

Allport, Gordon W.: *Becoming,* Yale University Press, New Haven, Conn., 1955.

————: *Personality,* Holt, Rinehart and Winston, Inc., New York, 1937.

Carmichael, Leonard: *Basic Psychology,* Random House, Inc., New York, 1957.

Eysenck, H. J.: *The Structure of Human Personality,* John Wiley & Sons, Inc., New York, 1953.

Hebb, Donald O.: *A Textbook of Psychology,* W. B. Saunders Company, Philadelphia, 1958.

Hilgard, Ernest R.: *Introduction to Psychology,* 3d ed., Harcourt, Brace & World, Inc., New York, 1962.

Keller, Fred S.: *The Definition of Psychology,* Appleton-Century-Crofts, Inc., New York, 1937.

Miller, George A.: *Psychology: The Science of Mental Life,* Harper & Row, Publishers, Incorporated, New York, 1962.

Munn, Norman L.: *Psychology,* 4th ed., Houghton Mifflin Company, Boston, 1961.

Murphy, Gardner: *Introduction to Psychology,* Harper & Row, Publishers, Incorporated, New York, 1951.

Postman, Leo: *Psychology in the Making,* Alfred A. Knopf, Inc., New York, 1962.

Snygg, Donald, and Arthur W. Combs: *Individual Behavior,* rev. ed., Harper & Row, Publishers, Incorporated, New York, 1959.

Woodworth, Robert S.: *Contemporary Schools of Psychology,* rev. ed., The Ronald Press Company, New York, 1948.

11. Social Science

Becker, Howard, and Alvin Boskoff: *Modern Sociological Theory,* Holt, Rinehart and Winston, Inc., New York, 1957.

Johnson, Harry M.: *Sociology: A Systematic Introduction,* Harcourt, Brace & World, Inc., New York, 1960.

Lipset, Seymour, and Neil Smelser: *Sociology, the Progress of a Decade,* Prentice-Hall, Inc., Englewood Cliffs, N.J., 1961.

Loomis, Charles P.: *Social Systems,* D. Van Nostrand Company, Inc., Princeton, N.J., 1960.

MacIver, Robert M., and Charles H. Page: *Society: An Introductory Analysis,* Holt, Rinehart and Winston, Inc., New York, 1949.

Mills, C. Wright: *The Sociological Imagination,* Oxford University Press, Fair Lawn, N.J., 1959.

Mises, Ludwig von: *Ultimate Foundations of Economic Science,* D. Van Nostrand Company, Inc., Princeton, N.J., 1962.

Rose, Arnold M.: *Sociology: The Study of Human Relations,* Alfred A. Knopf, Inc., New York, 1956.

Samuelson, Paul A.: *Economics: An Introductory Analysis,* 5th ed., McGraw-Hill Book Company, Inc., New York, 1961.

Soule, George: *An Introduction to Economic Science,* New American Library of World Literature, New York, 1948.

Tawney, R. H.: *The Acquisitive Society,* Harcourt, Brace & World, Inc., New York, 1920.

Weber, Max: *Basic Concepts in Sociology,* tr. by H. P. Secher, The Citadel Press, New York, 1962.

12. Music

Boyden, David D.: *An Introduction to Music,* Alfred A. Knopf, Inc., New York, 1956.

Cooper, Grosvenor: *Learning to Listen: A Handbook for Music,* The University of Chicago Press, Chicago, 1957.

Copland, Aaron: *What to Listen for in Music,* McGraw-Hill Book Company, Inc., New York, 1957.

Langer, Susanne K.: *Problems of Art,* Charles Scribner's Sons, New York, 1957.

Meyer, Leonard B.: *Emotion and Meaning in Music,* The University of Chicago Press, Chicago, 1956.

Morris, Reginald O.: *The Structure of Music,* Oxford University Press, Fair Lawn, N.J., 1935.

Murphy, Howard A.: *Music Fundamentals,* Chandler Publishing Co., New York, 1962.

Sessions, Roger: *The Musical Experience of Composer, Performer, Listener,* Princeton University Press, Princeton, N.J., 1950.

Stravinsky, Igor: *Poetics of Music,* Alfred A. Knopf, Inc., New York, 1956.

Zuckerkandl, Victor: *The Sense of Music,* Princeton University Press, Princeton, N.J., 1959.

13. The Visual Arts

Bell, Clive: *Art,* G. P. Putnam's Sons, New York, 1959.

Dewey, John: *Art as Experience,* G. P. Putnam's Sons, New York, 1959.

Fry, Roger: *Transformations,* Doubleday & Company, Inc., Garden City, N.Y., 1956.

Gombrich, E. H.: *The Story of Art,* Phaidon Publishers, Inc., New York, 1958.

Kuh, Catherine: *Art Has Many Faces,* Harper & Row, Publishers, Incorporated, New York, 1951.

Lowry, Bates: *The Visual Experience,* Prentice-Hall, Inc., Englewood Cliffs, N.J., 1961.

Panofsky, Erwin: *Meaning in the Visual Arts,* Doubleday & Company, Inc., Garden City, N.Y., 1955.

Pepper, Stephen C.: *The Work of Art,* Indiana University Press, Bloomington, Ind., 1955.

Read, Herbert: *Education through Art,* Pantheon Books, a Division of Random House, Inc., New York, 1958.

Santayana, George: *The Sense of Beauty,* Dover Publications, Inc., New York, 1955.

Taylor, Joshua C.: *Learning to Look: A Handbook for the Visual Arts,* The University of Chicago Press, Chicago, 1957.

14. The Arts of Movement

Chujoy, Anatole: *The Dance Encyclopedia,* A. S. Barnes and Co., Inc., New York, 1949.

Harthy, Ruth E., and others: *Understanding Children's Play,* Columbia University Press, New York, 1952.

Hayes, Elizabeth R.: *Dance Composition and Production,* A. S. Barnes and Co., Inc., New York, 1955.

H'Doubler, Margaret: *Dance: A Creative Art Experience,* 2d ed., The University of Wisconsin Press, Madison, Wis., 1959.

Huizinga, Johan: *Homo Ludens,* Beacon Press, Boston, 1955.

Lloyd, Margaret: *The Borzoi Book of Modern Dance,* Alfred A. Knopf, Inc., New York, 1949.

Martin, John: *Introduction to the Dance,* W. W. Norton & Company, Inc., New York, 1939.

Rogers, Frederick Rand (ed.): *Dance: A Basic Educational Technique,* The Macmillan Company, New York, 1941.

Sorell, Walter (ed.): *The Dance Has Many Faces,* The World Publishing Company, Cleveland, 1951.

15. Literature

Auerbach, Erich: *Mimesis,* Doubleday & Company, Inc., Garden City, N.Y., 1957.

Crane, Ronald S., and others (eds.): *Critics and Criticism: Ancient and Modern,* The University of Chicago Press, Chicago, 1957.

Fergusson, Francis: *The Idea of a Theater,* Princeton University Press, Princeton, N.J., 1949.

Goodman, Paul: *The Structure of Literature,* The University of Chicago Press, Chicago, 1954.

McGinn, Donald J., and George Howerton (eds.): *Literature as a Fine Art,* Harper & Row, Publishers, Incorporated, New York, 1959.

Read, Herbert: *The Nature of Literature,* Grove Press, Inc., New York, 1958.

Richards, I. A.: *Practical Criticism,* Harcourt, Brace & World, Inc., New York, 1929.

Schopenhauer, Arthur: *The Art of Literature,* The University of Michigan Press, Ann Arbor, Mich., 1960.

Wellek, René, and Austin Warren: *Theory of Literature,* Harcourt, Brace & World, Inc., New York, 1942.

Wimsatt, William K., Jr., and Cleanth Brooks: *Literary Criticism,* Alfred A. Knopf, Inc., New York, 1957.

16. Personal Knowledge

Allport, Gordon W.: *Becoming,* Yale University Press, New Haven, Conn., 1955.

Blum, Gerald S.: *Psychoanalytic Theory of Personality,* McGraw-Hill Book Company, Inc., New York, 1953.

Buber, Martin: *Between Man and Man,* Beacon Press, Boston, 1955.

————: *I and Thou,* Charles Scribner's Sons, New York, 1958.

Hendrick, Ives: *Facts and Theories of Psychoanalysis,* Alfred A. Knopf, Inc., New York, 1958.

Macmurray, John: *Persons in Relation,* Harper & Row, Publishers, Incorporated, New York, 1961.

Maslow, Abraham: *Toward a Psychology of Being,* D. Van Nostrand Company, Inc., Princeton, N.J., 1962.

May, Rollo (ed.): *Existential Psychology,* Random House, Inc., New York, 1961.

Montagu, M. F. Ashley (ed.): *The Meaning of Love,* The Julian Press, Inc., New York, 1953.

Moustakas, Clark E. (ed.): *The Self,* Harper & Row, Publishers, Incorporated, New York, 1956.

Mullahy, Patrick (ed.): *A Study of Interpersonal Relations,* Grove Press, Inc., New York, 1957.

Pfuetze, Paul E.: *The Social Self,* Bookman Associates, Inc., New York, 1954.

Polanyi, Michael: *Personal Knowledge,* The University of Chicago Press, Chicago, 1958.

————: *The Study of Man,* The University of Chicago Press, Chicago, 1959.

Sartre, Jean Paul: *Being and Nothingness,* Philosophical Library, Inc., New York, 1956.

Strauss, Anselm (ed.): *The Social Psychology of George Herbert Mead,* The University of Chicago Press, Chicago, 1956.

Sullivan, Harry Stack: *Conceptions of Modern Psychiatry,* W. W. Norton & Company, Inc., New York, 1947.

Tillich, Paul: *The Courage to Be,* Yale University Press, New Haven, Conn., 1952.

17. Moral Knowledge

Brandt, Richard B.: *Ethical Theory,* Prentice-Hall, Englewood Cliffs, N.J., 1959.

Childs, John L.: *Education and Morals,* Appleton-Century-Crofts, Inc., New York, 1950.

Edel, Abraham: *Ethical Judgment,* The Free Press of Glencoe, New York, 1955.

Edwards, Paul: *The Logic of Moral Discourse,* The Free Press of Glencoe, New York, 1955.

Garnett, A. Campbell: *Ethics: A Critical Introduction,* The Ronald Press Company, New York, 1960.

Lippmann, Walter: *A Preface to Morals,* Beacon Press, Boston, 1960.

Moore, George Edward: *Principia Ethica,* Cambridge University Press, New York, 1959.

Nowell-Smith, P. H.: *Ethics,* Penguin Books, Inc., Baltimore, 1954.

Phenix, Philip H.: *Education and the Common Good,* Harper & Row, Publishers, Incorporated, New York, 1961.

Pole, David: *Conditions of Rational Inquiry,* The Athlone Press, London, 1961.

Rice, Philip Blair: *On the Knowledge of Good and Evil,* Random House, Inc., New York, 1955.

Toulmin, Stephen: *The Place of Reason in Ethics,* Cambridge University Press, New York, 1960.

Urban, Wilbur Marshall: *Fundamentals of Ethics,* Holt, Rinehart and Winston, Inc., New York, 1930.

Wilson, John: *Reason and Morals,* Cambridge University Press, New York, 1961.

18. History

Butterfield, Herbert: *Man on His Past,* Beacon Press, Boston, 1960.

Childe, V. Gordon: *What Is History?* Abelard-Schuman, Limited, New York, 1953.

Cohen, Morris R.: *Meaning in Human History,* The Open Court Publishing Company, La Salle, Ill., 1947.

Collingwood, R. G.: *The Idea of History,* Oxford University Press, Fair Lawn, N.J., 1956.

Croce, Benedetto: *History as the Story of Liberty,* Meridian Books, Inc., New York, 1955.

Gottschalk, Louis: *Understanding History,* Alfred A. Knopf, Inc., New York, 1950.

Meyerhoff, Hans (ed.): *The Philosophy of History in Our Time,* Doubleday & Company, Inc., Garden City, N.Y., 1959.

Muller, Herbert J.: *The Uses of the Past,* Oxford University Press, Fair Lawn, N.J., 1952.

Nevins, Allan: *The Gateway to History,* Doubleday & Company, Inc., Garden City, N.Y., 1938.

Social Science Research Council, Committee on Historiography: *Theory and Practice in Historical Study*, Washington, 1946.

Stern, Fritz (ed.): *The Varieties of History*, Meridian Books, New York, 1957.

19. Religion

Burtt, Edwin A.: *Types of Religious Philosophy*, rev. ed., Harper & Row, Publishers, Incorporated, New York, 1951.

Eliade, Mircea: *The Sacred and the Profane*, Harper & Row, Publishers, Incorporated, New York, 1961.

Hutchison, John A.: *Faith, Reason, and Existence*, Oxford University Press, Fair Lawn, N.J., 1956.

James, William: *The Varieties of Religious Experience*, Modern Library, Inc., New York, 1902.

King, Winston L.: *Introduction to Religion*, Harper & Row, Publishers, Incorporated, New York, 1954.

Micklem, Nathaniel: *Religion*, Oxford University Press, Fair Lawn, N.J., 1948.

Otto, Rudolph: *The Idea of the Holy*, 2d ed., tr. by John W. Harvey, Oxford University Press, Fair Lawn, N.J., 1950.

Phenix, Philip H.: *Intelligible Religion*, Harper & Row, Publishers, Incorporated, New York, 1954.

————: *Religious Concerns in Contemporary Education*, Bureau of Publications, Teachers College, Columbia University, New York, 1959.

Sayers, Dorothy L.: *The Mind of the Maker*, Meridian Books, Inc., New York, 1956.

Tillich, Paul: *Systematic Theology*, The University of Chicago Press, Chicago, vol. 1, 1951; vol. 2, 1957; vol. 3, 1963.

Whitehead, Alfred North: *Religion in the Making*, The Macmillan Company, New York, 1926.

20. Philosophy

Ayer, Alfred Jules: *The Problem of Knowledge*, St. Martin's Press, Inc., New York, 1958.

Boas, George: *The Inquiring Mind*, The Open Court Publishing Company, La Salle, Ill., 1959.

Ebenstein, William: *Introduction to Political Philosophy*, Holt, Rinehart and Winston, Inc., 1952.

Hill, Thomas English: *Contemporary Theories of Knowledge*, The Ronald Press Company, New York, 1961.

Hocking, William Ernest: *Types of Philosophy,* 3d ed., Charles Scribner's Sons, New York, 1959.

Hospers, John: *An Introduction to Philosophical Analysis,* Prentice-Hall, Inc., Englewood Cliffs, N.J., 1953.

Montague, William P.: *Ways of Knowing,* The Macmillan Company, New York, 1925.

Russell, Bertrand: *The Problems of Philosophy,* Oxford University Press, Fair Lawn, N.J., 1912.

Stolnitz, Jerome: *Aesthetics and Philosophy of Art Criticism,* Houghton Mifflin Company, Boston, 1960.

21. The Scope of the Curriculum

Barzun, Jacques: *The House of Intellect,* Harper & Row, Publishers, Incorporated, New York, 1959.

Beck, Robert H., Walter W. Cook, and Nolan C. Kearney: *Curriculum in the Modern Secondary School,* 2d ed., Prentice-Hall, Inc., Englewood Cliffs, N.J., 1960.

French, Will, and Associates: *Behavioral Goals of General Education in High School,* Russell Sage Foundation, New York, 1957.

Harvard Committee: *General Education in a Free Society,* Harvard University Press, Cambridge, Mass., 1945.

Jacobson, Paul B., and others (eds.): *General Education in the American High School,* Scott, Foresman and Company, Chicago, 1942.

Jones, Howard Mumford: *One Great Society,* Harcourt, Brace & World, Inc., New York, 1959.

Kearney, Nolan C.: *Elementary School Objectives,* Russell Sage Foundation, New York, 1953.

Krug, Edward A.: *The Secondary School Curriculum,* Harper & Row, Publishers, Incorporated, New York, 1960.

McNerney, Chester T.: *The Curriculum,* McGraw-Hill Book Company, Inc., New York, 1953.

Parker, J. Cecil, T. Bentley Edwards, and William H. Stegman: *Curriculum in America,* Thomas Y. Crowell Company, New York, 1962.

Taba, Hilda: *Curriculum Development,* Harcourt, Brace & World, Inc., New York, 1962.

Thomas, Russell B.: *The Search for a Common Learning,* McGraw-Hill Book Company, Inc., New York, 1962.

22. The Logic of Sequence in Studies

Green, Edward J.: *The Learning Process and Programmed Instruction,* Holt, Rinehart and Winston, Inc., New York, 1962.

Hughes, J. L.: *Programmed Instruction for Schools and Industry,* Science Research Associates, Chicago, 1962.

23. Developmental Factors in the Sequence of Studies

Davis, W. Allison, and Robert J. Havighurst: *Father of the Man,* Houghton Mifflin Company, Boston, 1947.

Erikson, Erik H.: *Childhood and Society,* W. W. Norton & Company, Inc., New York, 1950.

Havighurst, Robert: *Human Development and Education,* Longmans, Green & Co., Inc., New York, 1953.

Hurlock, Elizabeth B.: *Child Development,* McGraw-Hill Book Company, Inc., New York, 1956.

Jersild, Arthur T.: *Child Psychology,* 5th ed., Prentice-Hall, Inc., Englewood Cliffs, N.J., 1960.

———— and Associates: *Child Development and the Curriculum,* Bureau of Publications, Teachers College, Columbia University, New York, 1946.

Kelley, Earl C., and Marie I. Rasey: *Education and the Nature of Man,* Harper & Row, Publishers, Incorporated, New York, 1952.

Livingstone, Sir Richard: *On Education,* Cambridge University Press, New York, 1956.

Murphy, Gardner: *Human Potentialities,* Basic Books, Inc., Publishers, New York, 1958.

Piaget, Jean: *The Child's Conception of Physical Causality,* Harcourt, Brace & World, Inc., New York, 1930.

————: *Judgment and Reasoning in the Child,* Harcourt, Brace & World, Inc., New York, 1928.

————: *The Language and Thought of the Child,* Meridian Books, Inc., New York, 1955.

Powell, John Walker: *Learning Comes of Age,* Association Press, New York, 1956.

Prescott, Daniel A.: *The Child in the Educative Process,* McGraw-Hill Book Company, Inc., New York, 1957.

Russell, David H.: *Children's Thinking,* Ginn and Company, Boston, 1956.

Strang, Ruth: *An Introduction to Child Study,* The Macmillan Company, New York, 1959.

Thomson, George G.: *Child Psychology,* 2d ed., Houghton Mifflin Company, Boston, 1962.

Whiting, John W. M., and Irvin Child: *Child Training and Personality,* Yale University Press, New Haven, Conn., 1953.

Witmer, Helen Leland, and Ruth Kotinsky: *Personality in the Making,* Harper & Row, Publishers, Incorporated, New York, 1952.

24. The Problem of Selection in the Curriculum

Chase, Francis S., and Harold A. Anderson (eds.): *The High School in a New Era,* The University of Chicago Press, Chicago, 1958.

Kimball, Solon T., and James E. McClellan, Jr.: *Education and the New America,* Random House, Inc., New York, 1962.

Machlup, Fritz: *The Production and Distribution of Knowledge in the United States,* Princeton University Press, Princeton, N.J., 1962.

Price, Derek J. DeSolla: *Little Science, Big Science,* Columbia University Press, New York, 1963.

25. The Use of the Disciplines

Alberty, Harold B., and Elsie J. Alberty: *Reorganizing the High School Curriculum,* 3d ed., The Macmillan Company, New York, 1962.

Dewey, John: *Democracy and Education,* The Macmillan Company, New York, 1916.

Douglas, Harl R: *The High School Curriculum,* 2d ed., The Ronald Press Company, New York, 1956.

Kitzhober, Albert R., and others: *Education for College,* The Ronald Press Company, New York, 1961.

Koerner, James D. (ed.): *The Case for Basic Education,* Little, Brown and Company, Boston, 1959.

Passow, A. Harry (ed.): *Curriculum Crossroads,* Bureau of Publications, Teachers College, Columbia University, New York, 1962.

Smith, B. Othanel, William O. Stanley, and J. Harlan Shores: *Fundamentals of Curriculum Development,* rev. ed., Harcourt, Brace & World, Inc., New York, 1957.

Stratemeyer, Florence B., and others: *Developing a Curriculum for Modern Living,* 2d ed., Bureau of Publications, Teachers College, Columbia University, New York, 1957.

26. Representative Ideas and 27. Methods of Inquiry

Bartlett, Sir Frederic: *Thinking,* Basic Books, Inc., Publishers, New York, 1958.

Bruner, Jerome S.: *The Process of Education,* Harvard University Press, Cambridge, Mass., 1960.

——— and others: *A Study of Thinking,* John Wiley & Sons, Inc., New York, 1956.

Bryson, Lyman: *The New Prometheus,* The Macmillan Company, New York, 1941.

Dewey, John: *How We Think,* D. C. Heath and Company, Boston, 1933.

Johnson, Wendell: *People in Quandaries,* Harper & Row, Publishers, Incorporated, New York, 1946.

Ohlsen, Merle M. (ed.): *Modern Methods in Elementary Education,* Holt, Rinehart and Winston, Inc., New York, 1959.

Sowards, G. Wesley, and Mary Margaret Scobey: *The Changing Curriculum and the Elementary Teacher,* Wadsworth Publishing Company, San Francisco, 1961.

Spearman, C.: *Creative Mind,* Appleton-Century-Crofts, Inc., New York, 1931.

Wertheimer, Max: *Productive Thinking,* Harper & Row, Publishers, Incorporated, New York, 1959.

Zeran, Franklin R. (ed.): *Life Adjustment Education in Action,* Chartwell House, New York, 1953.

28. The Appeal to Imagination

Chardin, Pierre Teilhard de: *The Phenomenon of Man,* Harper & Row, Publishers, Incorporated, New York, 1961.

Eiseley, Loren: *The Mind as Nature,* Harper & Row, Publishers, Incorporated, New York, 1962.

Getzels, Jacob W., and Philip W. Jackson: *Creativity and Intelligence,* John Wiley & Sons, Inc., New York, 1962.

Ghiselin, Brewster (ed.): *The Creative Process,* University of California Press, Berkeley, Calif., 1954.

Osborn, Alex F.: *Applied Imagination,* Charles Scribner's Sons, New York, 1953.

Parnes, Sidney J., and Harold F. Harding (eds.): *A Source Book for Creative Thinking,* Charles Scribner's Sons, New York, 1962.

Sinnott, Edmund W.: *Cell and Psyche,* Harper & Row, Publishers, Incorporated, New York, 1961.

Torrance, E. Paul: *Guiding Creative Talent,* Prentice-Hall, Inc., Englewood Cliffs, N.J., 1962.

Whitehead, Alfred North: *The Aims of Education, and Other Essays,* The Macmillan Company, New York, 1929.

Index

Index